Emerging Powers in a Comparative Perspective

Emerging Powers in a Comparative Perspective

The Political and Economic Rise of the BRIC Countries

EDITED BY VIDYA NADKARNI
AND NORMA C. NOONAN

BLOOMSBURY
NEW YORK • LONDON • NEW DELHI • SYDNEY

Bloomsbury Academic
An imprint of Bloomsbury Publishing Plc

175 Fifth Avenue   50 Bedford Square
New York   London
NY 10010   WC1B 3DP
USA   UK

www.bloomsbury.com

First published 2013

Library of Congress Cataloging-in-Publication Data
A catalog record for this title is available from the Library of Congress.

ISBN: HB: 978-1-4411-2803-4
PB: 978-1-4411-1986-5

Typeset by Fakenham Prepress Solutions, Fakenham, Norfolk NR21 8NN
Printed and bound in the United States of America

To our families

CONTENTS

CONTRIBUTORS

João Augusto de Castro Neves is an analyst at Eurasia Group's Latin America practice, focusing primarily on Brazil. He has conducted extensive research on Brazil's foreign policy, and has published papers and articles in books, newspapers, magazines, and academic journals. Joao has worked as an independent political consultant based in Washington, D.C., and is an editor of the journal *The Brazilian Economy*. He has lectured at several American and Brazilian universities, research institutes, and diplomatic academies. From 2007 to 2010, he worked as a political analyst at CAC Consultoria Politica, a political risk and analysis firm he co-founded in Brasilia. He also worked at Instituto Brasileiro de Estudos Politicos, one of Brazil's leading political think tanks and consulting firm, and at the Brazilian Congress.

David Fouse is Professor of Regional Studies at the Asia-Pacific Center for Security Studies (APCSS). Dr. Fouse's recent APCSS publications have dealt with Japan's dispatch of the Ground Self-Defense Force to Iraq, Japan's support for counterterrorism in Southeast Asia, and Japanese policies toward North Korea in the post-Cold War era.

Mary Troy Johnston was associate professor of political science at Loyola University New Orleans from 1988 until her retirement in May 2012. Her academic research has focused on the European Union and transatlantic relations, where her interests have ranged from decision-making studies to Europe's emerging security policy. As co-editor, with Janet Adamski and Christina Schweiss, of *Old Europe, New Security* (2006), she first contrasted US and EU security values and explored the concept of human security in more recent academic presentations. She has widely participated in conferences in Europe and the USA, presently continuing her work as an independent scholar and writer.

Vidya Nadkarni is Professor of Political Science and International Relations at the University of San Diego. From 1998 to 2006, she directed the Master's Program in International Relations at the University of San Diego. Her teaching and research interests are focused on international relations theory and the foreign policies of emerging powers. She has written numerous articles and book chapters on the Russian-Indian relationship, Russian foreign policy, and international relations theory. She is the author of *Strategic Partnerships in Asia: Balancing without Alliances* (2010).

Norma Corigliano Noonan is Professor of Political Science and Leadership Studies at Augsburg College. From 1993 to 2011 she directed the Master of Arts in Leadership Program at Augsburg College. She was the editor and co-author of *Russian Women in Politics and Society* (1996) and *Encyclopedia of Russian Women's Movements* (2001). She is the author of numerous articles on Russian foreign policy, international politics, political leaders, and women in leadership. Her interests in international politics have been eclectic, and she brings many years of reflection to her essay on the future of the USA as a global power.

Tatiana Shakleina serves as Head of the Foreign Policy Studies Department at the Institute of the USA and Canada Studies of the Russian Academy of Sciences, where she has worked since 1972. She has also taught at the State University of Humanities and at the Moscow State University of International Relations. Her most recent publications include *Russian Foreign Policy in Transition: Concepts and Realities* (2005); *Foreign Policy of the Bush Administration: Concepts and Practice* (2003); and *Russia and the United States in the New World Order* (2002).

Suisheng Zhao is Professor and Executive Director of the Center for China-US Cooperation at Josef Korbel School of International Studies, University of Denver. A founding editor of the *Journal of Contemporary China*, he is the author and editor of more than ten books. His most recent books are: *China and the United States; Cooperation and Competition in Northeast Asia; China-US Relations Transformed: Perspectives and Strategic Interactions; Debating Political Reform in China: Rule of Law versus Democratization;* and *A Nation-State by Construction: Dynamics of Modern Chinese Nationalism.*

LIST OF ABBREVIATIONS

ABM	Anti-Ballistic Missile
ARF	ASEAN Regional Forum
APEC	Asia Pacific Economic Cooperation
ASEAN	Association of South East Asian Nations
ASEAN+3	ASEAN + China, Japan and South Korea
BASIC	Brazil, South Africa, India, China
BIMST-EC	Bay of Bengal Initiative for Multi-Sectoral Technical and Economic Cooperation
BJP	Bharatiya Janata Party, India
BNDES	National Development Bank of Brazil
BRIC	Brazil, Russia, India, China
BRICS	Brazil, Russia, India, China, South Africa
CBDR	Common but differentiated responsibility
CEPA	Comprehensive Economic Partnership Agreement
CCP	Chinese Communist Party
CDS	South American Defense Council
CGPCS	Contact Group on Piracy off the Coast of Somalia
CHINALCO	China Aluminum Corporation
CIS	Commonwealth of Independent States
COP	Conference of the Parties
CNOOC	China National Offshore Oil Corporation
CSTO	Collective Security Treaty Organization
DFC	Dedicated Freight Corridor

DMIC	Delhi-Mumbai Industrial Corridor
DPJ	Democratic Party of Japan
ECB	European Central Bank
ECSC	European Coal and Steel Community
EEZ	Exclusive Economic Zone
EFSF	European Financial Stability Facility
EPA	Economic Partnership Agreement
ESS	European Security Strategy
ESM	European Stability Mechanism
EU	European Union
FDI	Foreign Direct Investment
FTA	Free Trade Agreement
FTAA	Free Trade Area of the Americas
GATT	General Agreement on Tariffs and Trade
G2	Group of 2
G7	Group of 7
G8	Group of 8
G20	Group of 20
G77	Group of 77
GDP	Gross Domestic Product
GNI	Gross National Income
IBSA	India, Brazil, South Africa
ICC	International Criminal Court
IMF	International Monetary Fund
IR	International Relations
JETRO	Japanese External Trade Organization
JOGMEC	Japan's Oil, Gas and Metals National Corporation
ITEC	Indian Technical and Economic Cooperation
LIEO	Liberal International Economic Order

LOC	Lines of Credit
MEA	Ministry of External Affairs, India
MERCOSUR	(Also MERCOSUL) Common Market of the South (Spanish: Mercado Comun del Sur)
MINUSTAH	United Nations Peacekeeping Mission in Haiti
MOD	Ministry of Defence, India
MTCR	Missile Technology Control Regime
NAM	Non-aligned Movement
NATO	North Atlantic Treaty Organization
NDPG	National Defense Program Guidelines
NGO	Non-Governmental Organization
NIEO	New International Economic Order
NPT	Non-Proliferation Treaty
ODA	Official Development Assistance
OECD	Organization for Economic Cooperation and Development
PLA	People's Liberation Army
PNE	Peaceful Nuclear Explosion
PRC	People's Republic of China
R2P	Responsibility to Protect
R&D	Research and Development
RAO UES	Unified Energy System of Russia
RF	Russian Federation
ROSATOM	Russian State Nuclear Energy Corporation
SAARC	South Asian Association for Regional Cooperation
SAFTA	South Asian Free Trade Area
SAPTA	SAARC Preferential Trading Arrangement
SCAAP	Special Commonwealth Assistance for Africa Program
SCO	Shanghai Cooperation Organization
SIPRI	Stockholm Peace Research Institute
SOE	State Owned Enterprise

START	Strategic Arms Reduction Treaty
TCS	Technical Cooperation Scheme
TIG	Trade in Goods
UESR	Unified Energy System of Russia
UN	United Nations
UNASUR	Union of South American Nations
UNCTAD	United Nations Conference on Trade and Development
UNFCCC	United Nations Framework Convention on Climate Change
UNGA	United Nations General Assembly
UNSC	United Nations Security Council
US/US	United States
USA	United States of America
USSR	Union of Soviet Socialist Republics
WMD	Weapons of Mass Destruction
WTO	World Trade Organization

CHAPTER ONE

Introduction

Vidya Nadkarni

China's rapid emergence as a major power became a subject for scholarly speculation as early as the mid-1990s.[1] By the turn of the twenty-first century, the combined effect of China's remarkable economic performance, its rising military capabilities, and its growing global presence was reflected in unqualified acceptance in the world's major capitals of China's "arrival" as a great power. China is viewed as the nearest peer competitor of the United States of America (USA). Russia, India, and Brazil rank in the next tier of powers. India's potential as a great power began to be noted in the early years of the twenty-first century. While lagging behind China in economic growth rates and military strength, India's global profile has benefited from US endorsement of its role as a great power in-the-making.[2] Brazil and Russia have, as has India, sought to become regionally and globally assertive. In his 2001 paper titled "Building Better Global Economic BRICs," Goldman Sachs economist Jim O'Neill popularized the BRIC acronym to bring attention to the rising economies of Brazil, Russia, India, and China and inaugurated serious scholarly efforts devoted to understanding the impact of these countries on world affairs.[3]

This book represents one such attempt by bringing together a group of scholars who examine the coming power-shift from the perspective of established (the USA, Europe, and Japan) and rising (China, India, Russia, and Brazil) powers and the roles that these powers are likely to play in the twenty-first century. While there has been much scholarly debate and discussion over the nature, implications and durability of American global preeminence, there have been few systematic inquiries into the nature of the challenges the USA may face from likely competitors. In the globalized world of the twenty-first century, power is diffused among multiple state and non-state actors and the challenges to security are multifaceted. Thus, questions related to the rise and decline of powers have to range beyond a mere tally of the hard capabilities of states.

For most of the second half of the twentieth century, West European countries and Japan were able to forge a new path to power based on pursuing trade and commerce—a circumstance enabled by the security umbrella provided by the USA. The Cold War had generated a very specific set of norms that underpinned a competitive international security order guided largely by the dictates of East-West strategic and ideological rivalry. The East-West thaw brought an end to an almost half-century of assiduous US-Soviet efforts to devise elaborate measures to compete while avoiding the escalatory dangers inherent in any direct military confrontation between the nuclear-armed powers. While fears of apocalyptic nuclear war have receded in the twenty-first century, the rise of transnational problems like terrorism and climate change has brought to the forefront normative questions about the kind of global leadership required for multilateral cooperation.

The collapse of the Soviet Union and demise of its East European Empire expanded the boundaries of the European Union (EU) within the institutional ambit of which former East European satellite states could be socialized into EU norms. As a "civilian power," the EU seeks to project global influence based on the concept of international responsibility by fostering multilateral cooperation in achieving its objectives.[4] The success of this global socialization project is likely to hinge to a large degree upon the role that Russia will seek to play in Eurasia and elsewhere. Japan's twenty-first century role will be intimately bound up with the nature and form of China's rising power. The latter, in turn, will be affected by the tempo of India's rise in Asia and the world. Brazil's emerging role will create a new center of power in the Americas. The international political, security, and economic implications of these developments are of great significance in anticipating the nature of the coming international order.

As China, Russia, India, and Brazil assume a larger role in the global economy, these countries will, as a consequence of their economic weight and political aspirations, become vital players in addressing the transnational challenges of globalization, climate change and terrorism. Additionally, their emergence begs answers to several interesting questions about traditional inter-state security concerns: How will the coming power transition affect the preeminent role of the USA? Will the rising powers seek to revise the international order or work within it? How will the salience of transnational global problems affect questions of international and world order? Understanding the national aspirations of China, India, Russia, and Brazil will be of great significance in answering these questions and in understanding the shape of the twenty-first century world.

In the sections below, we examine themes that will allow us to construct the conceptual scaffolding for the arguments presented in the chapters that follow. These sections cover the nature of the anticipated power transition; the significance of the international hierarchy of power; the importance of national role conceptions; the impact of globalization; and the effect of demographic pressures on established and rising powers.

The Coming Power Transition

A protracted process of power transition is underway from long dominant centers of power in the west to countries in the eastern and southern hemispheres. The gradual rise of the West in the sixteenth century was prefaced by seafaring voyages spearheaded by Portugal and Spain that began in the early fifteenth century, which opened up the promise of trade and settlement in territories previously uncharted by Europeans.[5] In time, due largely to their military and technological superiority and willingness to use force, most of the major European powers colonized vast regions in the Americas, Australasia, and Africa. Growing European ascendancy received an added fillip from the rise of the industrial revolution in the eighteenth century. By the nineteenth century, major European capital cities had become colonial metropolises and the epicenters of global commerce. European dominance continued until the mid-twentieth century, when World War Two (1939–45) devastated the European continent. The process of decolonization, which unfolded in the latter half of the twentieth century, further crippled Europe's big powers. The post-1945 emergence of a bipolar world led by a preeminent USA, with the Soviet Union in the role of a challenging power, ended the period of European dominance.

Until the turn of the nineteenth century, the continent of Asia had cut a high economic profile in the world. Asia produced much of the global wealth and accounted for a significant percentage of world trade. According to Angus Maddison, China and India together accounted for 48.9 percent of world GDP (gross domestic product) in 1820 compared to 23 percent for Western Europe.[6] By 1913, Western Europe accounted for 33 percent of world GDP compared to a China-India total of 16.3 percent.[7] If the twenty-first century is an Asian century, one may therefore more aptly refer to the "return" of Asia after centuries of dormancy during which the Asian continent had ceded its position of primacy first to European powers and later to the USA. While the relative positions of currently dominant states is declining vis-à-vis the emerging powers, it will most likely be decades before rising Asian states will have the capacity to eclipse the combined economic and military might of the USA, the European countries and Japan. China and India are joined by Russia and Brazil as contesting claimants to great power status.

The problem of change in world politics continues to vex scholars and policy makers alike. If, as realists argue, dominant powers shape the international order to conform to their particular interests and value preferences, then two important questions arise: (1) what is the process by which dominant powers rise and decline; and (2) how may we ascertain the nature and likelihood of normative changes to the international order following periods of power transition? These considerations are of critical relevance in the twenty-first century during which the USA with its European and Japanese allies have to assess the implications of the rising global reach of China, of the ascending trajectories of India and Brazil, and of the resurgence of Russia.

Power transition literature has suggested that the process of international systemic change is fraught with violence. A readjustment in the power hierarchy of states in the international system that reorders earlier patterns of relations between super-ordinate and subordinate states comes about when there is a significant change in the distribution of power. The rise of new powers, dissatisfied with the status quo and possessing the capabilities to challenge the prevailing order, creates disequilibrium in the system. Such a state of affairs often results in efforts by the new powers to challenge the position of the dominant state(s).[8] Writing from a realist perspective, Robert Gilpin noted that power shifts have occurred when the international system is in disequilibrium and rising powers calculate that the benefits accruing from challenging the dominant power exceed the costs.[9]

Surveying the historical rise and decline of great powers, Gilpin noted that while a peaceful adjustment of systemic disequilibrium is possible, hegemonic war has been the primary driver of transformative international political change.[10] Other scholars have recognized the possibility of peaceful change in world politics.[11] However, hegemonic war was considered to be the primary catalyst of power transitions until the peaceful end of the bipolar order led several scholars to challenge the conclusions of the realist-oriented power transition school. These scholars argued that because state identities and interests are malleable (rather than fixed, as realists tend to assume), socially constructed and subject to redefinition in light of new ideas and norms, the probability of peaceful systemic change cannot be easily dismissed.[12] They pointed to Soviet leader Mikhail Gorbachev (1985–91) who rejected rigid and anachronistic Cold War doctrines and strategies and adopted notions of universal security and common global interests, which "free[d] the Soviet Union from the coercive social logic of the cold war."[13]

Gilpin attributed the decline of dominant powers to a triumvirate of variables: the heavy burdens of leadership; rising domestic consumption; and the diffusion of technology.[14] Such a characterization focuses largely on the impact of hard military and economic capabilities in assessing power but also implies the influence of intangible factors in the rise of challengers, such as their desire to achieve great power status and their will to act as great powers. For liberal international relations scholars, normative factors figure prominently in gauging great power status. The social conferral of great power status by dominant powers upon rising powers is contingent upon the latter acting "responsibly" in the world by upholding norms of the international order.[15] The impact of power transitions on the norms underlying international order is a salient concern for dominant powers because prevailing norms reflect their preferences. For instance, after the victory of the Bolshevik revolution in Russia in October 1917, early Soviet leaders had hoped to overturn an international order based on states with one based on international working class solidarity. The failure of the world socialist revolution to materialize led to the gradual socialization of the Bolshevik Soviet state into the norms of an inter-state societal order.[16]

Immediately after World War Two, the major powers sought to tame the use of force by states through the creation of the United Nations (UN). International norms based on respect for state sovereignty coupled with the doctrine of collective security were designed to "save succeeding generations from the scourge of war."[17] The bipolar division of the Cold War world, however, negated the promise of an international order based on collective security by fostering the creation of a dual order. East-West ideological divisions had created a US-sponsored security order that centered on the North Atlantic Treaty Organization (NATO) in Europe and bilateral security alliances with Japan and South Korea in Asia and an international economic order underpinned by the Bretton Woods system.[18] On the Soviet side, the Warsaw Treaty Organization (Warsaw Pact) and the Council for Mutual Economic Assistance respectively underwrote the rules of the security and economic order for countries in the socialist bloc.

Soviet President Mikhail Gorbachev's inauguration of "new thinking" in foreign policy in the late 1980s led to a gradual Soviet withdrawal from its outer empire in Eastern Europe followed by a peaceful denouement to the Cold War. The unilateral exit of the Soviet Union from its Eastern European sphere of influence meant that norms of the international economic and security order established by Western powers remained uncontested and gained greater standing. On security matters, the Soviet Union under Gorbachev proved willing to support collective security norms. Thus, when Iraq invaded Kuwait in August 1990, the Soviet Union joined the USA, the United Kingdom, and France in November 1990 to pass United Nations Security Council Resolution 678 supporting military action against Iraq in the absence of an Iraqi withdrawal from Kuwait by 15 January 1991.[19] But such superpower accord was short-lived.

As NATO and the EU expanded to incorporate former socialist bloc countries in Eastern Europe, Russia remained an outsider. Under President Yeltsin, Russia balked at supporting military intervention efforts in the Balkans in the 1990s that were spearheaded by the USA and Europe. Post-Yeltsin era Russian leaders generally have been opposed to humanitarian interventions that violate the sovereignty of third countries. Among Western countries, however, the norm of sovereignty, interpreted in its tight version as the freedom of states from external interference, has come to be challenged. Western concern over the protection of human rights led to the enunciation in the year 2001 of the doctrine of "responsibility to protect" (R2P). R2P is founded on a new security and human rights norm, which qualifies the right of a state to sovereignty by asserting that the international community has the right to intervene in countries where the government is unable or unwilling to protect its citizens from wanton physical harm.[20] Russia and China have strongly resisted the practical application of this doctrine. Their lack of support is evident in the exercise of their veto power in the United Nations Security Council against resolutions calling for military interventions for humanitarian purposes.

As regards the international economic order, membership in the Bretton Woods institutions became nearly global and policies of economic liberalization were adopted by a greater numbers of countries. China's liberalizing economic reforms predated the end of the Cold War. China began its engagement with the global economy in 1978 under the post-Mao leadership of Deng Xiaoping. Liberal economic reforms in India, Russia, and Brazil began in earnest in the early 1990s. But the new powers of the twenty-first century have been selectively supportive of the norms underpinning a liberal international economic order based on the promotion of open trade and have lobbied for a greater voting share in decision-making in the World Bank and the IMF.

The Rising Powers in the International Hierarchy of Power

In the international hierarchy of power, states may be stratified according to whether they are superpowers, great powers, regional powers, or middle powers. This categorization is often based on a particular state's level of hard (military and economic) capabilities, the geographical scope of its influence, and the acknowledgment by other states of its power status. The term "superpowers" came into the international relations lexicon toward the end of World War Two to apply to the dominant positions of the USA and the Soviet Union, which had overwhelming and mobile military capabilities and the will to use force, if necessary, in order to project power globally, often in multiple regions simultaneously.[21] "Great power plus great mobility of power" was how William T. R. Fox defined a superpower.[22] During the Cold War, both the USA and the Soviet Union deployed military, economic, political, and cultural instruments of power and influence to promote their interests and ideological preferences around the world. With the end of the Cold War and the subsequent dissolution of the Soviet Union, the USA emerged as the only global superpower with an unmatched military, an unrivaled economy, and a stable polity.

Great powers, not unlike superpowers, are global players with a reach and interest in projecting influence beyond their immediate region. While great powers may not possess overwhelming dominance in all areas of power—military, economic, political and cultural, and may not have the capacity or be able to sustain the costs of bringing military power to bear in several theaters of conflict simultaneously—they do have the capacity and desire for exercising influence in global domains. Regional powers are able and willing to exert dominant influence in their respective geographical regions but do not have the capacity to project power globally. Regional powers have traditionally been viewed as middle powers, occupying a position somewhere between great powers and other states. However, since 1998, with the launching of the Middle Powers Initiative by Douglas Roche, a former Canadian Senator and Ambassador, middle powers have also come to be defined as "politically and economically significant, internationally respected countries that have renounced the nuclear arms race."[23]

Using the typology above, the USA is the only country that can lay claim to the title of superpower, although given the diffusion of power in the twenty-first century, no single country can achieve all its international objectives without the cooperation of other major powers. In spite of their buffeting in the 2008 financial crisis, the European Union and Japan remain major economic powers that are regionally dominant and globally consequential actors. China is an acknowledged great power, and its leaders see their country as being in a league of its own, second only to the USA. Russia, India, and Brazil dominate their respective regions, are recognized as important players at the global table, and have aspirations to great power status.

Given the relative positions of major states in the power hierarchy, the central thread in the twenty-first century power transition narrative is the role of China. China's global rise has important geostrategic implications for all other powers and is potentially consequential for the nature of the future international order. On the one hand, China has benefited economically from engaging with a globalization process anchored largely in the rules of a liberal international economic order, particularly as regards open trade. On the other hand, a rising China has often challenged what its leaders perceive as US dominance over the post-World War Two economic order. Chinese leaders have also expressed dissatisfaction with the norms of the international security order. The stability of prevailing norms will hinge upon whether China, in particular, will seek to adapt to or revise the international order in accordance with its interests and value preferences.

There are additional areas of uncertainty, which relate to how China accommodates the domestic tensions arising from the clash between a modern and increasingly prosperous society and an authoritarian polity, and between the wealthy and the economically disadvantaged segments of the population. Moreover, even as we contemplate a world in which a rising China will play an increasingly prominent role, we cannot overlook the fact that continued high rates of economic growth in the future are a matter of conjecture. A marked slowdown in the Chinese economic growth rate could spark domestic unrest and the resultant socio-political instability could complicate China's aspirations to global leadership.

Such questions apply with equal force to Russia, as demonstrated by the popular demonstrations against the perceived irregularities in the December 2011 Duma (Russian Parliament) elections and the March 2012 presidential elections.[24] As democratic polities, Brazil and India have strong civil societies but have to contend with the pressures that arise from the rising demands of their disadvantaged populations for a more equitable distribution of their countries' growing share in global wealth. How political leaders position their states as they negotiate the tortuous path between the external demands of great power status and the internal needs of a developing society rests largely on their self-image of the role they envisage for their countries.

National Role Conceptions

Role theory examines the attitudes and behavior of state actors in terms of the self-defined role expectations of policy makers and the signals they receive from the outside. According to K. J. Holsti,

> A *national role conception* includes the policy makers' own definition of the general kinds of decisions, commitments, rules and actions suitable to their state, and of the functions, if any, their state should perform on a continuing basis in the international system or in subordinate regional systems.[25]

National role conceptions are supported or challenged by "role prescriptions" that have their source in the external environment, whether deriving from the structure of the international system, international norms and traditions, or the weight of world public opinion.[26] The environment thus confers a particular role upon a state that may or may not correspond to the self-defined national role conception of the state in question.

The position of a given state in a hierarchically stratified international system often provides a vantage point for role definition both by that state's policymakers and by other states. While prevailing elite and leadership

views often weigh heavily when national role conceptions are considered
in "freeze frame" fashion, such "roles" often emerge through a process
of contestation among elites and between elites and the public. Roles are
dynamic and subject to appraisal and reappraisal. Domestic sources of
dynamism come during periods of domestic leadership transition or in
the wake of domestic social and economic upheavals. In addition, global
or regional geopolitical and geoeconomic changes often serve as external
triggers for role reappraisals. In each of the countries under consideration,
national image is subject to contestation in response to signals from the
internal and external environments.

The US self-image as a global leader was forged in the crucible of the
World War Two experience. Prior to the attack on Pearl Harbor in 1941,
the USA was content to serve as a regional hegemon and gatekeeper of
the Western hemisphere. US entry into the First World War, for instance,
came in response to German attacks on neutral US merchant ships in the
Atlantic and a growing belief that Germany represented a direct threat
to US security. Soon after the war, the USA, even as a fast rising power,
intentionally retreated from European and global involvement and refused
to join the newly created League of Nations. Only with the end of World
War Two in 1945, when faced with an eclipsing British Empire and the
menace of Soviet communism, did American security planners gradually
begin to envisage the establishment of a global system of naval bases to
protect strategic interests and markets. The move toward internationalism
came after a vigorous domestic debate during the interwar period about
the global role of the USA in which the internationalists prevailed over the
isolationists. The threat of expanding Soviet influence in Europe and the
fragility of governments in Europe and Asia strengthened the hand of the
internationalists.

Formerly dominant European powers began the process of reinventing
the basis of their power after the military and economic devastation of the
World War Two and the gradual unraveling of European empires in Asia
and Africa after 1945. The continent, which was the site of great power
competition based on alliances and balances of power from the eighteenth
to the early twentieth centuries, moved to develop new norms for the joint
pursuit of peace and prosperity in Europe, which were formalized in many
documents over the next five decades. The EU today defines its role as
the purveyor of a new type of global power. As the official website of the
EU notes: "The sheer size of the European Union in economic, trade, and
financial terms makes it a world player."[27]

The EU seeks to fulfill this role not through the use of force but
by promoting human rights and democracy, spreading prosperity, and
supporting the enforcement of the rule of law and good governance.[28] As
with European countries in the aftermath of World War Two, Japan's defeat
in that war ended its quest of an Asian hegemony. Japan refashioned its

image from that of a traditional great power to that of a trading state and soon became the second largest global economy after the USA. The end of the Cold War and the rising power of China have re-opened debate in Japan over the foundation of the country's power and status in the twenty-first century.

In terms of its national self-image, China, after the communist revolution in 1949, saw itself as a member of the communist world joined with the Soviet Union in a battle against American imperialism. After the Sino-Soviet split became public in 1960, Mao began to characterize both the Soviet Union and the USA as imperialist states and China as part of a third world of developing states fighting against imperialism and colonialism.[29] In 1978, under the leadership of Deng Xiaoping, China made a gradual transition from being an ideologically driven actor to a pragmatic and involved participant in the international community of states. With high rates of economic growth fueled by a move to state-led capitalism and a deepening engagement with the international economy, China has come to view itself as an important global player in the same league as the world's great powers. However, China also sees itself as a developing country that must strive to mitigate persisting economic inequalities and is therefore entitled to reduced international burden sharing in addressing problems like climate change.

Russia has undergone several transformations in its national self-image in recent centuries. During the imperial phase the tsar saw his role as protector of the vast Russian empire, Slavism and Orthodoxy. During the Communist period, the Bolsheviks saw their mission as spreading communism to all corners of the globe. Based on its size and considerable resources, post-communist Russia continues to view itself as a great power and seeks to reclaim its earlier level of global influence. Resentful of western skepticism about Russia's democratic credentials, Russian leaders have promoted the notion of Russia as a sovereign democracy and resisted multilateral efforts to "police" the democratic standing of countries.

India's view of its role and place in the world traversed the European journey in reverse. From a self-perception after independence in 1947 as a purveyor of a new path to peace and prosperity based on non-violent norms, India moved to add a muscular view of power to buttress its claims to global leadership and complement what the country's leaders saw as the inherent international appeal of its democracy and age-old civilization. Since the beginning of the twenty-first century, Brazil, likewise, based on its massive territorial size and noteworthy economic gains, has moved from seeing itself as a regional power to being part of the league of global players.[30] With a figurative foot each in the economically developed North and the developing South, India and Brazil "sit uneasily between the attitudes and interests of the North and the South."[31]

Globalization

What is undeniable is that the economic rise of China, India, and Brazil in particular has been greatly facilitated by the conscious decision of their leaders to engage robustly with the process of globalization. India and Brazil were founding members of the General Agreement on Tariffs and Trade (GATT) in 1947 and joined the World Trade Organization (WTO) at its inception in January 1995. The USA played a vital role in the global economic integration of China by backing Chinese entry into the WTO in December 2001. Russia, since 1992, has become engaged in the international economy and was granted membership in the WTO in December 2011. All these countries are also members of the International Monetary Fund (IMF) and the World Bank. Although buffeted by the 2008 financial crisis, globalization has been nurtured and sustained by the post-World War Two institutionalization of liberal economic norms in the context of the US-sponsored Bretton Woods system.

These norms, designed to promote international monetary stability and reduce barriers to the free flow of trade and capital, were formalized in the trio of Bretton Woods institutions established under US leadership after World War Two: The IMF, the GATT (transformed into the WTO in 1995), and the International Bank for Reconstruction and Development (the largest bank in the World Bank Group). Liberal economic principles assumed unquestioned primacy after the demise of Soviet-style communism. These principles formed the basis for the 1989 introduction by economist John Williamson of the term "Washington Consensus" and informed the international lending practices of multilateral development aid agencies.[32]

In the wake of the 2008 financial crisis, the Washington Consensus came under severe criticism and the post-Cold War faith in the virtues of an untrammeled free market was shaken. Some scholars began to tout the "Beijing Consensus" (the China model) based on state capitalism as a more effective route to development.[33] But the Chinese way is not the only extant model on the menu of economic policy choices. As economist David Rothkopf observed, we are "entering . . . an era of competing capitalisms." The "Anglo-American model of economic Darwinism" is facing competition from rival models: "capitalism with 'Chinese characteristics'"; "Eurocapitalism"; and "the 'democratic development' capitalism of India and Brazil, with their strong social agendas to go with their growth aspirations."[34] More significantly, as Rothkopf pointed out, "[h]istory teaches us that as economic power shifts, intellectual influence follows." Thus, he noted that "a global consensus is likely to emerge that there should be a greater role for the state in the marketplace."[35]

The most concrete manifestation of such change came at the Group of 20 (G20) summit meeting in London in April 2009 when US President

Barack Obama "acknowledged that the 'Washington Consensus' of unfettered globalisation (sic) and deregulation was now outmoded, and called for a more balanced approach to regulating markets rather than letting them run free."[36] More importantly, a new Financial Stability Board that includes all G20 members was set up to serve as a global financial regulator. China and India were given greater voting shares in the IMF.[37] The IMF leadership was made open to all members rather than the earlier practice of restricting the top position to Europeans, leading one observer to ask whether this represented "the beginning of a new world economic order."[38] But China's reticence in pushing for a Chinese candidate to head the IMF after the resignation in May 2011 of its leader Dominique Strauss-Kahn demonstrated yet again the country's unwillingness to be thrust prematurely into a position of global responsibility. India, China, and Russia, after initial hesitation, supported the candidacy of Christine Lagarde of France for the post of IMF's Managing Director.

Demographic Challenges

All the countries in this study are undergoing significant demographic transformations that will materially affect their ability to project power and influence in the world. While population numbers cannot be overlooked as an important resource in calculations of a country's military potential and economic capacity, numbers alone do not tell the whole story. Indicators of health, income, education, technological sophistication, and civic mindedness add to or detract from mere population figures. In general, the graying of populations in the US, Japan, Europe, and China; the precipitous decline in population numbers and public health in Russia; and the hundreds of millions in India who live below the poverty line of US$1.25 a day all represent hurdles that call for remedial action.

The USA is in a relatively better position both in terms of population numbers and on measures of health and education, but has to contend with the challenges associated with the demographic pressures on its European and Japanese allies. Demographic expert Nicholas Eberstadt explains US demographic "exceptionalism" as stemming from two factors: continued receptivity to newcomers and immigrants, and fertility patterns that are atypical for the developed world. The USA registers 2.0 births per woman in contrast to the norm of 1.5 in Western Europe, 1.4 in Eastern Europe, and 1.3 in Japan. Japan and China are also culturally more resistant to immigration.[39]

China and India are the world's most populous states with populations numbering 1.34 billion and 1.2 billion respectively.[40] In China, a slower birth rate and an aging population raise the prospect of a diminishing demographic dividend.[41] On the positive side, a significant proportion of China's people are urban dwellers and college-educated and therefore better equipped to deal with the demands of a post-industrial society.[42] An educated populace, however, could demand avenues for greater political participation, thereby raising legitimacy problems for China's authoritarian polity and a challenge to the "core interest" of regime survival. That the Chinese leaders worry about such challenges is evident in their speedy efforts to clamp down on social media networks promoting an Arab Spring-style jasmine revolution and moving with haste to disperse public demonstrations.

With a growing population, albeit at a slowing growth rate, India in 2030 is expected to have 1.5 billion people with a working age population (ages 15–64) of 68 percent—a demographic dividend that would be an economic boon for the country were literacy levels to rise and high poverty levels to plummet. But the corruption-ridden and fractious democratic political process complicates the Indian government's ability to be effective in the allocation of resources both to infrastructural and human resource needs. If India is unable to reverse poverty and illiteracy rates significantly and rapidly, economic growth rates will decline. Demographic issues represent daunting domestic challenges that have the potential to derail India's great power aspirations.

Between 1993 and 2010, Russia's population fell from 148.6 million to about 142 million. Accompanying this downward spiral were more worrisome trends captured in declining health and education standards. According to Eberstadt,

> By 2008, Russian authors were publishing far fewer scientific papers than the authors of Russia's BRIC peers—Brazil, China, and India. In effect, Russia stands as the new and disturbing wonder in today's globalized world: a society characterized by high levels of schooling but low levels of health, knowledge, and education.[43]

According to a World Bank report on demographic trends, Brazil is at the mid-point of a "profound socioeconomic transformation driven by demographic change."[44] By 2020, the country will reach the end of its "inflection point" for a short "demographic bonus" when the working age population outnumbers the dependent population.[45] But Brazil's achievement in reducing rates of poverty is remarkable. Poverty rates declined from 53 percent in 1981 to 9.5 percent in 2008 calculated on a per person average of US$2.00 per day. Brazil thus has a short-term window to create sufficient opportunities in the labor market to boost economic productivity and increase international competitiveness before a growing aging population resulting from declining fertility rates and lower mortality rates will begin to claim a significantly larger share of the country's resources.

Extrapolating from global demographic data, Eberstadt concludes that population trends may in a "limited but tangible" way "contribute to the calculus of American strategic preeminence in the Asia Pacific region, and indeed around the world."[46]

The Structure of the Book

How the rise of China is viewed by established and emerging powers alike constitutes one of the central unifying questions of the book. China, as was noted earlier, is well ahead of the pack of rising powers and is the primary potential challenger to the global preeminence of the USA. The nature of the US-China nexus affects the bilateral interactions between all other dyads of countries considered in this study.

In Chapter 2, Norma Noonan notes that while the USA is a preeminent power and a global leader, there is a wide-ranging debate over whether American power is on the decline or whether the USA will be "the major exception to the 'decline and fall' syndrome." Whatever the outcome of this debate, however, Noonan states that the USA has to craft a strategy to deal with other rising powers. Of these rising powers, China is the country with which the USA is "most intricately" involved. The close intertwining of their economies and China's global economic presence have meant that China is "competing in traditional US spheres of influence" in Latin America and is impinging on US interests in the Asia Pacific region. As with China, US relations with Russia are "complicated." Russia has slipped to "second-level status" in the view of US policy makers and Noonan suggests that greater attention to this bilateral relationship may be warranted. US ties with Europe and Japan benefit from their history as allies. Based on shared values and interests, Noonan argues that a "close partnership with India" is "in the best interests of the USA." Noonan concludes that while the future role of the USA remains an "open question," the USA may have to develop the "diplomatic skills" necessary to operate in a world where it is no longer the dominant power.

Mary Troy Johnston (Chapter 3) sees a collective Europe as representing a new type of power. The EU projects itself as a "normative power" that has "developed multi-level governance" structures to promote its "soft power." Europe's global role, she argues, must be seen through the prism of "new power currencies." European countries have moved beyond traditional notions of state sovereignty and security. Europe has "embraced the concept of human security" replacing *raison d'état* with *raison humaine*, which is founded on respect for human rights, the rule of law and democratic governance. But she sees the continued ricocheting effects of the 2008 global financial crisis with the sovereign debt problems of Greece,

Portugal, and other European countries as representing a challenge for EU policymakers. Whether or not the EU model will be applicable elsewhere, Johnston argues that Europe will have a seat at the global table. Above all, she notes, "Europe has shown a facility for adaptation and innovation, recognizing the reality of change and the need for accommodation in a multi-polar world."

Japan, David Fouse (Chapter 4) remarks, rose "from the ashes of World War Two to become the second largest global economic power in 1968." Japan accomplished this economic feat by forging a "consensus around a strategy of pursuing rapid economic development while maintaining a low diplomatic and military profile." In the post-Cold War period, Japanese policy makers are divided between progressives who tout Japan as a "global civilian power" and conservatives who "see Japan in more traditional terms of great power status." This debate, however, was overshadowed by a prolonged period of economic stagnation that began in the early 1990s and lasted until 2010. By 2010, China had overtaken Japan as the world's second largest economy. Japan's debt problems and a rapidly aging population have imposed a "growing burden" on the economy and left the country with "very little room for maneuver" vis-à-vis its "deepening dependence on the surging Chinese economy." As its economic clout has decreased, Japan has become diplomatically more assertive. This more "open" approach has "moved Japanese foreign policy closer in line with the USA." Additionally, Japan has built "new strategic partnerships in order to counter China's influence." Fouse concludes by arguing that Japan views its role as both "complex and limited, aimed at sustaining the US-centered liberal international order while building pathways to integrate China."

Suisheng Zhao (Chapter 5) describes China as a "reluctant global power in search of its rightful place" in the world. Zhao argues that increased Chinese assertiveness vis-à-vis the USA and European countries in protecting the "core interests" of regime survival, economic development and territorial integrity followed the global economic downturn which severely affected the economies of Western powers. But, he observes, Beijing has not articulated a "broader vision" of its role as a rising power and is wary about assuming international responsibilities that may adversely affect core interests. Accompanying this reluctance to shoulder global responsibilities is a strong leadership and popular consensus that China rightfully belongs to the great power club and frustration stemming from a perception that there is a "Western conspiracy" aimed at slowing down China's rise. He concludes that China has neither completely "abandoned its low profile policy" nor has shown full readiness to assume a global leadership role.

Nadkarni (Chapter 6) states that India has sought to maintain "strategic autonomy" through "engagement with all centers of power" as a deliberate strategy in its twenty-first century "quest for wealth, power and status." India's extended neighborhood policy has enlarged the country's presence in its home continent beyond the sub-region of South Asia. From a global leadership role in the 1950s that was largely symbolic, Nadkarni notes, India moved in the 1960s to develop stronger military capabilities. India's economic growth took off in the early 1990s with the adoption of liberal economic reforms. By the early 2000s, India had added "economic heft to its growing military power." With hard capabilities complemented by the magnetism of its culture and the vibrancy of its democracy, India has enhanced its credentials for seeking entry into the great power club. However, there are numerous obstacles in the path of India's rise. High rates of poverty and illiteracy, official corruption, and a weak infrastructure detract from the country's foreign ambitions. Furthermore, Nadkarni argues, India has not yet shown a willingness to play a great power role in multilateral venues.

According to Shakleina (Chapter 7), contemporary Russia is not so much a rising power as one in process of preserving and consolidating its great power potential. Arguing that the Slavophile vs. Westernizer categorization of Russian scholars is obsolete, she states that Russian foreign policy discourse is conducted on the one hand by liberal internationalists and liberal realists and on the other by conservative internationalists and traditional conservatives. Liberal internationalists accept American global leadership and the entire panoply of Western values and call for greater attention to the resolution of domestic issues. Liberal realists share the faith in Western values but "emphasize the importance of foreign rather than domestic policy." Liberal conservatives "support the concept of a polycentric world order." They are intellectual liberals who "adhere to realism in politics" and to ideas of "strong statehood." By 2011, Shakleina observes, liberal realists and liberal conservatives were "close to equal" in terms of their influence on policy. She concludes by noting that Russia possesses many of the traditional elements of great power status but also has a long-standing historical culture of autonomy in the pursuit of domestic and foreign policy and of "thinking globally."

Writing about Brazil, de Castro Neves (Chapter 8) observes that size and abundance of natural resources have led the country to believe in the "inevitability of its great power role in the world" since "the heyday of its monarchic imperium in the nineteenth century." With the end of the Cold War, the country has begun anew to consider that idea. In the 1990s, Brazil's preoccupation with the challenges of democratization and with achieving economic stability left its leaders "little leeway to operate actively in global affairs." But since the turn of the twenty-first century, Brazil has become "more assertive regionally and globally." De Castro Neves argues that this expansion of influence will occur along three "overlapping and often bumpy tracks"—one track focused on building regional consensus on global affairs; the second track aimed at updating the bilateral relationship between the USA and Brazil, the two largest democracies of the Western hemisphere; and finally, the multilateral international institutions track designed to increase Brazil's global leverage. De Castro Neves notes in conclusion that Brazilian leaders emphasize autonomy as an important attribute of foreign policy but the concept is interpreted in many different ways, which leaves open the question of whether Brazil will act as a satisfied power or move to a "more explicitly revisionist foreign policy."

What follows from these accounts is the story of a world in flux. The global preeminence of the USA is on a slow decline. But while US global leadership may be showing signs of flagging, none of the other great power contenders has yet shown the readiness to assume the burdens and responsibilities of great power status.

Endnotes

1 For a listing of the mid–1990s literature on China's rise, see Samuel S. Kim, "China's Path to Great Power Status in the Globalization Era," *Asian Perspective*, Vol. 27, No. 1. (2003), 35–75.

2 See Chapter 6 for details.

3 Jim O'Neill, "Building Better Economic BRICs," Goldman Sachs, Global Economics Paper, No. 66, 30 November 2001, http://www2.goldmansachs. com/our-thinking/brics/brics-reports-pdfs/build-better-brics.pdf

4 Andrea Ciambra, "'Normative Power' Europe: Theory and Practice of EU Norms," Jean Monnet Working Paper No. 64, July 2008, http://www.fscpo. unict.it/EuroMed/jmwp64.pdf

5 Daron Acemoglu, Simon H. Johnson, and James A. Robinson, "The Rise of Europe: Atlantic Trade, Institutional Change and Economic Growth," Sloan School of Management, Massachusetts Institute of Technology, Working Paper No. 4269–02, 25 November 2002. Social Science Research Network, http:// papers.ssrn.com/sol3/papers.cfm?abstract_id=355880

6 Calculated from figures in Table 8b in Angus Maddison, *The World Economy: Historical Statistics*. (Paris: OECD, 2003), 261.

7 Ibid.

8 Ronald L. Tammen, et al, *Power Transitions: Strategies for the twenty-first Century*. (New York: Chatham House, 2000), 21–33.

9 Robert Gilpin, *War and Change in World Politics*. (Cambridge: Cambridge University Press, 1981).

10 Ibid., 44.

11 Charles A. Kupchan, Emmanuel Adler, Jean-Marc Coicaud, and Yuen Foon Khong (ed.) *Power in Transition: The Peaceful Change of International Order*. (New York: United Nations University Press, 2001).

12 Jeffrey W. Legro, *Rethinking the World: Great Power Strategies and International Order*. (Ithaca: Cornell University Pres, 2005).

13 Alexander Wendt, "Anarchy Is What States Make of It: The Social Construction of Power Politics," *International Organization*, Vol. 46, No. 2 (Spring 1992), 421.

14 Robert Gilpin, *War and Change in World Politics*. (Cambridge: Cambridge University Press, 1981).

15 Hedley Bull, *The Anarchical Society: A Study of Order in World Politics*. (New York: Columbia University Press, 1977), 202.

16 David Armstrong, *Revolution and World Order: The Revolutionary State in International Society*. (Oxford: Clarendon Press, 1993).

17 See Preamble to the United Nations Charter on the official UN website, http:// www.un.org/en/documents/charter/preamble.shtml

18 The Bretton Woods system anchored liberal economic principles of an open international economy in three institutions: the International Monetary Fund; the International Bank for Reconstruction and Development (the largest bank in the World Bank Consortium); and the World Trade Organization created in 1995 as a successor to the General Agreement on Tariffs and Trade. For brief official histories of each of these organizations, see the websites of the IMF, the IBRD, and the WTO: http://www.imf.org/external/about/history.htm, http:// web.worldbank.org/WBSITE/EXTERNAL/EXTABOUTUS/0,,contentMDK:20653 660~menuPK:72312~pagePK:51123644~piPK:329829~theSitePK:29708,00.html, http://www.wto.org/english/thewto_e/whatis_e/inbrief_e/inbr01_e.htm

19 The text of Resolution 678 is available at http://www.un.org/docs/scres/1990/ scres90.htm

20 At the 60th session of the United Nations General Assembly in September 2005, 191 states endorsed a resolution upholding this doctrine. See, "History and Timeline of R2P," The Responsibility to Protect Coalition, http:// r2pcoalition.org/content/view/22/48/

21 William T. R. Fox, *The Superpowers: The USA, Britain, and the Soviet Union—Their Responsibility for Peace*. (New York: Harcourt, Brace & Co., 1944). Fox believed that Britain with its vast overseas empire qualified as a superpower, but very soon after the end of World War Two, an economically devastated Britain began to divest itself of its colonies, with India, the "jewel in the crown," gaining independence in August 1945. Britain, after World War Two, could no longer be counted as a superpower.

22 William T. R. Fox, "The Super-powers: Then and Now," *International Journal*, Vol. 35, No. 3. (Summer 1980), 417.

23 See, http://www.middlepowers.org/about.html

24 See John Watts, "Putin cracks down on protesters after election victory," *Human Events*, Vol. 68, No. 9. (12 March 2012), 7.

25 K. J. Holsti, "National Role Conceptions in the Study of Foreign Policy," *International Studies Quarterly*, Vol. 14, No. 8. (September 1970), 245–6.

26 Ibid., 246.

27 "External Relations: A Global Task," Europa—the official Website of the European Union, http://europa.eu/pol/ext/index_en.htm

28 See the official EU website, http://eeas.europa.eu/policies/index_en.htm

29 Chen Zhimin, "Nationalism, Internationalism, and Chinese Foreign Policy," *Journal of Contemporary China*, Vol. 14, No. 42. (February 2005), 45.

30 Julia E. Sweig, "A New Global Player: Brazil's Far-flung Agenda," *Foreign Affairs*, Vol. 89, No. 6. (November/December 2011), 173–84.

31 Fen Osler Hampson and Paul Heinbecker, "The 'New' Multilateralism of the Twenty-First Century," *Global Governance*, Vol. 17, No. 3. (2011), 302.

32 John Williamson, "A Short History of the Washington Consensus," Institute for International Economics, September 2004. http://www.iie.com/publications/papers/williamson0904-2.pdf

33 John Williamson, "Is the 'Beijing Consensus' Now Dominant?" *Asia Policy*, No. 13. (January 2012): 1–16. As Williamson explains, Joshua Cooper Ramo coined the term "Beijing Consensus" in 2004. See Ramo, *The Beijing Consensus* (London: Foreign Policy Centre, 2004).

34 David Rothkopf, "Free-market evangelists face a lonely fate," *Financial Times*, 31 January 2012, http://www.ft.com/cms/s/0/09aa8e5a-4919-11e1-954a-00144feabdc0.html#axzz1npPztVuY

35 Ibid.

36 Steve Schifferes, "G20 leaders seal US$1tn global deal," *BBC News*, 2 April 2009, http://news.bbc.co.uk/2/hi/business/7980394.stm

37 See "Leaders' statement from G20 summit in London," *BBC News*, 2 April 2009, http://news.bbc.co.uk/2/hi/business/7979606.stm

38 Steve Schifferes, "G20 leaders seal US$1tn global deal."

39 Nicholas Eberstadt, "Power and Population in Asia: Demographics and the Strategic Balance," Policy Review No. 123, Hoover Institution Publications, Stanford University, February 1, 2004, http://www.hoover.org/publications/policy-review/article/6298

40 World Bank data from the official website, http://data.worldbank.org/country/china and http://data.worldbank.org/country/india

41 A demographic dividend refers to the economic advantages accruing to countries with a rising number of working-age adults in the total population.

42 Michael Wines and Sharon LaFraniere, "New Census Finds China's Population Growth Has Slowed," *The New York Times*, 28 April 2011, A11.

43 Nicholas Eberstadt, "The Dying Bear," *Foreign Affairs* Vol. 90, No. 6 (November/December 2011): 100.

44 Michele Gragnolati et al, "Becoming Old in an Older Brazil: Implications of Population Aging on Growth, Poverty, Public Finance, and Service Delivery," Report of the World Bank's Brazil Human Development Team, Development Department, Latin America and the Caribbean Region, April 2011:1 http://siteresources.worldbank.org/BRAZILINPOREXTN/Resources/3817166-1302102548192/Brazil_Aging_Full_Eng_final.pdf

45 Ibid., iii.

46 Nicholas Eberstadt, "Power and Population in Asia: Demographics and the
    Strategic Balance," op. cit.

Bibliography

Acemogu, Daron, et al. "The Rise of Europe: Atlantic Trade, Institutional Change
    and Economic Growth." Sloan School of Management, Massachusetts Institute
    of Technology, Working Paper No. 4269–02 (November 2002). http:// papers.
    ssrn.com/sol3/papers.cfm?abstract_id=355880
Armstrong, David. *Revolution and World Order: The Revolutionary State in
    International Society.* (Oxford: Clarendon Press, 1993).
BBC News. "Leaders' statement from G20 summit in London." 2 April 2009.
    http://news.bbc.co.uk/2/hi/business/7979606.stm
Bull, Hedley. *The Anarchical Society: A Study of Order in World Politics.* (New
    York: Columbia University Press, 1977).
Ciambra, Andrea. "'Normative Power' Europe: Theory and Practice of EU
    Norms." Jean Monnet Working Paper No. 64. (July 2008). http://www.fscpo.
    unict.it/EuroMed/jmwp64.pdf
Eberstadt, Nicholas. "The Dying Bear." *Foreign Affairs*, Vol. 90, No. 6.
    (November/December 2011), 95–108.
—"Power and Population in Asia: Demographics and the Strategic Balance."
    Policy Review No. 123, Hoover Institution Publications, Stanford University
    (1 February 2004). http://hoover.org/publications/policy-review/article/6298
European Union. "External Relations: A Global Task." http://europa.eu/pol/ext/
    index_en.htm
—http://eeas.europa.eu/poliices/index_en.htm
Fox, William T. R. *The Superpowers: The United States, Britain, and the Soviet
    Union—Their Responsibility for Peace.* (New York: Harcourt, Brace & Co., 1944).
—"The Super-powers: Then and Now." *International Journal*, Vol. 35, No. 3.
    (Summer 1980), 417–36.
Gilpin Robert. *War and Change in World Politics.* (Cambridge: Cambridge
    University Press, 1981).
Gragnolati, Michele, et al. "Becoming Old in an Older Brazil: Implications of
    Population Aging on Growth, Poverty, Public Finance, and Service Delivery."
    Report of the World Bank's Brazil Human Development Team, Development
    Department, Latin America and the Caribbean Region (April 2011). http://
    siteresources.worldbank.org/BRAZILINPOREXTN/Resources/3817166–
    1302102548192/Brazil_Aging_Full_Eng_final.pdf
Hampson, Fen Osler and Paul Heinbecker. "The 'New' Multilateralism of the
    Twenty-First Century." *Global Govenance*, Vol. 17, No. 3. (2011), 299–310.
Holsti, K. J. "National Role Conceptions in the Study of Foreign Policy."
    International Studies Quarterly, Vol. 14, No. 8. (September 1970), 233–309.
International Monetary Fund. "Brief History." http://imf.org/external/about/
    history.htm
Kim, Samuel S. "China's Path to Great Power Status in the Globalization Era."
    Asian Perspective, Vol. 27, No. 1. (2003), 35–75.

Kupchan, Charles A. et al. (eds) *Power in Transition: The Peaceful Change of International Order*. (New York: United Nations University Press, 2001).

Legro, Jeffrey W. *Rethinking the World: Great Power Strategies and International Order*. (Ithaca: Cornell University Press, 2005).

Maddison, Angus. *The World Economy: Historical Statistics*. (Paris: OECD, 2003).

Middle Powers Initiative. http://www.middlepowers.org/index.html

O'Neill, Jim. "Building Better Economic BRICS." Global Economics Paper No. 66 (November 2001). http://www2.goldmansachs.com/our-thinking/brics/brics-reports-pdfs/build-better-brics.pdf

Ramo, Joshua Cooper. *The Beijing Consensus*. (London: Foreign Policy Centre, 2004).

Responsibility to Protect Coalition. "History and Timeline of R2P." http://r2pcoalition.org/content/view/22/48/

Rothkopf, David. "Free market evangelists face a lonely fate." *Financial Times*. (31 January 2012). http://www.ft.com/cms/s/0/09aa8e5a–4919–11e1–954a–00144feabdc0.html#axzz1npPztVuY

Schifferes, Steve. "G20 leaders seal $1tn global deal." *BBC News*, 2 April 2009. http://news.bbc.co.uk/2/hi/business/7980394.stm

Sweig, Julia. "A New Global Player: Brazil's Far-flung Agenda." *Foreign Affairs*, Vol. 89, No. 6. (November/December 2010), 173–84.

Tammen, Ronald L. et al. *Power Transitions: Strategies for the 21st Century*. (New York: Chatham House, 2000).

United Nations Charter, Preamble. http://www.un.org/en/documents/charter/preamble/shtml

United Nations Resolution 678. http://www.un.org/docs/scres/1990/scres90.htm

Watts, John. "Putin cracks down on protesters after election victory." *Human Events*, Vol. 68, No. 9. (12 March 2012), 7.

Wendt, Alexander. "Anarchy is What States Make of It: The Social Construction of Power Politics." *International Organization*, Vol. 46, No. 2. (Spring 1992), 391–425.

Williamson, John. "A Short History of the Washington Consensus." Institute for International Economics (September 2004). http://www.iie.com/publications/papers/williamson0904–2.pdf

Wines, Michael and Sharon LaFraniere. "New Census finds China's Population Growth Has Slowed." *The New York Times*, 28 April 2011: A11.

World Bank. "Brief History." http://web.worldbank.org/WBSITE/EXTERNAL/EXTABOUTUS/0,,contentMDK:20653660~menuPK:72312~pagePK:51123644~piPK:329829~theSitePK:29708,00.html

—"Data on China." http://data.worldbank.org/country/china

—"Data on India." http://data.worldbank.org/country/india

World Trade Organization. "Brief History." http://www.wto.org/english/thewto_e/whatis_e/inbrief_e/inbr01_e.htm

Zhimin, Chen. "Nationalism, Internationalism, and Chinese Foreign Policy," *Journal of Contemporary China*. Vol. 14, No. 2. (February 2005), 35–53.

CHAPTER TWO

The Global Leadership of the USA and the Emerging Powers

Norma C. Noonan

Perhaps the most important strategic question for the USA in the twenty-first century is whether it will remain the preeminent global leader or even among the top five global leaders by mid-century. American power and influence remain but are perhaps on a slow decline. Some scholars view the financial crisis of 2008 as a pivotal moment in the unraveling of the American era.[1] Others believe that the American-led era ended earlier as a result of longer trends rather than any single crisis.[2] The rapidly emerging powers, such as China, India, Brazil, and Russia (BRIC), have garnered considerable attention. China in particular is often mentioned as the next preeminent global superpower, because of its economic growth rate and huge population. India is also mentioned as a possible global superpower because of its rapid growth and highly educated, technologically sophisticated stratum within its huge population. Some argue that the USA will stay the course as the leading power but needs to make major strategic and tactical corrections to restore and maintain global leadership.[3] Thomas Barnett maintains that the USA must come up with a new strategic plan in order to remain a global leader and lays out a twelve step strategy to achieve that goal.[4] Thomas Friedman and Michael Mandelbaum are also among fervent advocates of a redefined US strategy to maintain its preeminence.[5] Fareed Zakaria argues that the USA is not in decline but believes others are rising so that the international arena is changing.[6] Robert Kagan questions whether the USA is declining and believes that the decision as to its future as a global power remains in American hands.[7] Zbigniew Brzezinski argues that the "waning of the American dream" has implications for the global power of the US; he argues effectively that America's global power may depend on its ability to solve its many problems at home.[8] Joseph Nye argues that "America is not in absolute decline, and, in relative terms, there is a reasonable probability that it will remain more powerful than any other country in the coming decades."[9] No one has all the answers, and recommended solutions vary. Innovation and creativity are often cited as keys to revitalization of the economy and to rebirth of the American spirit in the years to come.

Most of the dialogue about the future of the USA has occurred among analysts and strategists who suggest possible courses of action for the USA to pursue. Little of the dialogue can be heard among policymakers who tend to focus on immediate problems and crises. The debates about the decline of American power, the rising power of China, the growing technological presence of India, and the evolving nature of globalization, have not deeply penetrated the consciousness of the American public. One is reminded of the United Kingdom after World War Two when it was no longer a dominant power, but the British public thought of the British Empire as secure and steadfast.

The concept of American "exceptionalism" also clouds popular judgment. Although there are various interpretations of exceptionalism, the term conveys the image of a USA that is special, unique, and not subject to the normal trajectories which have affected other historically great powers such as the Roman Empire or the British Empire. Michael Hunt argues that powerful countries are not likely to reflect on their possible decline.[10] Exceptionalism also influences the way the USA behaves in the international arena. The USA usually accepts international norms of behavior but sometimes sees itself as the final arbiter of acceptable behavior in the international arena.[11] Madeline Albright offers an interesting perspective on American views of the right of the USA to decide on its own standards of international behavior; she concludes: "Though America may be exceptional, we cannot demand that exceptions be made for us."[12]

Mark Hertzgaard has called the USA a "parochial superpower."[13] This label fits well the indifference of a majority of Americans to the rest of the world. Although Americans engage in tourism, only a relatively small percentage of the population travels to foreign destinations.[14] Although American introspection about its "decline" has been present for decades, there is little attempt by average Americans to discover what is happening in the rest of the world or to examine how the rest of the world perceives international developments. Many Americans are unconcerned about events in the world except when there is an international catastrophe, such as a tsunami or earthquake, or when the USA is directly involved in a foreign country, such as Iraq or Afghanistan. Americans willingly buy inexpensive foreign-made products, and they may wonder why manufacturing of consumer goods seems to have declined in the USA but give little thought to the connection between the two phenomena.

The historic isolation of the nineteenth century also plays a role in American parochialism. When Mark Twain spoke of "innocents abroad," he was thinking of the nineteenth century tendency of Americans to remain aloof from the world. When they emerged from their cocoon in the early twentieth century, they were surprised by what they found.[15] After World War Two, the USA engaged with the rest of the world to combat the spread of communism. But, after the collapse of the Soviet Empire, the USA became more ambivalent about collaboration. The "go-it-alone" approach of the George W. Bush administration (2001–9) reflects the legacy of isolationism combined with a desire to maintain US primacy in the world. Policy focused on military supremacy and, not infrequently, reflected indifference to the will or wishes of allies.[16] The Obama administration (2009–) has been more inclined toward a multilateral approach, but elements of a "go-it- alone" approach persist. Evidence of greater emphasis on multilateralism can be found in the efforts to tackle the global financial crisis of 2008. The USA and other leading economic powers in the Group of 8 (G8) expanded consultations to include the Group of 20 (G20) states, an acknowledgement that the crisis was too severe to be handled by only a few states.[17] Whereas earlier the G20 was primarily a meeting of finance ministers and governors of central banks, after 2008 the G20 held summits at which heads of government or heads of state represented the members.[18]

Arguments about the USA's decline as a superpower rest not only on the changing world but also on American attitudes. Friedman and Mandelbaum maintain that Americans have become complacent about declining conditions in the country and argue that the USA must overcome that mindset if it is to remain a superpower.[19] Acquiescence to decline can also be found in US predictions about when China will overtake the USA as the world's largest economy.[20] Although some analysts predict and lament the decline of the USA, others see the USA as the major exception to the "decline and fall" syndrome. Only the unfolding reality in the decades to come will reveal the accuracy of the contradictory predictions. Whether or not the United States is in decline is not certain, but other states are rapidly emerging as global powers, changing the dynamics of the international order. The focus of this chapter is an overview of US relations with rising and established powers.

The Post-World War Two Context of US Superpower Status

Most Americans alive in the twenty-first century have lived virtually their entire lives in the era when the USA has been a superpower, a role it assumed after World War Two. Prior to that time, the USA was relatively passive in the global arena, although active in the western hemisphere, the Philippines, and a few other areas. The USA emerged from World War Two, as the pre-eminent power in the world. Most of the great powers of Europe were greatly weakened by two major wars over the span of thirty years. The closest rival was the USSR, which emerged as a military power after 1945, even though its economy lagged behind its military capabilities.

The Cold War was a competition for the allegiance of states throughout the world. The competition was bipolar: a struggle between the leading democratic, capitalist state (the USA) and the leading Marxist-Leninist socialist state (the USSR). Although numerous second rank powers associated with either the USA or the USSR, some important states remained non-aligned, including India. There were no clearly ascendant rivals to the two military superpowers. Some newly independent states used the dynamics of the Cold War to play the two superpowers against each other in order to maximize aid to their countries. Although the Cold War posed military and political risks, there was simplicity in the bipolar world, particularly during the first decade when tight bipolarity existed. Americans often viewed the world in stark terms: states were either with us or against us. The term "Unamerican" arose within the USA and was used to denounce those who appeared to oppose or question the American way of life. In a mirror-image, the Soviet Union also saw the world in stark terms and sometimes classified states either as "*nashi* (ours)" or "*vashi* (yours)." The bipolarity of the Cold War, already attenuated by the 1960s and 1970s, eroded further during the Gorbachev era of "new thinking" in Soviet foreign policy and *perestroika* and *glasnost* within the USSR.[21] Bipolarity abruptly ended when the USSR imploded at the end of 1991. Although the Russian Federation (RF), created in 1991, inherited the military weapons of the USSR and arguably Soviet military might, it was faced with greatly diminished economic resources and a reduced population. Russia remained a military superpower, but its overall status declined, especially during the extreme economic reverses of the tumultuous 1990s.

In the early 1990s, Americans were lulled into complacency, believing that the USA was the sole, surviving superpower. Charles Krauthammer referred to this as a "unipolar moment."[22] Secretary of State Madeline Albright was quoted as stating that the USA was the one "indispensable power."[23] It was a fleeting moment. Arguably, the 1990s may have been the highpoint for the USA as a superpower, although others point to the period between 1945 and 1970 as the "golden era" of American power.[24]

But the world was rapidly becoming more complex in several ways: (1) the rise of new economic powers, (2) increasing globalization and interdependence, and (3) the growing threat of terrorism from extremist groups around the world. Most advanced countries, including the US, have experienced serious terrorism within their borders, whether the massive destruction of the Twin Towers in New York on 9/11/01 or periodic terror in large cities such as Moscow and London. Terrorism has struck countries in Asia as well as in Europe and the US. No area is immune from such attacks. As the chapter explores the relationship between the USA and the rising power, it is important to keep in mind the complexity of the contemporary world.

US-China Relations in the Twenty-first Century

Among the rising powers, China is the country with which the USA is most intricately engaged. China is also the state considered most likely to assume preeminent superpower status in the near future. Robert Shapiro argues that China and the USA are presently the two indispensable powers.[25] Kagan and others have referred to the "G2" (China and the US).[26] China's economic growth has been one of the great success stories of the late twentieth and early twenty-first centuries. In the late 1970s, after the death of Mao Zedong, China, under the leadership of Deng Xiaoping, injected capitalist elements into its socialist economy. The USA was one of the first Western states to open its doors to Chinese manufacturing and products, but only after Japan had pioneered an economic relationship with China. China's economic expansion was initially fuelled by its cheap labor and ability to manufacture goods that appealed to consumers in Japan and the USA. By the first decade of the twenty-first century, the American and Chinese economies were intricately intertwined. Americans bought Chinese consumer products, and China invested its profits in the USA. By 2010, China's annual exports to the USA exceeded imports by US$273 billion.[27] China's trade with the USA tops that with all other countries by a wide margin.[28] The runner-up is Japan, whose 2010 trade with China totaled US$297.8 billion (as contrasted with US$385.3 billion with the USA).[29] Perhaps more significant is the fact that Japan has a positive trade balance with China. US-China trade statistics can be interpreted from differing perspectives. In 2005, Susan Shirk noted that 40 percent of US consumer goods came from China.[30] Taking a broader definition of consumer goods that includes services and durable goods, a 2011 study indicated that only about 2.7 percent of US expenditures for consumer goods come from China.[31]

China has had a positive trade balance for two decades; by the early twenty-first century, China had the largest foreign currency reserves in the world—an estimated US$1 trillion.[32] China invested profits from foreign exports in financial products, such as US treasury bonds as well as direct foreign investment in the USA and other states. As of June 2012, China possessed almost ¼ of US foreign-held debt, rendering it America's largest single foreign creditor, with approximately US$1.16 trillion.[33]

China's economic growth rate in the first decade of the twenty-first century eclipsed that of most Western countries, which were treading water or growing very slowly, especially after the 2008 global recession. China's growth has also been impacted by the 2008 fiscal crisis; China may even have a negative trade balance in 2012.[34]

Shapiro has argued that the USA and China are likely to "set much of the course of globalization" in the near future; he states that "globalization will have an eastern and a western pole."[35] Although China's engagement with the global economy transformed China within a relatively brief period, Shapiro notes China's uneven development and the fact that the most advanced industries tend to be foreign owned. Most of the economic growth has occurred in the key coastal regions and major cities; the interior lags far behind its urbanized eastern and southern regions. Domestic production tends to focus on basic goods, which are not of the caliber of export production manufactured mostly at foreign-owned firms.[36] China has become the first- or second-ranked trading partner of advanced and developing nations, a formidable achievement.[37] Shapiro casts a critical eye on China's perhaps overstated accomplishments; he also notes that American problems such as an aging population, growing economic inequality, a low savings rate, and a reliance on foreign capital cloud the US future.[38]

The interdependence of the USA and China is well understood. Both would suffer if trade and investment were cutback or curtailed. As of 2010, China had more than US$11.2 billion in direct investments in the US.[39] Although China is extending its economic outreach to other regions of the world, most other countries are modest trading partners when compared with the USA. Although American pundits may lament dependence on China, some analysts believe that beneath the seemingly unstoppable rise of China lies a relatively weak country. Quinlan argues: "The fact that one of the poorest nations in the world…exports its savings to one of the richest nations on earth has to rank as one of the greatest economic anomalies of all time."[40] There are potential issues which may impede China's rapid economic growth in the future. International firms are finding that the Chinese government has imposed regulations which adversely affect them, and some firms are relocating.[41] Shirk points out that foreign trade constitutes 75 percent of China's GDP, making it "dependent on other countries for its domestic prosperity and stability."[42] Shirk also points to China's problems such as a weak banking system, an increasingly independent educated middle class, growing inequality, and pollution among factors that may threaten the viability of its political system.[43] Despite these problems, China continues to progress as a global economic power.

With its growing power, China is increasingly setting the tone and scope of its interactions with the USA; China is more assertive than earlier.[44] As Quinlan phrased it, "The world's largest debtor nation has less clout when dealing with the world's largest creditor nation…"[45] In the final joint statement of the Hu-Obama Summit in early 2011, China reaffirmed its sovereignty in defining human rights in China and strongly reasserted its perennial claim that Taiwan is part of China.[46] The joint statement reflected a major compromise on the advocacy of human rights in China and of US support for Taiwan. Since formal recognition of the People's Republic of China (PRC) in the 1970s, the USA has walked on a tightrope: officially the USA recognizes only the PRC but maintains extensive unofficial relations with Taiwan. The USA remains the leading champion of Taiwan. The economies of China and Taiwan are increasingly intertwined, even though Taiwan functions politically as if an independent country.[47]

China's foreign outreach has expanded far beyond East Asia, its historic sphere of influence. China is now competing in traditional US areas of influence, including Latin America. The USA has had a strong presence in Asia and in the Pacific Rim and intends to remain a Pacific power. US-China relations are likely to remain an important part of each other's foreign policy focus, but with growing wariness on both sides.

The USA and the New Russia

Late twentieth century American history was intertwined with that of the Union of Soviet Socialist Republics. When the USSR collapsed in December 1991, a new relationship had to be forged with the Russian Federation and with the fourteen other states that emerged from the Soviet Union. Even though Russia is included in the BRIC, doubts persist whether in fact it is a rising power. Russia has many strengths, such as natural resources, a highly developed military, and a well-educated population, but its economic development since 1992 has been checkered and disappointing.[48] The major cities are showplaces, but the rest of the country is unevenly developed. Despite a well-educated population, Russia has not achieved distinction in manufacturing or innovation in the post-Soviet era. Russia has found it difficult to attract foreign investment.[49] Some of its work in science and software development is peerless, but those strengths have not been translated into making the country a technological giant. President Dmitri Medvedev (2008–12) aspired to modernize the economy and bring it more fully into the technological age despite obstacles such as political cronyism, corruption, a weak judicial system, and a slowly developing parliamentary system, but remained optimistic.[50] Vladimir Putin, President (2000–8), Prime Minister (2008–12) and President (2012–), has laid out an ambitious plan for Russia's future development to make it more competitive in the rapidly changing world. Russia has considerable potential as an emerging power, but weak property rights legislation, corruption, and the paucity of exportable consumer goods have limited its attractiveness for investment by developed countries. Plans for development of a center of innovation at Skolkovo, sometimes called Russia's "Silicon Valley," offers hope for future progress.[51] Optimism and plans by the leadership have not sufficed to persuade observers that Russia will be a major player in the twenty-first century.

The relationship between the USA and the Russian Federation is complicated, which is not surprising given the Cold War. Although both countries aspired to build a new relationship in the 1990s and early twenty-first century, results have been disappointing. There have been ups and downs, but on balance relations have been at best lukewarm. Cooperation exists in specific areas, such as nuclear arms reduction and arms control, joint scientific projects, and space exploration, but broadly-based collaboration in the international arena is absent. Russia is part of Europe but not a member of NATO or the EU. The Russian Federation is represented in both bodies, and its views are respected, but it has no direct voice in decision making. The USA has less interest in Russia than in China, both because of China's rapid growth and because the two economies are conjoined. American policy pundits view Russia as an important regional power with which cooperation is possible in defined areas. Although they sometimes act in concert, Russia and the USA differ in their approach to important international issues, including Iran, Syria, Israel and other Middle Eastern countries. Since 1992, Russian leaders have sought to be equal partners with the USA and have been frustrated by their second-level status among American policymakers. Nonetheless, the USA was the prime mover in the inclusion of Russia into the Group of 7 (G7), thus transforming it into the G8.

Russia's greatest assets in the international arena are its natural resources, especially gas and oil. These contribute to its being a valuable partner for energy-hungry European states, but not as much for the USA. Russia supplied the EU with 31 percent of its total crude oil in 2010.[52] In contrast, Russia ranks 8th among countries from which the USA buys crude oil.[53] The US oil imports from Canada are more than six times greater than from Russia. Trade between the RF and the USA in 2010 totaled US$31.7 billion, of which US imports from Russia constituted US$25.7 billion and exports to Russia only US$6 billion.[54] Russia is ranked 32nd among countries to whom the USA exports. Those statistics explain some reasons why the USA has not viewed Russia as a crucial partner. Russia's status as a rising power, if it can address some of its problems, will render it an important player in the twenty-first century.

The USA and the European Union

Historic and continuous ties with the countries of Europe, especially those in the EU, are often taken for granted in the USA. Although not a member of the EU, the US economy is connected with the EU through joint ownership of various enterprises and direct foreign investment. At the end of 2009, the USA had approximately US$2 trillion of direct investment in Europe.[55] Germany, France, and the United Kingdom, in particular, have substantial direct foreign investment in the USA. Through NATO the USA has military cooperation with most EU members. The EU, as a whole, constitutes a formidable economic and political presence, despite the economic reverses some members have suffered since the 2008 global financial crisis.[56] Some EU members, most notably Germany, have recovered since 2008.[57] In the early 2000s, differences over policy, especially in respect to the Iraq War, damaged the US working relationship with several EU governments, but policy and governmental changes have resolved some earlier disagreements. Among the twenty-seven EU member states, the United Kingdom is perhaps the closest ally of the USA, followed by Germany and Italy. Relations with France, the oldest ally of the USA have sometimes been checkered, but during the administration of President Nicolas Sarkozy (2007–12), the climate improved. Although some analysts dismiss the power and significance of the EU, T. R. Reid views the EU as a formidable economic machine.[58] Quinlan, on the other hand, is inclined to view Europe as a region with declining power and influence; according to Quinlan, "… the twilight of Europe and Japan and their diminished capacity to affect the global agenda is just as important as the much-told story of the rise of China and India…"[59]

The US and Japan: Long-term Allies

The Japanese-US relationship moved from enmity in World War Two to a close alliance in the post-war era. Japan is a key Asian partner for the USA. Like China, Japan has invested heavily in the USA and ranks second only to China in the total value of its American debt holdings.[60] Over the years, the partnership had some discordant notes, mostly due to trade issues, but the partnership is firm and likely to remain very important in the twenty-first century. Both countries have had, and seek to retain, a major role in Asia. Japan, China, and the USA are the most prominent players in East Asia, and their interactions, even when bilateral, have significant implications for all three countries. China and the USA have an important partnership and also a developing rivalry. Japan's relationship with China is complicated by their history and has deteriorated in recent years because of territorial issues and because of Japan's refusal to apologize, in a way acceptable to China, for its aggression in the 1930s and 1940s. Japan was one of the first major powers to launch a strong economic relationship with the PRC in the 1970s; Japan pioneered the path which the USA followed. As Chinese economic and political power expands, US-Japanese cooperation may be essential to keeping Chinese influence in check. Japan has suffered numerous setbacks since the 1990s that cloud its political and economic future. Most recently, the earthquake, tsunami, and nuclear accident of 2011 have adversely affected Japan's rebounding economic system.[61] Overall, the Japanese-US strategic partnership remains important for both states in the years ahead.

The USA and Other Potential Global Powers: India and Brazil

India, the world's largest democracy, is another rising power of the twenty-first century. India has an enormous population; India's well-educated millions are among the most technologically advanced people in the world, but India also has millions of people who live in poverty and are poorly educated. India manufactures products the world wants, but not to the extent of the Chinese economy.

Despite shared democratic ideals, India and the USA did not always have a smooth relationship after India's independence from Britain in 1947. In recent years, India and the USA have been reliable partners, but have differences on several issues, including India's development of nuclear power and US policy toward Pakistan and Afghanistan.[62] Trade grew steadily in the first decade of the twenty-first century as did direct foreign investment in each other's country. Ties between India and the USA are especially strong in technology, which Prime Minister Manmohan Singh (2004–) identified as a focal area of cooperation.[63] Many Indians are employed by US corporations within the USA and within India.[64] Indian firms are expanding their hiring of Indian talent, and American students have gone to India to pursue internships in technology, management, and other fields sponsored by a program called "Passport to India."[65] Although many analysts believe that China is the rising superpower, some analysts suggest that India will win the race in the long run.[66] Both for strategic reasons and for their commitment to democracy, it would be incumbent on the USA and India to maintain a strong relationship.

For a long time, the USA has been the single most powerful country in the western hemisphere. Since the Monroe Doctrine was pronounced in the early nineteenth century, the USA has been an influential force in Latin America. Brazil in recent years has emerged as a significant power, although not yet a superpower. Brazil's economic growth in recent decades has been impressive. With a population of almost 200 million, Brazil's possibilities should not be underestimated. Brazil's economy weathered well the global recession of 2008 and has continued to grow at an impressive annual rate. Brazil is able to attract foreign direct investment, and over the years the USA has been the largest foreign investor in Brazil.[67] Brazil and the USA have generally cordial relations but have disagreements over specific issues such as nuclear non-proliferation and the non-return of American-born children taken to Brazil by a non-custodial parent.[68] Argentina is probably the only South American neighbor that may be able to check the rise of Brazil, although Argentina has faced many internal problems. Brazil may play a role in China-US relations in the future. China has expanding interests in South America, a region the USA has long taken for granted. In 2010, China surpassed the USA as Brazil's leading trade partner.[69]

The Evolving Role of the USA in World Affairs: Prospects and Perspectives

The USA has played a dominant role in world affairs since 1945. Its future role is in question. It would not be easy for the USA to disentangle itself from global obligations, nor does the USA appear to want disentanglement. Politicians debate the future role in world politics at the same time that analysts predict the changing role of the USA in a world of rising powers.[70] Kori Schake believes that globalization as experienced until the early twenty-first century was an American phenomenon.[71] Now globalization has assumed new forms as the world becomes increasingly "flat" in Thomas Friedman's famous description.[72]

Schake offers one of the most articulate summaries of why the USA may retain her superpower status into the foreseeable future:

American power is of a unique kind, converging as it does economic, military, diplomatic, linguistic, and cultural elements in a self-reinforcing mix. It has been a juggernaut of influence, advancing the globalization and Americanization of the international order. The dynamism of American power has the potential to remain at the apogee of the international order, setting rules and ensuring the well-being of Americans for the foreseeable future.[73]

This optimistic prediction may be challenged by declinists or skeptics. Barnett, for example, believes that the USA can continue as a superpower only if it develops a master plan for the future.[74] Quinlan argues that the American-led era of globalization ended in 2007 when the global financial crisis began to erupt and then spread in 2008.[75] Some analysts see the 2008 financial crisis as a watershed in the decline of US global supremacy.

In particular, Michael Mandelbaum argued that the events of 2008 would change forever the amount the USA would invest in foreign policy, especially in foreign wars. Mandelbaum calculated the cost of US military involvement in Iraq and Afghanistan in the years since 9/11/2001 and concluded that such expenditures were unlikely to occur in the future.[76]

Michael Hunt, writing in 2007 before the financial crisis, argued that the USA was likely to remain a hegemonic power, although he too did not rule out decline.[77] Hunt pointed out the risks for the USA of continuing a dominant role and of diminishing its role. Although critical of US hegemony, he warned of objective dangers such as the proliferation of nuclear weapons, global environmental damage, and other issues that might necessitate a continuing active role. Hunt strongly recommended that the USA act in collaboration with other partners instead of alone as it did during the G.W. Bush administration.[78] On balance, Hunt recommends an active, yet more limited and collaborative, US presence in world affairs.

Is a new, multipolar globalization on the horizon? Meetings of the G8 and G20 testify to ongoing consultations among the world's major economic powers. Consultation and collaboration can take many forms. In the recent past, the USA has been the leader of the G8. The enhanced role of the G20 attests to the recognition that a few well-established powers cannot resolve issues in isolation. In 2009, it was agreed that the G20 would become the main economic council of the major states, in effect diminishing the power of the G8.[79] The G20 members (nineteen states plus the EU) represent 90 percent of the global GDP and 80 percent of the world's production.[80] It may be harder to get consensus among the larger G20, than among the G8, because of differences in priorities and objectives among established and rising powers. Kagan, for example, warns that a multipolar world may be a less stable world.[81] Brzezinski similarly warns that the world after an American decline is likely to be a more chaotic world.[82]

In the past half century, the USA has led from a position of pre-eminence in world affairs. It is not easy to share power after one has been a dominant superpower. It will necessitate a reconceptualization of positions and attitudes. President Barack Obama (2009–) received considerable criticism, especially from Republican rivals, for his accommodating stance in international relations. Obama has been more cognizant of the changing global situation than some of his Republican contemporaries. Several declared Republican presidential contenders in 2011 and early 2012 advocated a de facto return to the Bush era "go-it-alone" practice.

Whether another dominant power will emerge in the near future is uncertain. China, the most likely candidate, has several weaknesses, including uneven development, reliance on foreign trade, and an archaic political system. If the USA is part of a multipolar world, as a significant but not dominant power, it may have to rely on its diplomatic skills more than in the past. Negotiating with equals is perhaps more difficult than leading as the unchallenged superpower. The USA has had an "ambivalent attitude" toward negotiation in the past, but good negotiating skills may be invaluable in the multipolar world. Richard Solomon and Nigel Quinney state that composite American negotiating behavior is perceived by others as four-faceted: business-like, legalistic, moralistic, and hegemonic.[83] American negotiators, on the other hand, perceive themselves as "pragmatic and fair-minded."[84] The dissonance in perception may be a significant problem once the USA is no longer the dominant superpower and needs to be willing to compromise more than in the past. The USA may also have to improve its diplomatic skills if it wants to become a mediator among competing powers in a multipolar world. Brzezinski, in particular, thinks that USA must become "the *balancer* and the *conciliator*" among the major powers in Asia.[85]

A key to US future leadership in the world may lie in developing new technologies which maintain a competitive advantage even as other powers increase their power. Shapiro argues that although the USA may not invest more than other states in new technology, it has been more skillful in implementing its use; he points to the rise in American productivity vis-à-vis other developed areas, including Europe and Japan.[86] In contrast, Friedman and Mandelbaum point to the areas in which the USA is lagging behind, including math, physics and numerous technological developments.[87] The arguments about the US future position in the world are not easily resolved, since analysts tend to rely primarily on evidence which supports their perspective. There are many variables that may affect the USA and each of the rising powers. It is likely that the USA will remain a major player on the world stage but will be joined by other important powers. The competition is strong as we move through the twenty-first century.

Endnotes

1 Joseph P. Quinlan, *The Last Economic Superpower, The Retreat of Globalization, the End of American Dominance and What We Can Do about It.* (New York: McGraw Hill, 2011), 82.

2 Paul Starobin, *Five Roads to the Future: Power in the New Global Age.* (New York: Penguin Books, 2009), 6–7. Starobin believes that the world "after America" has already come into being.

3 Joshua Kurlantzick, "The Asian Century: Not Quite Yet," *Current History*, Vol. 110, No. 732 (January 2011), 26–31.

4 See Thomas Barnett, *Great Powers: America and the World after Bush.* (New York: G. P. Putnam, 2009), 1 and Ch. 2.

5 See Thomas Friedman and Michael Mandelbaum, *That Used To Be Us: How America Fell Behind the World We Invented and How We Can Come Back.* (New York: Farrar, Strauss, and Giroux, 2011).

6 See Fareed Zakaria, The Post American World: Release Two. (New York: Norton, 2012).

7 See Robert Kagan, *The World America Made.* (New York: Norton, 2012).

8 See Zbigniew Brzezinski, *Strategic Vision: America and the Crisis of Global Power.* (New York: Basic Books, 2012), 37ff.

9 Joseph Nye, http://www.project-syndicate.org/commentary/nye104/English

10 Michael H. Hunt, *The American Ascendancy: How the USA Gained and Wielded Global Dominance.* (Chapel Hill, N.C.: University of North Carolina Press, 2007), 315.

11 For a thorough review of US exceptionalism and international law, see Natsu Taylor Saito, *Meeting the Enemy: American Exceptionalism and International Law.* (New York: New York University Press, 2010).

12 Madeline Albright, *The Mighty and the Almighty: Reflections on America, God, and World Affairs.* (New York: Harper Collins, 2006), 32.

13 Mark Hertsgaard, *The Eagle's Shadow: Why America Fascinates and Infuriates the World.* (New York: Farrar, Strauss, and Giroux, 2002), 3–24.

14 http://www.nomadicmatt.com/travel-blogs/why-americans-dont-travel-overseas/ Only 15 percent of Americans held passports prior to legislation that required passports for Canada and the USA. After that the total was 21 percent.

15 See Mark Twain, *Innocents Abroad.*

16 Barnett, *Great Powers: America…*, 12ff.

17 www.g20.org/en/g20/what-is-g20. The G8 states include Canada, France, Germany, Italy, Japan, Russia, United Kingdom, and the USA, with special representation for the European Union. The G20 include the G8states plus Argentina, Australia, Brazil, China, India, Indonesia, Mexico, Saudi Arabia, South Africa, Republic of Korea, and Turkey, plus special representation for the European Union. The twenty states represent 90 percent of the GDP in the world.

18 One summit was held in 2008, two in 2009, two in 2010, and one in 2011.

19 See Friedman and Mandelbaum, *That Used to Be Us…*, Ch. 1.

20 Charles Kenny, "The Case for Second Place," *Bloomberg BusinessWeek.* (17–23 October 2011), 14–15.

21 *Perestroika* referred to the economic and political restructuring of the USSR undertaken during the Gorbachev years; *glasnost* referred to the more open cultural and political climate, as well as to the revelation of selected political secrets of the Soviet era.

22 Cited in Barnett, *Great Powers: America…*, 12.

23 Madeline Albright as cited in Barnett, 229, and by Dieter Farwick, "The USA of America —Still an Indispensable Power?" World Security Network,

11 December 2007. http://www.worldsecuritynetwork.com/showArticle3. cfm?article_id=15234

24 Quinlan, *The Last Economic Superpower*, 7–10.

25 Robert J. Shapiro, *Futurecast: How Superpowers, Populations, and Globalization Will Change Your World by the Year 2020.* (New York: St. Martin's Griffin Press, 2008), 158.

26 Kagan, *The World America Made*, 68–9.

27 www.census.gov/foreign trade/balance/c5700.html; and https://www.uschina. org/statistic/tradetable.html

28 https://www.uschina.org/statistics/tradetable.html

29 Ibid.

30 Susan L. Shirk, *China: Fragile Superpower*. (New York: Oxford University Press, 2007), 16.

31 http://thinkprogress.org/yglesias/2011/08/09/09/292128/made-in-China-accounts-for-less-than-three-percent-of-American-personal-consumption-expenditures/ The argument is based on the fact that the consumer goods category includes services and durable goods which tend to be made in the US Consumer goods from China tend to include clothing, shoes, and toys.

32 Shirk, *China: The Fragile Superpower*, 6

33 http://www.treasury.gov/resource-center/data-chart-center/tic/Documents/mfh. txt (2012)

34 http://www.reuters.com/article/2011/11/22/us-china-economy-xia-idUSTRE7AL0MK20111122

35 Shapiro, 128.

36 Ibid., 128.

37 Ibid., 129.

38 Ibid., 130–1. Although Shapiro's book was written before 2008, he anticipates well the problems the US faced and was likely to face in the future.

39 Forbes magazine, http://www.forbes.com/sites/toddwoody/2011/05/06/chinas-direct-investment-in-the-us-doubled-in–2010/

40 Quinlan, *The Last Economic Superpower*, 49.

41 Ibid., 77. Quinlan offers quotes from American and European firms about their difficulties in China. Quinlan sees this as part of a growing trend, after the crisis of 2008, for countries to prefer their domestic businesses; see 74–80.

42 Shirk, *China: The Fragile Superpower*, 24.

43 Ibid., 26–34.

44 Yuan-Kang Wang, "China's Growing Strength," http://www.brookings.edu/papers/2010/11_china_taiwan_wang.aspx

45 Quinlan, *The Last Economic Superpower*, 48.

46 Chen-Sen J. Yen, "Sovereignty, Human Rights and China's National Interest," http://www.fpri.org/enoes/201102.yen.china.html

47 For a discussion of the economic relationship, see Scott Kastner, "Does Economic Integration Augur Peace in East Asia," *Current History*, Vol. 110, No. 737, 223ff.

48 See Gulnaz Sharfutdinova, *Political Consequences of Crony Capitalism inside Russia*. (Notre Dame, IN: Notre Dame University Press, 2010).

49 Shapiro, *The Last Economic Superpower*, 158–9.

50 Lyubov Pronina, "Dreams of an iPad Economy," *Bloomberg Business Week*. (7–11 February 2011), 11.

51 www.masterrussian.com/russia/skolkovo.htm

52 European Commission Energy. http://ec.europa.eu/energy/observatory/oil/doc/import/coi/eu-coi-from-extra-eu–2011–01–03.pdf

53 See US Energy Information Administration. Crude Oil and Total Energy Imports. http://205.254.135.24/pub/oil gas/petroleum/data publications

54 See US Department of State. Background Note: Russia. http:/www.state.gov/r/pa/ei/bgn/3183.htm

55 Congressional Research Service: http://www.fas.org/sgp/crs/misc/RS21118.pdf

56 See T. R. Reid, *The United States of Europe*, for discussion of the power of Europe.

57 See Martin Orth, "Economic Recovery in Germany," *Magazin-deutschland.de*, E5, No.6, 2010, 17–20.

58 See Reid, *The United States of Europe*.

59 Quinlan, *The Last Economic Superpower*, 143.

60 http://www.treasury.gov/resource-center/data-chart-center/tic/Documents/mfh.txt (2012)

61 Steven Vogel, "Japan's Post Catastrophe politics," *Current History*, Vol. 110, No. 737. (September 2011), 217–22.

62 See Evan A. Feigenbaum, "India's Rise, America's Interest," *Foreign Affairs*. (March-April 2010).

63 Carnegie Endowment, "Prospects and Challenges for US-India Technology Cooperation": http://carnegieendowmen.org/2010/06/23/prospects-and-challenges-US-india-technology-cooperation/ffi

64 See Thomas Friedman, *The World Is Flat, 3.0: A Brief History of the twenty-first Century*. (New York: Picador, 2007), 126–36 for a detailed discussion of the symbiotic relationship in technology and customer service between the two countries.

65 http://blogs.state.gov/index.php/site/entry/passport_to_india

66 See Daniel Lak, *India Express*. Lak offers extensive arguments why India will emerge as the superpower rather than China.

67 US Department of State: http://www.state.gov/r/pa/ei/bgn/35640.htm

68 It is estimated that there are over sixty children in Brazil who were taken there by a non-custodial parent and not returned to their legal domicile in the USA.

69 See the chapter on Brazil for further discussion of China-Brazil relations.

70 For two differing perspectives, see Kori Schake, *Managing American Hegemony: Essays on Power in a Time of Dominance.* (New York: Oxford University Press, 2007), 135 ff. for a refutation of US decline and Friedman and Mandelbaum, *That Used To Be Us,* for discussion of US complacency about its diminishing status.

71 Schake, *Managing American Hegemony,* 77ff.

72 Friedman, *The World Is Flat: 3.0.*

73 Schake, *Managing American Hegemony,* 187–8.

74 Barnett, *Great Powers: America…,* Ch. 2.

75 Quinlan, *The Last Economic Superpower,* 20.

76 Michael Mandelbaum, *The Frugal Superpower: America's Global Leadership in a Cash-Strapped Era.* (New York: Public Affairs Press, 2010), Ch. 1.

77 Michael H. Hunt, *The American Ascendancy,* 308–15. Hunt prefers the term "hegemony" to other descriptors of the US role.

78 Ibid., 320–24.

79 The G8 states represent about 60 percent of world GDP.

80 No Author, "About G20." http://www.g20.org/about what is g20.aspx.

81 Kagan, *The World America Made,* 83.

82 Brzezinski, *Strategic Vision,* 75ff.

83 Richard Solomon and Nigel Quinney, *American Negotiating Behavior: Wheeler-Dealers, Legal Eagles, Bullies, and Preachers.* (Washington, D.C.: USA Institute of Peace, 2010), 19–45.

84 Ibid., 19–20.

85 Brzezinski, *Strategic Vision,* 185. The italics are Brzezinski's, not this author's.

86 Shapiro, *Futurecast,* 155–7.

87 See Friedman and Mandelbaum, *That Used To Be Us.*

Bibliography

Albright, Madeline. *The Mighty and the Almighty: Reflections on America, God, and World Affairs.* (New York: Harper Collins, 2006).

Bacevich, Andrew J. *The Limits of Power: The End of American Exceptionalism.* (New York: Metropolitan Books, 2008).

Barnett, Thomas J. *Great Powers: America and the World after Bush.* (New York: G. P. Putnam, 2009).

Brzezinski, Zbigniew. *Strategic Vision: America and the Crisis of Global Power.* (New York: Basic Books, 2012).

Carnegie Endowment. "Prospects and Challenges for US-India Technology Cooperation:" http://carnegieendowmen.org/2010/06/23/

prospects-and-challenges-u.s.-india-technology-cooperation/ffi www.census.gov/foreign trade/balance/c5700.html

Congressional Research Service. http://www.fas.org/sgp/crs/misc/RS21118.pdf

European Commission Energy. http://ec.europa.eu/energy/observatory/oil/doc/import/coi/eu-coi-from-extra-eu-2011-01-03.pdf

Farber, David. *What They Think of Us: International Perceptions of the United States since 9/11.* (Princeton, N.J.: Princeton University Press, 2007).

Farwick, Dieter. "The United States of America –Still an Indispensable Power?" World Security Network, December 11, 2007. http://www.worldsecuritynetwork.com/showArticle3.cfm?article_id=15234

Feigenbaum, Evan A. "India's Rise, America's Interest," *Foreign Affairs*, March-April 2010.Vol. 89, No. 2, 76–91.

Friedman, Thomas. The World Is Flat: 3.0: *A Brief History of the 21st Century.* Revised. (New York: Picador, 2007).

Friedman, Thomas and Michael Mandelbaum. *That Used To Be Us: How America Fell Behind the World We Invented and How We Can Come Back.* (New York: Farrar, Strauss, and Giroux, 2011).

Hertsgaard, Mark. *The Eagle's Shadow: Why America Fascinates and Infuriates the World.* (New York: Farrar, Strauss, and Giroux, 2002).

Hunt, Michael H. *The American Ascendancy: How the United States Gained and Wielded Global Dominance.* (Chapel Hill, N.C.: University of North Carolina Press, 2007).

Kagan, Robert. *The World America Made.* (New York: Knopf, 2012).

Kastner, Scott L. "Does Economic Integration Augur Peace in East Asia?" Current History, Vol. 110, No. 737. (September 2011), 223–8.

Kenny, Charles. "The Case for Second Place." *Bloomberg BusinessWeek.* 17–23 October 2011, 14–15.

Kurlantzick, Joshua. "The Asian Century: Not Quite Yet." *Current History*, Vol. 110, No. 732 (January 2011), 26–31.

Kurlantzick, Joshua. "A False Brigade." *Bloomberg BusinessWeek.* 7–13 November 2011, 6–7.

Lak, Daniel. *India Express: The Future of the New Superpower.* (New York: Palgrave MacMillan, 2008).

Ledeneva, Alena V. *How Russia Really Works: The Informal Practices That Shaped Post-Soviet Politics and Business.* (Ithica, N.Y.: Cornell University Press, 2006).

Mandelbaum, Michael. *The Frugal Superpower: America's Global Leadership in a Cash-Strapped Era.* (New York: Public Affairs, 2010).

N. A. http://blogs.state.gov/index.php/site/entry/passport_to_india

—http://www.forbes.com/sites/toddwoody/2011/05/06/chinas-direct-investment-in the u-s-doubled-in–2010/

—http://www.Masterrussian.com/Russia/skolkova.htm

—www.g20.org/en/g20/what-is-g20.

—http://www.reuters.com/article/2011/11/22/us-china-economy-xia-idUSTRE7AL0MK20111122

—http://thinkprogress.org/yglesias/2011/08/09/09/292128/made-in-China-accounts-for-less-than-three-percent-of-American-personal-consumption-expenditures/

—http://www.treasury.gov/resoruce-center/data-chart-center/tic/Documents/mfh. txt (2012)

—https://www.uschina.org/statistics/tradetable.html

—http://usgovinfo.about.com/od/moneymatters/ss/How-Much-US-Debt-Does-China-Own.htm

Nye, Joseph. http://www.project-syndicate.org/commentary/nye104/English

Orth, Martin. "Economic Recovery in Germany." *Magazin-deutschland.de*. E5, No. 6, 2. (December-January 2010), 17–20.

Pronina, Lyubov with Ryan Chilcote. "Dreams of an iPad Economy in Russia." *Bloomberg BusinessWeek*. (7–13 February 2011), 11–12.

Quinlan, Joseph P. *The Last Economic Superpower: The Retreat of Globalization, the End of American Dominance and What We Can Do about It.* (New York: McGraw Hill, 2011).

Reid, T. R. *The United States of Europe: The New Superpower and the End of American Supremacy.* (New York: Penguin Press, 2005).

Saito, Natsu Taylor. *Meeting the Enemy: American Exceptionalism and International Law.* (New York: New York University Press, 2010).

Schake, Kori N. *Managing American Hegemony: Essays on Power in a Time of Dominance.* (Stanford, C.A.: Hoover Institution Press, 2009).

Shapiro, Robert J. Futurecast: *How Superpowers, Populations, and Globalization Will Change Your World by the Year 2020.* (New York: St. Martin's Griffin Press, 2008).

Sharafutdinova, Gulnaz. *Political Consequences of Crony Capitalism inside Russia.* (Notre Dame, IN.: Notre Dame University Press, 2010).

Shirk, Susan L. *China: Fragile Superpower.* (New York: Oxford University Press, 2007).

Solomon, Richard H. and Nigel Quinney. *American Negotiating Behavior: Wheeler-Dealers, Legal Eagles, Bullies, and Preachers.* (Washington, D.C.: United States Institute of Peace Press, 2010).

Starobin, Paul. *Five Roads to the Future: Power in the New Global Age.* (New York: Penguin Books, 2009).

US Department of State. Background Note: Russia. http:/www.state.gov/r/pa/ei/bgn/3183.htm

—http://www.state.gov/r/pa/ei/bgn/35640.htm

US Energy Information Administration. Crude Oil and Total Energy Imports. http://205.254.13.24/pub/oil gas/petroleum/data publications

Vogel, Steven. "Japan's Post-Catastrophe Politics." *Current History*, Vol. 1001, No. 737. (September 2011), 217–22.

Wang, Yuan Kang. "China's Growing Strength, Taiwan's Diminishing Options." http://www.brookings.edu/papers/2010/11_china_taiwan_wang.aspx

Yen Chen-shen J. "Sovereignty, Human Rights and China's National Interest: A Non-Zero Sum Game." http://www.fpri.org/enotes/201102.yen.china.html

Zakaria, Fareed. *The Post-American World: Release Two.* (New York: Norton, 2012).

CHAPTER THREE

Europe: Global Power in the Making

Mary Troy Johnston

What type of a power-in-the-making is Europe? Europe can be viewed as an emerging power, in the sense that it is the first time Europe as a collective power is on the rise. Historically, Europe has been a collection of states, albeit powerful and established ones, since absolutism reached its height in sixteenth- century France and spread to other European countries through the seventeenth century. The Peace of Westphalia in 1648 settled the question that Europe would consist of individual nation states. This construct prevailed until two world wars devastated Europe in a span of just over three decades. The advent of nuclear weapons and their use at the end of World War Two enforced the logic that future wars could be nuclear wars. Europe's resulting existential crisis spurred the decision to create the European Coal and Steel Community (ECSC) in 1952, the first European project that challenged traditional state-bound governmental forms. Six nation-states recast themselves as members of the ECSC, the first supranational organization in history, with the intention of transforming Franco-German rivalry into cooperation. Belgium, the Netherlands, Luxembourg, Italy, France, and Germany (the "Original Six") agreed to surrender sovereignty to an institution named the High Authority which was invested with the authority to make binding decisions on a narrow and legally restricted range of issues related to the coal and steel sector. More than a half-century later, Europe has created a vast array of practices, forms and structures to give flesh to its collective identity, a project that has also served the cause of regional peace.

As a power whose essence is innovation, the practice of statecraft in contemporary Europe does not conform to traditional power models.

Europe does not aspire to military superiority or even to "balancing" power and thus diverges from the well-worn path of other ambitious states. In its quest for reinventing the conduct of international relations, Europe is in the process of challenging a range of preconceptions that condition the reflexes and actions of the USA, and states seeking hegemonic power.[1] To assess the impact of Europe's global role, one must consider the new power currencies of Europe. Thus, this chapter focuses on the theoretical and policy shifts in Europe that reject power projection through military force in favor of utilizing soft power and economic assistance to pursue non-traditional security goals. Is it generally advantageous that Europe has developed multi-level governance to affect its soft power, creating capacities to engage in a variety of decision-making contexts? Does Europe's new currency, the euro, give it an advantage in the global economy? The question of whether Europe is a power in international relations must be adjusted to European preferences. The measure is what kind of standing relative to other emerging powers and the USA does Europe hope to attain with its new approaches? The following analysis addresses the problems and prospects of Europe's unique pursuit of new power capabilities.

For a variety of reasons, the reality of the EU as a global power is hard to grasp. Its international role is so segmented, its power ambitions so non-traditional, its manifestations so numerous that it is possible to miss the cumulative picture and dwell more on its sketchy nature. Ginsberg perceives the difficulty of sizing up "the EU as an international actor," stating that, "...its place in international affairs is new, unorthodox, sui generic (sic), and counterintuitive to those who only see a world of Westphalian states."[2] With so much of its diplomatic work conducted in the background of international relations and the absence of a physical display of an EU military force, and the incremental nature of change in the EU, it is easy to dismiss Europe as pretentious rather than serious. This chapter takes an integrative and dynamic approach to comprehend a Europe that is more than the sum of its parts. The EU exists as a multidimensional international actor which exercises power in a variety of contexts and on a range of issues. Europe has to be viewed in a multi-level context, consisting of states, the regional organization of the EU, a variety of European formations in international relations, for example, Europe in NATO and as a member of different informal groupings, such as the Quartet (Russia, USA, United Nations and EU) that negotiates behind closed doors since 2002 on issues related to the Middle East peace process. Europe comprehends a vast network of relations criss-crossing, double-backing, and circling the globe along national, regional, and international levels, which enhance, both formally and informally, the range of decision-making options and geopolitical influence. The unification of Europe is also an idea that has motivated EU enlargement, inspiring visions of an expansive Europe potentially expanding to Russia and Turkey.

Observers cannot get the full sense of the impact of Europe if they try to categorize or approach the subject with traditional concepts. The concept of the nation-state, even though Europe gave it birth, does not have relevance for multi-ethnic states that submit themselves to regional and international laws. The state is no longer the only, or even the primary source of law on a range of issues. Innovative concepts, like supranationalism, integration, pooled sovereignty, multi-level governance, effective multilateralism and human security, suggest the extent to which Europe is immersed in innovation.

Perhaps the most fundamental difference separating the EU from the USA and emerging powers surrounds understandings of sovereignty. Europeans have been trying to transcend the notion of territorially defined states since Jean Monnet described the "first principle" of the Schuman Proposals in 1950 as "the abnegation of sovereignty in a limited but decisive field," and the resultant ECSC in 1952 as "the first European Community, merging part of its members' sovereignty and subordinating it to the common interest."[3] National sovereignty remains very important for the USA, especially as it relates to external sovereignty. The USA is very keen to project power abroad to protect its sovereign interests and insists on the respect of other countries for its actions taken in "self-defense," even if such actions are controversial, such as the use of drones in countries not at war with the USA. For the newly emerging powers in Asia, Africa, and Latin America, the understanding of sovereignty also tends to be defensive. Sovereignty for them is a principle to establish their independence vis-à-vis powers in a position to block their rise. These countries, as the USA, are very sensitive when it comes to what they see as interference in their internal affairs. For their part, Europeans have been able, relatively speaking, to maintain their lifestyles and free societies, by "pooling sovereignty," a term that conveniently glosses over the fact that member states have given up a significant measure of national sovereignty, even if ostensibly, to gain greater external sovereignty for the European region. The European perspective takes the traditional state-centric approach as an impediment to problem-solving, to the extent that sovereignty concerns undermine international cooperation. Europeans see an excessive preoccupation with sovereignty concerns as working counter to the norms of global responsibility and policies of self-help taking precedence over common cause. Keohane aptly characterizes the significance of the space Europeans have created for innovation for themselves, and just as importantly, in their external relations:

The separation of sovereignty from success creates an opening for innovative institutional thinking, free from the straitjacket of sovereignty. In particular, the fact that European states no longer cling to their external sovereignty provides an opportunity to design new institutional structures for troubled societies, whose structures have failed to provide order and create the basis for economic growth.[4]

The Meaning of Power

In addition to rethinking sovereignty, its innovative approach to security characterizes the New Europe. In no realm more than in the area of security do we see the clearest expression of Europe as a power in the making, presenting a vivid contrast to the attachment of the USA to traditional military notions of security. Varying concepts and preferences as they relate to power are at the root of differences between the USA and Europe. In the wake of public responses to the 2003 Iraq War, Kagan drew the lines provocatively between Europe and the USA in assessing the fallout from the Iraq War, stating, "Opinion polls taken before, during, and after the war have shown two peoples living on separate strategic and ideological planets."[5] He also tapped into the popular vein, reflecting the divergent views of many Americans and Europeans who were drawing upon different security perspectives.

Americans tend to see power in more monolithic terms whereas Europeans see it in more relative terms. The core of the US view is the belief in the importance of preponderant military force in assessing power. As the USA has military superiority, and because US decision-makers tend to understand power as a function of military capability in the tradition of political realism, the idea of power being an absolute arbiter of outcomes does not seem beyond the pale. The unprecedented military strength of the USA reinforces the country's sense of its own exceptionalism. From that unique vantage point, the world is unipolar; the USA is hegemonic.

Europeans tend to see power more in multidimensional terms. De facto power consists of different types. For example, Joseph Nye identifies hard, soft and economic power.[6] Nye's concept of soft power has gained currency in military circles under the rubric of "winning hearts and minds" in the battlefield.[7] Nye has provided an accurate description of the power ambitions of Europeans, to the extent they depend on their diplomatic ties, their "connectedness," to get the outcomes they want.

Europeans have become very skilled at developing soft power resources, fostering relations with other countries by willingly participating in multilateral institutions and creating new ones. Nye, writing during the George W. Bush presidency, described Europeans as "more comfortable with and more adept at using multilateral institutions than Americans."[8] On the initiative of European countries, the International Criminal Court (ICC) came into being in 1998, celebrated as "an historic milestone" with 120 states signing the foundational Rome Statute. The ICC can be seen not only as a soft power outcome but, if it functions well, a generator of soft power. The USA decided to forego this opportunity by refusing to participate in the ICC. Europe's pursuit of "soft power" is especially evident in relations with emerging powers. For example, Europe now engages in regular contact with emerging powers at the summit level, building on the tradition of institutionalized EU summitry, dating back to 1974. When Europe gave up two of its seats on the Executive Board of the IMF to emerging powers, this move must be seen, not as a diminution of Europe's presence but a conscious attempt to trade seats for more influence in that organization, as well as an opportunity to build relations with emerging powers to facilitate cooperation in other multilateral fora.

India now considers itself a soft power, vesting in the European approach to international relations. Russia and China newly seem to be aware of the political advantage that soft power confers. Uncharacteristically, Russia lodged a complaint with the Kyrgyz government over its censorship of Internet coverage of political corruption in Kyrgyzstan, a former Soviet Republic.[9] Despite its own questionable record defending freedom of expression, Russia was able to side with the international lobby opposing government control of media. *The Economist* reported in 2011 that, "over the past decade building soft power has emerged as a new party priority in China." Furthermore, Chinese elites first embraced soft power at an official level, as early as 2003, and the Central Committee noted in 2011, the "conspicuous gains" made as a result of its efforts.[10] China has been promoting the attractiveness of its culture, "softening" language about its power ambitions, investing in a Chinese presence in international media. The press coverage pointedly noted that these efforts stem from these leaders and not, as Nye conceived the source of soft power, from "individuals, the private sector and civil society."[11]

The ability of the EU to wield power depends on how much of these different kinds of power have accumulated in Europe's basket in relation to the "power baskets" of other countries.[12] Effective power also depends on the relevance of the different kinds of power that the EU and USA possess. If military force is the power currency in the world, the USA is a "hyper-power."[13] But, the use of force must be operationalized by the "will" to use force, which in a democracy requires both popular support for and leaders' commitment to wars and other kinds of military interventions. Europeans leaders do not place the same confidence in the use of force to achieve their goals, and their publics do not accord much legitimacy to the use of military approaches to solve the world's problems. In fact, Europeans are more inclined to accept the evolution of a multipolar world as new power contenders emerge onto the world stage. They hold this view in common with BRIC countries, which are determined to realize their opportunities in a world in which power equations are not static. From the European perspective, if power is becoming more widely dispersed, it makes sense to share power.

The European Emphasis on Human Security

Europeans have gleaned different security lessons, based on threats they experienced in their own backyard. The death and destruction throughout the 1990s that ensued with the break-up of the former Yugoslavia impressed the realization that Europeans needed regional security capacities. Certainly, that tragedy was a formative event for Europe, comparable with the psychological reckoning with vulnerability that the USA faced after 9/11. The chaotic state disintegration in the Balkans presented a large-scale humanitarian crisis of a level of horror that Europe had not seen since World War Two. Europeans, as did Americans after 9/11, also had equal reason to revise security conceptions after the break-up of the former Soviet Union, which imploded almost overnight into a plethora of fragile states in close proximity to Europe. Whereas the collapse of the Soviet Union was seen by many in the USA as a victory and as vindication of the Reagan administration policy of outspending the USSR on arms and defeating the Cold War enemy, the fracturing of the Soviet bloc posed huge security challenges for Western Europe, threatening to flood the region with economic refugees, infiltrate the area with criminal networks, unleash the dangers of "loose nukes," and wreak widespread political instability. In October 1991, the EU Commission warned "the new freedoms achieved in central and eastern Europe may lead to such a desire to emigrate as to overwhelm the economic and legal structures of the host countries" in Western Europe.[14] Reflecting on the coup attempt launched by conservative elements of the Communist Party in August 1991, which ended Soviet President Gorbachev's rule and eventually ushered in Yeltsin's presidency, the Commission was uncharacteristically forthcoming, stating:

> The collapse of the Soviet Empire and the abrupt revival of nationalities (for some of whom diaspora is in prospect), introduces an additional element of uncertainty. The collective subconscious is increasingly taking note of these events, with uncertainty quickly giving way to fear.[15]

The potential spill-over effects of political instability in the East could have dealt a death blow to the European post-World War Two order inspired by integration. In face of this profound uncertainty, Europe constructed the threat as emanating from state disintegration in place of the military threat previously posed by the Soviet Union.[16]

The Balkan crisis and Soviet break-up profoundly affected European thinking about security at the same time that European leaders were struck by their lack of capacity for safeguarding regional security. Experientially, Europeans had developed a strong emphasis on human security in contrast to the American stress on national security, which is consistent with a traditional state-based approach. The primacy of human rights in European security thinking elicited a natural negative reaction to human rights abused in the former Yugoslavia. That emphasis can also be understood as having derived from the lessons Europeans learned from their past history of coloni alism and the crimes against humanity committed by several European countries, such as Germany and Italy, during World War Two. To the extent that the USA was a half-hearted participant in colonialism, the country did not embrace human rights primacy as did Europeans attempting to atone for their past. The USA could also insulate itself, relatively speaking, from the atrocities committed during World War Two because Americans, as a whole, were so far removed from the actual scene of the Nazi death camps. In contrast, the primacy of human rights for Germany has been a way for the country to enact socially constructive policies while rescuing its legacy and rehabilitating its image. In stark contrast to Germany, for example, the USA frequently explains its resistance to internalizing international human rights law in terms of the exceptionalism of the country's human rights regime, touting its solid domestic legal foundation and the superiority of its own legal protections. This conviction was so strong during the George W. Bush administration that the USA was willing to press the claim that the USA does not torture prisoners of war or "enemy combatants" as they were officially designated when indeed most of the world recognized US-sanctioned actions, such as water-boarding, as nothing if not torture.

The EU has embraced the concept of human security.[17] Essentially, the concept means that the reason for security actions should be to benefit individuals; *raison humaine* replaces *raison d'état*. This approach is inherently critical of the pursuit of security based on national interests, because of the potentially disastrous humanitarian consequences when each country pursues its own objectives based on the national interest. Proponents of this view reject as flawed the security judgment that war is an effective instrument against terrorists and other "enemies," especially through the unilateral use of force. According to Gropas, "In effect, military alliances and balance of power tactics are no longer considered sufficient" in the 2003 European Security Strategy (ESS); rather the emphasis is on cooperative security.[18] She refers us instead to the EU "triptych" of, "human rights, rule of law, and democratic governance."[19] The notion of human security also subjects war to the test of how much harm is done to individuals. A consensus has begun to emerge in Europe that the USA failed to protect civilians in wars in Afghanistan and Iraq from insurgents and fighters as well as from the accidental and excessive use of force by US military personnel. Consequently, the very population the USA had hoped to mobilize for its cause became alienated. Systematic neglect of the effects of war on the peoples of Iraq and Afghanistan could not be more strongly reinforced than by the failure of the Pentagon to maintain and make public an accurate count of war casualties among Iraqi and Afghan civilians and thus for Americans to be kept in the dark about the human costs of these wars to non-Americans.

The human toll can be measured in more than the loss of life. The 2003 ESS could have served as a warning label for US military policy, "Conflict not only destroys infrastructure including social infrastructure; it also encourages criminality, deters investment and makes normal economic activity impossible."[20] That the opium trade in Afghanistan still thrives with its proceeds supporting terrorists and other criminals, after US troops have been trying to stabilize the country since October 2001, shows the ramp-up of crime in the dark shadows of military interventions. Gretchen Peters makes the case that cooperation between "extremists and narco-traffickers" compromised war efforts, as the failure to stop opium production in Afghanistan led to a deteriorating security situation there. For Peters, "this conflict wasn't about religion, or a clash of civilizations. It was about criminal money, and lots of it."

Protecting the environment also constitutes a human security issue for Europeans. Making the linkage between security and the wellbeing of the environment has taken the USA much longer than Europe. In fact, the BP oil spill in the USA continued for weeks before President Obama framed it as a "security" crisis. As Europeans are prone to assess war in terms of human costs, they tend to be more aware of its environmental impact. Meanwhile, the American public, which tends to support war policy, does not exhibit a consensus on environmental issues. Climate change became a divisive issue in transatlantic relations when the USA did not participate in the Kyoto process to conclude a legally binding regime to reduce carbon emissions to mitigate global warming. Europe has long regarded protecting the environment as a critical security focus for politics. For example, the Green movement in Europe is now more than a quarter of a century old, and most European political parties embrace environmentalism. This is especially true in Germany, which is Europe's leading economy. For followers of eco-politics, whereas the pursuit of power tends to be an abstraction, saving the Earth is not only a harsh reality, but also perhaps a hopeless reality known too late.

Wary of war, Europeans strictly limit their support for military intervention and, when they do use force, justify their actions in human terms. They seek legitimacy by engaging in "cooperative security." Significantly, cooperation includes BRIC countries. The EU India Naval Operation, launched in December 2008, mainly in response to criminality and piracy along the Somali coast, combines defense of international shipping lanes with a humanitarian mission, that of protecting food shipments and assistance to needy Somalis. In March 2011, France and the United Kingdom spearheaded the use of military force to remove Libyan leader Muammar Gaddafi (which this chapter will discuss in more detail later) and framed it as a cooperative security action with humanitarian objectives.

The Euro: A Currency of Power or of Liability?

A new source of economic power for Europe has been the rise of the euro as an international currency. The euro has steadily been competing with the dollar as a transaction and reserve currency. The case of Russia moving its currency reserves into euros is a striking one. The Russian Central Bank reported to the State Duma (Russia's parliament) in 2009 that "about 47.5 percent of the currency assets of the Russian Central Bank were based on the euro, whereas the dollar-based assets made up 41.5 percent."[21] The European Commission Directorate for Economic and Financial Affairs estimated in November 2010 that approximately 329 million individuals in the EU conduct their business in euros. Furthermore, when the use of the euro outside the EU is taken into account, for example by countries that are preparing to join the eurozone, the regional currency has passed up the dollar in some respects. The Commission mentions that the cash value of euro currency holdings around the world has surpassed that of the dollar.[22] Those facts are all the more telling when one considers that the euro as a currency was introduced only in 2002. The euro presents an option besides the dollar as an international currency and offers leverage to central bankers hoping to influence US monetary policy. Other emerging economies have sent signals that they too would like to become less dependent on monetary policy made in Washington, as they float trial balloons suggesting a shift to non-dollar currencies. For example, they have proposed denominating oil transactions in currencies other than the dollar.[23]

The days are over when the USA dictates monetary policy to eurozone countries. European decision-makers have shown autonomy in the policies they have pursued to cope with global financial instability, which hit crisis point in the USA with the collapse of Lehman Brothers on 11 September 2008, and spread quickly to Europe. The USA convinced that liquidity had to be maintained, pursued a "stimulus" policy of pumping money into the American economy and putting pressure on the eurozone countries to do the same. With Germany in the lead, Europeans have pursued a different policy course, refusing to increase money supply at the levels desired by the USA. Nonetheless, they responded to the financial crisis by taking a range of measures. Less than a month after the Lehman Brothers' bankruptcy, EU Finance Ministers met on 7 October 2008, and sought to reassure bank depositors by putting into effect an EU guarantee of bank funds to help stabilize the international financial system. The near collapse of the US financial system and its negative global impact had emboldened European decision-makers. Uncharacteristically, they publicly questioned the US approach. In October 2010, German Economics Minister Rainer Bruderle pointedly criticized the USA when he remarked, "excessive, permanent money creation in my opinion is an indirect manipulation of an exchange rate."[24] Europeans have refused to mute their concern, as they would have done in pre-euro times, over the weak dollar and the artificial advantage it gives to US exports.

Ever since the first signs of their sovereign debt crisis showed up in late 2009, Europeans have insisted on making their own decisions even as financial uncertainty persists. Facing the potential collapse of the eurozone from the Greek debt crisis and fears verging on panic that it would spill-over to other deeply indebted EU countries, the European Central Bank (ECB) took measures to stabilize the situation. Its response, however, was widely criticized for being inadequate. But, Europeans saw themselves as devising solutions to an unprecedented situation, especially their ability to improvise an institutional response from scratch. The ECB managed the crisis by giving troubled banks access to emergency financing and backing. In May 2010, the EU moved forward with a rescue package (bailout), for Greece amounting to 110 billion euros, put together in collaboration with the IMF. Then, it proceeded to create a complex of institutions, to increase the capacities of the EU to prevent future crises, including the European Financial Stability Facility (EFSF), a temporary fund meant to guarantee liquidity in troubled economies while their leaders stabilized their financial situations. The long-term plan hinges on the creation of the European Stability Mechanism (ESM), a permanent fund to replace the EFSF, modeled on the IMF. On 11 July 2011, Finance ministers from the 17 eurozone countries successfully concluded the treaty to establish the ESM. Once the treaty has been ratified by each county, it is expected to go into effect in July 2013. The institution will serve as a prime lender with the contingencies that such assistance is "necessary to ensure the financial stability of the euro area as a whole" and that borrowers are subject to strict conditionality arrangements.[25] The finalization of a second Greek bailout occurred on 14 March 2012. An additional 130 billion euros were approved for Greece by national governments and parliaments in the eurozone, showing the extent to which earlier efforts to resolve the crisis had fallen short.[26]

Throughout the crisis, the EU capitalized on its strengths to coordinate with a variety of institutions at every level with national banks, national governments, and international institutions, including the IMF and the Group of 20. Europeans engaged in multilevel decision-making (in EU parlance "effective multilateralism"), a decisional approach they have helped devise and that they recommend for complex transnational issues. Then IMF Managing Director Dominique Strauss-Kahn made the following assessment in March 2009, "The IMF has also partnered very effectively with the European Union during the crisis-jointly providing balance of payments support to countries in the region."[27] Despite the measures central bankers, international lenders and politicians took to contain the crisis to Greece, it spread next to Ireland, which required a bailout that climbed in seven months to 90 billion euros in November 2010. Meanwhile rating agencies in the USA downgraded the credit worthiness of debt-ridden member countries of the EU.[28] Speculation abounded that Europe's contemptuously named PIIGS, Portugal, Ireland, Italy, Greece and Spain would swamp the eurozone with debt, putting downward pressure on the euro. Speculators continued to push up the costs of government borrowing in the countries they suspected most of financial flagrancy. Fears were rampant that a bond crisis in Europe could precipitate a banking crisis. Politicians in Europe became wedged between domestic political demands and those of the eurozone, leaving German Chancellor Angela Merkel awash in criticism that Germany defaulted in its regional leadership, trying to put off big decisions, while local elections proceeded.

Europe's financial crisis shows that a multilevel context provides both flexibility and an entangling complex of demands. The involvement of the IMF in the crisis can be seen as both positive and negative. To the extent that the IMF could be seen as imposing stiff conditionality arrangements on EU borrowers, criticism could be deflected away from EU decision-makers. However, passing the ball to the IMF, at a time when it was critical to convince markets that EU leaders were competent to manage the strains on the eurozone, proved a negative. Europe did not muster the independence and solidarity that monetary union implies and requires. Furthermore, domestic politics complicated the regional response to the crisis. Anxious markets in Europe spread their volatility to the USA in the first week of September 2011, while nervous governments and global investors awaited a decision by the German Federal Constitutional Court on whether the bailouts that Germany had provided to debtor countries in the EU were constitutional.[29] Germany's highest Court decided affirmatively, but conditioned future aid on the approval of the German parliament, the Bundestag. Eurozone leaders met at summit level, 26 October 2011, with the goal of convincing markets that Europe had a plan in place to bring Greece back to stability and keep financial distress from spreading, a strategy widely reported as "ring fencing."[30] Global markets repeated what had become a familiar pattern, spiking in anticipation of a resolution to the debt crisis and then plunging upon disappointment as the agreement confronted political problems. The summit had produced bold measures, described by the London *Financial Times*, as "a three pronged strategy to put Greece's public finances back on a sustainable basis, to strengthen European banks' balance sheets, and to beef-up the European Financial Stability Facility (EFSF) as a multi-functional rescue vehicle..."[31] Optimism was short-lived when then Greek Prime Minister Papandreou announced that he would hold a national referendum on the terms Europe offered to his country, introducing the prospect of rejection by Greece of a complex rescue package. One headline in October 2011, "Markets surge after eurozone summit deal," was replaced in four days by another, "Greek referendum plan causes global stock market panic."[32]

Relevant to this study is that the summit agreement envisioned consulting with Russia, China and India in an effort to get these countries to contribute to a newly created fund backing up the EFSF, with the idea of leveraging Europe's lending capacity with resources from emerging economies. Initially, "…Beijing, like Moscow, reiterated it would likely take an important role in boosting the European rescue fund through the IMF, in a sign that emerging economies plan on assuming a larger role in the world economy."[33] Once the Greek government was seen to be reneging on its commitments, Chinese and Indian leaders were not hesitant about expressing their concerns. Indian Prime Minister Manmohan Singh observed that "much more needs to be done" for Europe to address its uncertain investment environment.[34]

The continuing crisis demonstrated the failure of political decision-making in Europe to keep pace with the speed of global financial transactions. Capital takes flight with electronic speed whereas consensus building depends on painstaking negotiations fraught with conflicting interests and ideologies. EU officials and politicians have lauded the complex politics of accommodation, counting "the European way" of resolving issues as among its proudest achievements. Delays in taking decisions until trade-offs are made and offering up interim solutions of a partial nature are hallmarks of the EU process, fine-tuned by European politicians as they cobbled together agreements among 27 governments still pursuing distinct national interests with governments accountable to their own electorates. Markets reacted negatively to fractious and reactive decision-making in Europe during the financial crisis, just as they punished the US government for failing to reach a consensus on the debt ceiling in July 2011 with a subsequent downgrading of US debt by ratings agency Standard & Poors on 5 August 2011. The white noise of intra-European and transatlantic political division drowned out the positive signals European decision-makers intended to send as they tried to cope incrementally with what the European press dubbed "the contagion."

At the center of the crisis, Germany tried to hold fast to its economic model based on an economic doctrine of stability, a lesson learned from the hyperinflation of the early 1920s of the Weimar Republic. Conservative German Chancellor Angela Merkel presided over a coalition government whose junior partners were even more opposed to exposing the German economy to the dysfunction of peripheral eurozone economies than members of her own party. A series of rulings by the German Constitutional Court and the Bundestag were legally required to allow the German government to increase its contribution to the eurozone bailout fund. Democratic processes in Germany and the EU produced the uncertainty that unsettled markets. US Secretary of the Treasury Timothy Geithner attended a summit of eurozone leaders to try to convince them to "leverage" their bailout fund by increasing ECB guarantees to the fund, basically increasing its lending capacity. Geithner stressed the US administration view that strong action was needed to calm markets and, optimally, to reduce the costs of borrowing in struggling European economies to buy them time to address their financial problems. In Geithner's proposal, Germany saw the potential of a reaction from US financial ratings agencies that could potentially downgrade the Triple A ratings enjoyed by France, Germany, Austria, and Finland of the eurozone if these countries were judged to have over-extended their debt obligations, even if only on paper. Despite the precautions they took, France and Austria could not prevent a downgrade by Standard and Poor's to double A-plus status in January 2012.[35] US ratings agencies consider the fundamentals of economies in determining ratings, which in turn influence investors. It is significant that, despite high rates of economic growth, none of the BRIC countries have earned the highest ratings enjoyed by the European countries named above.[36]

The German Chancellor also had to consider that she could not generate support domestically for bailouts if she failed to convince Germans that Europe's debtor countries would adopt policies leading to financial stability. "Austerity," the term *du jour* for adopting debt-reduction measures, became another contentious issue in transatlantic relations. The USA maintained that economies could not recover without financial stimulus (based on the US experience with its own financial crisis in 2009) whereas Germany, among other European countries, was convinced that debt was the reason for the loss of consumer confidence. "Austerity" meant something altogether different to leaders in the European context than for the Obama administration which insisted that spending and loosening fiscal constraints would give Europe an economic boost. The Germans, in particular, refused to come to the rescue of flailing economies in Europe, if that meant sanctioning the status quo of overspending in debtor countries. Therefore, Greece, Italy, Spain, Ireland, and Portugal had to enact austerity policies while the UK did so voluntarily. These plans were modeled after the "conditionality arrangements the IMF had imposed on borrowing countries, the "rule book," so to speak, of the international economic system in the post-World War Two era, although it had rarely been applied to developed countries in Europe. If the eurozone were going to survive, other countries could not be allowed to follow policies that electorates in payer countries could not support. Germany's main "leverage" during the crisis was exerted through the measure of placing conditions on borrowing, in concert with the IMF. As of March 2012, Europe is still plagued by financial problems, political uncertainties and prospects of slow economic growth. The following statement nonetheless remains true, "The eurozone remains a long way from a fiscal union-but steps towards a greater pooling of sovereignty have already been made that would have been unimaginable even a few years ago." Perhaps, most important among these steps is that the region's leaders are considering "measures that would see European authorities, in effect, taking control of the domestic policies of eurozone member states that failed to follow its rules."[37]

The issue on which Europe desperately needs a consensus in order to maximize influence is determining a sure way out of the financial crisis. Seventeen eurozone countries have already set themselves apart from the ten remaining EU members who have either opted out of the euro or wait to qualify. The solution to Europe's financial woes weighs heavily on the core 17 with currency fluctuations. These countries have tilted to policies that include more regulation of capital markets under the leadership of German Chancellor Angela Merkel, along with more eurozone integration to make certain that common policies are followed. Meanwhile, the British government champions American style economic liberalization and tries to figure out ways of being even more loosely connected to Europe. Relatively speaking, European integration used to occupy a safe position "above politics" being seen by the public (with the exception of the British) as neither Left nor Right ideologically. The sovereign debt crisis has fully "politicized" the EU, drawing it into economic debates, intra-European and transatlantic, debates that are deeply polarizing in terms of the widening spectrum of political views and fuelling nationalistic tensions. Political solidarity and the future of the euro depend on resolution to Europe's sovereign debt crisis.

The US and Europe: Worlds Apart?

The USA and Europe operate on the basis of divergent political cultures. Very different core values affect their discrete security orientations. Scholars are prone to argue that Europeans have a broader conception of security, casting a wider net to enfold a multiplicity of threats to the stability of states, from protection against sharks, migrations of fish, and water pollutants. The transatlantic gap over the use of force does not show signs of closing. Despite the fact that in 2010 Europeans were more favorable to American President Obama than Americans themselves, admiration does not spill over into American war policies.[38] When Europeans are polled as to whether "war is necessary to obtain justice under some circumstances," 27 percent of Europeans compared to 77 percent of American respondents support this statement.[39] Furthermore, "49 percent of Americans and only 8 percent of EU respondents agree strongly" with this reason for war.

The question of *guns v. butter* is passé for Europeans; the more pressing question is preserving the welfare state during a global economic downturn in which economic growth spurred initially by globalization has now sputtered almost to a halt. According to Europeans, the question that befits a mature power is *how to spread the butter*. To their credit, Europeans have helped move failed states to the center of security concerns and drawn attention to the link between economic development and security. Economist Joseph Stiglitz lauds Europe for the social emphasis of its development assistance policies: "Not only has Europe been more vocal in articulating the concerns of the poor in developing countries, but many of the European countries have actually put their money where their mouth is."[40] According to the Organization for Economic Cooperation and Development (OECD) statistics in 2009, the USA contributed 0.21 percent of the country's gross national income (GNI) to development assistance. All of the EU members of the OECD with the exception of two, Italy and Greece, contributed a greater percentage of GNI than the USA, and of those, ten EU countries contributed at least twice as much, with Sweden contributing more than five times as much.[41] The national contributions were augmented by a separate total for EU institutions of US$13,444 million as compared to the total for the USA, US$28,831 million. These statistics bear out the criticism the USA faces for not contributing enough in percentage of GNI, although the total dollar amount of US contributions exceeds that of any other single country. Wars on two fronts in the USA have assured that security considerations take precedence over other external policy goals.

War fatigue and budget constraints have made the US public question the need for more aid to Afghanistan. The subject of foreign assistance is an unpopular one for politicians, indeed a subject that candidates seeking the presidency do not broach. At present in the USA, the political climate does not favor "articulating" global welfare policies, which is an extension of the polarization that marks national debates on questions of spending on the have-nots (or shifting income away from the rich through taxes). The politics of overseas development aid are extremely complicated and would require a separate in-depth analysis. However, a few general observations reveal the different spending patterns of the USA and Europe. Data on foreign aid often obscure significant factors. For example, the way the OECD calculates foreign aid does not include military aid, an inclusion that would better capture US priorities. Neither does it include aid to countries that fall in the category between rich and poor countries. Thus OECD figures did not include the aid the USA gave to Russia after the collapse of communism or that the EU gave to Central and Eastern European countries during their democratic and market transitions, including the amounts that Germany spent on unification.[42]

Aside from asserting different values in foreign policy, the USA and EU also seem to weigh differently the importance of having their values determine their foreign policies. In this respect, Americans tend to be able to compartmentalize their foreign policy goals from aspirations tied to political values. Political realism that has dominated US foreign policy thinking "maintains that universal moral principles...must be filtered through the concrete circumstances of time and place."[43] Values tend to be more conditional in US foreign policy, producing inconsistencies. Alternatively, a clear-cut and well-defined set of values constitute a more stable foundation of the emerging European international identity, as they are expected to inform international law and political representation in international forums. Europe pursues power in the world by trying to "universalize" its values.

Europeans tend to see a wider divide than Americans do in their relations with the Chinese. As they tend to perceive constructive foreign relations to be a function of common of values, 63 percent of Europeans in public opinion polls in 2010, "agreed that China and Europe have such different values that cooperating on international problems is impossible" whereas a smaller percentage of Americans, 47 percent, have that concern.[44] In support of European skepticism that China poses a real challenge to Europe as a "normative" power, observers have noted that China has asserted leadership in the UN General Assembly to set back European positions. Dempsey recently reported, that "with the radical shifts in global influence led by China, Europe's influence is waning, and fast."[45] Meanwhile, those countries on which Europe has counted in the past to participate in the international value system that the EU sees as its mission to construct, have often exercised their independence in voting. For example, Brazil, India and South Africa increasingly echo China's concern with the importance of "non-interference" in their internal affairs.[46] Europeans suffered a major setback in the UN Security Council in October 2011 when France, Germany, Portugal, and the UK prepared a draft resolution strongly opposing "the continued grave and systematic human rights violations and the use of force against civilians by the Syrian authorities."[47] Russia and China vetoed the draft while Brazil, India, Lebanon and South Africa abstained. The reality of a multipolar world has definitely dimmed Europe's prospects for decisive leadership in international organizations. Nonetheless, EU, along with those countries "attracted" to its values and potential EU member states, still has the representation to check the aspirations of any other single power or bloc hoping to prevail in international decision-making without European backing.

Challenges to Europe's Global Leadership

The Arab Spring of 2011 has brought Europe face to face with the problems posed by its embrace of soft power. Having long prided itself on being the biggest aid donor, the EU has had to come to terms with the fact that money can be the root of much evil. That the EU gave the most regional aid among Mediterranean countries to Tunisia, the first of the strongman regimes taken back by the people in the pro-democracy movements that swept the Arab

world, forced the European Commission to reexamine the way it targets
financial assistance. The EU was also the most important trading partner
of Tunisia. As a US State Department report issued in September 2011
noted, "Tunisia is very closely linked to Europe."[48] The country's privileged
position vis-à-vis Europe, led one critical observer to conclude that, "The
events in Tunisia are a bitter lesson for the EU's indulgent policy towards
Ben Ali's repressive regime."[49] The relevance of the EU's soft power will be
tested as newly democratic Arab regimes make their transitions to more
popular forms of government and will be decided on the basis of political
values and the structure of foreign relations the new leaders embrace.

The Arab Spring has also meant that European countries have had to
revisit the utility of hard power in the military intervention against the
Libyan ruler Muammar Gaddafi, in which the use of force was officially
sanctioned, in March 2011, under UN Security Council Resolution 1973,
mandating the protection of civilians. Significantly, the UN Security
Council, in October 2011, unanimously agreed to end the military action
(with abstentions from India, China, Brazil, Russia, and Germany) once
Gaddafi had been effectively removed from power and killed by members of
the popular rebellion. That decision signaled the limited nature of so-called
"humanitarian interventions," which may prove to be a defining condition
of the use of force for the European countries that participated in the action.
Nonetheless, the use of force, even if limited, was divisive for Europe with
individual countries, most notable among them being Germany, refusing
to participate in the military aspects of the mission while avowing their
support for the mission and giving non-military assistance.[50]

The role Europeans played in ousting the Libyan leader seemed to suggest
that Europe had become more willing to become the strategic player the
USA has wanted it to be. Although more willing to use force, Europeans
demonstrated once again their dependency on the USA in instances of
military action. In this context, Biscop emphasizes that "the well-known
European deficiencies, especially as concerns strategic enablers—90 percent
of which had to be provided by the US" during the Libyan intervention.[51]
Consequently, Europe is faced again with a difficult dilemma: how to
respond to US pressure to develop the military assets that the region needs
to provide security in its neighborhood while Europeans continue to need
convincing about the utility of military force and diverting scarce resources to
defense budgets. Furthermore, Europeans have to resolve among themselves
whether their interests will best be served by building up defense through
NATO or under the EU framework of the Common Security and Defense
Policy. Biscop favors the latter course: "The European autonomy which their
new strategy requires cannot be achieved without a platform for European
coordination, for which NATO is not now configured," noting that any new
capabilities could be utilized by the Alliance.[52] At present, the USA is forced
to rely on partners in Europe, with varying levels of strategic assets.

Europe mainly strives to emerge as a "leading" power, through its soft power style of leading by example, engendering trust by institutionalizing relations and networking with a myriad of states, organizations, and informal groupings. It seeks to gain a more universal acceptance of its vision of a world integrated around a European value-set. Although this aim is lofty, the less Europe speaks with one voice, the less impact it can expect to have on global political issues. Foreign policy differences in the EU have always plagued common decision-making, the most damaging split coming in the wake of the Iraq War in 2003 when then US Secretary of Defense Donald Rumsfeld famously labeled countries in support of the US effort as "New Europe" and those against as "Old Europe," in an especially prickly reference to France and Germany. The heightened political rhetoric actually distracted from the situation on the ground in which a majority of Europe's citizens were against the war, their ranks swelling over time, with most countries eventually withdrawing their troops from the battlefield.[53]

Conclusion

The collectivist view of Europe as a stabilizing bloc in a world in which the tectonic plates of economic and political power are rapidly shifting has been badly damaged by the national interests at stake during a time of slowing economic growth and amidst the uncertainties of competing against emerging economies for fiscally constrained markets of the future. The strength of collective Europe at the beginning of this century is that it could remain an economic player among the giants, whether rising powers as China, emerging powers like Brazil and India, or the USA, which is a preeminent power but perhaps descending from its behemoth status.

In the political realm, Europe's goal was to have a "normative" advantage, having learned from its own mistakes during earlier centuries of projecting power to pursue narrow national interests.[54] After the end of World War Two, Europe turned its attention to the spillover effects of wars, imperialism, and economic deprivation. This vision has become cramped as the region's capacity to conduct international relations has been undercut by financial and political strains. Europe's greatest challenge has radically changed into a domestic one, that of bringing the next generation into the political fold and winning back citizens increasingly disaffected by politics seen in the recent popularity of rejectionist parties. These parties described as "anti-muslim, anti-elite, anti-globalisation and increasingly anti-Brussels" exacerbate the political malaise spreading across Europe.[55] The space "above politics" is untenable in the information age. Participants in the Arab Spring, the Occupy Movement in the USA, and in the street protests and riots in the UK, Spain, Italy, and Greece demand new forms of political influence.

Europe's strength in innovative politics and institution-building is also the source of its weakness. As a pioneer in developing its boldest experiments (i.e. the euro and multi-level governance) Europe has had to learn in the process of doing, instead of being able to rely on lessons from the past. What started out as innovation has tended to get bogged down in the "muddling through" modus that has come to characterize European governance. For example, Europe's normative feat, assisting the democratization, market transitions, and reorientation of security and political values in Eastern and Central Europe through enlarging the EU has encountered practical problems. Europe has become a much-expanded area for the free movement of persons, goods, and services, with new access routes for criminal networks, posing new challenges for policing. But the opposite view is that Europe has been able to project stability and expand the area of shared values. In the final analysis, Europe is not the foremost power, or the foremost of emerging powers, but it has a seat at the global table. Its power stems from a hybrid of traditional and non-traditional means. Far from being in a decrepit and retrenching mode, Europe has shown a facility for adaptation and innovation, recognizing the reality of change and the need for accommodation in a multi-polar world.

Endnotes

1 I am grateful to my colleague, Dr. Peter Burns, at Loyola University, New Orleans, for suggesting that the policies of the EU challenge assumptions of existing international relations theories.

2 Roy H. Ginsberg, 2nd edn, *Demystifying the European Union: The Enduring Logic of Regional Integration.* (Lanham, M. D.: Rowman & Littlefield Publishers, Inc., 2010), 246.

3 Sherrill Brown Wells, *Pioneers of European Integration and Peace 1945–1963: A Brief History with Documents.* (Boston: Bedford/St. Martin's, 2007), 99, 13.

4 See Keohane's insightful analysis of this transatlantic divergence in Robert O. Keohane, "Ironies of Sovereignty: The European Union and the USA," *Journal of Common Market Studies*, Vol. 40, No. 4. (2002), 743–65.

5 See Robert Kagan, *Of Paradise and Power: America and Europe in the New World Order.* (New York: Vintage Books, 2004), 43.

6 Joseph Nye, *Soft Power: The Means to Success in World Politics.* (New York: PublicAffairs, 2004). See chart on types of power, 31.

7 The shift to "winning hearts and minds" in Afghanistan is described by Anna Mulrine, "How Petraeus has changed the Afghanistan war," *The Christian Science Monitor.* (31 December 2010), http:www.csmonitor.com/USA/ Military/2010/1231/How-Petraeus-has-changed-the-Afghanistan-war.

8 Nye, *Soft Power,* p. 81.

9 Andrew E. Kramer, "Before Kyrgyz Uprising, Dose of Russian Soft Power," (18 April 2010), *New York Times* online, http://www.nytimes.com/2010/04/19/world/asia/19kyrgyz.html?_r=1

10 "Sun Tzu and the art of soft power," *The Economist.* (17–30 December 2011), 71, 72, 74.

11 Ibid., p. 72.

12 The author's idea of "baskets" of power was adapted from the theory of basket sovereignty in Michael Ross Fowler and Julie Marie Bunck, *Law, Power, and the Sovereign State: The Evolution and Application of the Concept of Sovereignty.* (University Park, P.A.: The Pennsylvania State University Press, 1995).

13 Kagan, *Of Paradise and Power.* According to Kagan, French Foreign Minister Hubert Vedrine characterized US power at the time of the Clinton administration as *hyperpuissance* or hyperpower, 43.

14 Commission of the European Communities, "Commission Communication to the Council and the European Parliament on Immigration," SEC (91) 1855 final, (23 October 1991), http://aei.pitt.edu/1260/

15 Ibid.

16 To further understand the problem of failed states, see Ashraf Ghani and Clare Lockhard, *Fixing Failed States: A Framework For Rebuilding A Fractured World.* (London: Oxford University Press, 2008).

17 See Mary Kaldor, New and Old Wars: Organized Violence in a Global Era, 2nd edn. (Cambridge: Polity Press, 2006).

18 Ruby Gropas, "What role for Human Rights in the European Security Strategy?," 64. www.consilium.europa.eu/uedoc&/cm&Upload/78367.pdf

19 Ibid.

20 Ibid.

21 "Dollar stops being Russia's basic reserve currency," (19 May 2009), www.english.pravda.ru/business/finance/19–05–2009/107581-dollar_russia–0/19.05.2009.

22 European Commission Economic and Financial Affairs official site, www.ec.europa.eu/economy_finance/euro/index_en.htm

23 According to Fisk, "Brazil has shown interest in collaborating in non-dollar oil payments, along with India. Indeed, China appears to be the most enthusiastic of all the financial powers involved…" See Robert Fisk, "The demise of the dollar," (6 October 2009), www.independent.co.uk/news/business/news/thedemise-of-the-dollar.1798175.html

24 "G20 Vows to Avoid Currency War and to Share I.M.F. power," (23 October 2010), www.nytimes.com/2010/10/24 business/global/24g20.html?_r=1&hp

25 European Commission Economic and Financial Affairs, Treaty establishing the European Stability Mechanism (ESM), http://ec.europa.eu/economy_finance/articles/financial_operations/2011–07–11-esm-treaty_en.htm

26 Stephen Castle, "With Details Settled, a 2nd Greek Bailout Is Formally Approved," *New York Times online*. (14 March 2012), http://www.nytimes.com/2012/03/15/business/global/greece-gets-formal-approval-for-second-bailout.html

27 Dominique Strauss-Kahn, "After the Global Financial Crisis-The Road Ahead for Europe," Address at the Warsaw School of Economics, Warsaw, Poland. (29 March 2010), http://www.imf.org/external/np/speeches/2010/032910.htm

28 Andrew Willis, "Merkel Backs European Credit Rating Firm," *Bloomberg Businessweek*. (5 May 2010), http://www.businessweek.com/print/globalbiz/content/may2010/gb2010055_734001.htm

29 "German Court Rejects Challenges to Euro Bailouts," Spiegel Online, http://www.spiegel.de/international/germany/0,1518,druck–784859,00.html

30 For example, the British Chancellor called for the three Rs (ring-fencing, resolution, and recapitalisation) to resolve the crisis. See Allegra Stratton, "George Osborne calls on Europe to be decisive over Greece crisis," *The Guardian*. (10 October 2011), http://www.guardian.co.uk/politics/2011/oct/10/george-osborne-europe-greece-crisis

31 Ralph Atkins, "Eurozone options: Rescue raises doubts over details and deeper issues," *Financial Times* online. (2 November 2011), http://www.ft.com/intl/cms/s/0/4abb70d6–014c–11e1-ae24–00144feabdc0.ht

32 "Markets surge after eurozone summit deal," Agence France-Presse, 27 October 2011, http://www.montrealgazette.com/story_print.html?id=5613972&sponsor=; Jill Treanor and Katie Allen, "Greek referendum plan causes global stock market panic," *The Guardian*. (1 November 2011), http://www.guardian.co.uk/world/2011/nov/01/greek-referendum-global-stockmarket-panic

33 Ibid, Agence France-Presse.

34 "Bailout money witheld from Greece," *BBC News*. (2 November 2011), http://www.bbc.co.uk/news/business–15550422?

35 Gerrit Wiesmann, Peter Spiegel, & Robin Wigglesworth, "S & P Downgrades France and Austria," Financial Times online. (14 January 2012), http://www.ft.com/intl/cms/s/0/78bf6fb4–3df6–11e1–91f3–00144feabdc0.html#axzz1qASIwI2D

36 According to the Sovereign Ratings List for local currencies by Standard & Poors, the following ratings apply to China AA-, Russia BBB+, Brazil BBB+, India BBB-, USA AA+, http://www.standardandpoors.com/ratings/sov (Accessed 4 November 2011).

37 Ralph Atkins, "Eurozone options: Rescue raises doubts over details and deeper issues," *Financial Times*. (2 November 2011), http://www.ft.com/intl/cms/s/0/4abb70d6–014c–11e1-ae24–00144feabdc0.ht

38 Transatltantic Trends Key Findings 2010, www.flad.pt/documentos/1284748741S1IJ9ablBq18RQ0.pdf

39 Ibid.

40 Joseph E. Stigilitz, *Freefall: America, Free Markets, and the Sinking of the World Economy*. (New York: W. W. Norton & Company, 2010), 236.

41 As a percentage of GNI, Sweden contributed 1.12 percent, Luxembourg 1.04 percent, Denmark 0.88 percent, and Netherlands 0.82 percent, Belgium 0.55 percent, Ireland 0.54 percent, UK 0.52 percent, Finland 0.54 percent, France 0.47 percent, Spain 0.46 percent, Austria 0.30 percent, Germany 0.35 percent, Portugal 0.23 percent See DAC Members' Net Official Development Assistance in 2009, http://www.oecd.org/document/9/0,3746,en_26

42 Larry Nowels, "Foreign Aid: Understanding Data Used to Compare Donors," *Congressional Research Service Report for Congress*, Order Code RS22032.

43 Hans J. Morgenthau, "Political Power: A Realist Theory of International Politics," in John A. Vasquez (ed.), Classics of International Relations, 3rd edn. (Upper Saddle River, N.J.: Prentice Hall, 1996), 26.

44 Transatlantic Trends, op.cit.

45 Judy Dempsey, "For Europe, A Challenge to make Its Voice Resonate," New York Times online. (13 October 2010), www.nytimes.com/2010/10/14/world/europe/14iht-letter.html?pagewanted=2&_r=1&sq=europefinancialcrisis&st=cse&scp=9

46 Ibid.

47 *Russia and China veto draft Security Council resolution on Syria*, UN News Service, http://www.un.org/apps/news/printnews.asp?nid=39935

48 "Background Note: Tunisia," US State Department. (22 September 2011), http://www.state.gov/r/pa/ei/bgn/5439.htm

49 Moritz Schneider, "The Crumbling Facade of Europe's Bulwark of Stability-Tunisia's Revolution unmasks the EU's misguided approach in the Southern Backyard," *Europe's World*. (19 January 2011), http://www.europesworld.org/NewEnglish/Home_old/CommunityPosts/tabid/809/PostID/2207/language/en-US/Default.aspx

50 Those countries preferring to affiliate only with the civilian side included Croatia, Czech Republic, Estonia, Hungary, Latvia, Lithuania, Luxembourg, Poland, Portugal, Slovakia, Slovenia, Iceland, and Germany. Meanwhile, European countries contributing militarily included France, the country which actually initiated putting together the coalition to use force against Gaddafi, UK, Belgium, Norway, Denmark, Italy, Spain, Netherlands, Albania, Bulgaria, Greece, and Romania. Among the former, Italy, Spain and Netherlands conducted reconnaissance flights only whereas Albania, Bulgaria, Greece, and Romania gave "some military support." See "Libya: Where do NATO countries stand?" *BBC News*. (12 April 2011), http://www.bc.co.uk/news/world-africa–134092451?

51 Sven Biscop, "As the EU Said at the NATO Summit," *Security Policy Brief*, No. 33. (February 2012), http://www.egmontinstitute.be/papers/12/sec-gov/SPB33.pdf

52 Ibid.

53 Earlier European troop withdrawals from Iraq include Spain in April 2004, Portugal in February 2005, Hungary in March 2005, The Netherlands in March 2005, Italy in November 2006, and Slovakia in January 2007. See *Iraq*

Coalition Troops. (February 2007), http://www.globalsecurity.org/military/ops/iraq_orbat_coalition.htm

54 Nathalie Tocci employs the concept of the EU as a normative actor. See "The European Union as a Normative Foreign Policy Actor." *CEPS Working Document*, No. 281. (January 2008).

55 I am grateful to my former student, Caleb Carr, for bringing this article to my attention and for highlighting the quote, "What the EU lacks is not democracy but popular engagement." See "Beyond the fringe: The rise of populists is a threat both to the euro and to the EU as a whole," *The Economist.* (12 November 2011), http://www.economist.com/node/21536873/

Bibliography

Atkins, Ralph. "Eurozone options: Rescue raises doubts over details and deeper issues." *Financial Times* online. (2 November 2011), http://www.ft.com/intl/cms/s/0/4abb70d6-014c-11e1-ae24-00144feabdc0.ht

"Background Note: Tunisia." US State Department. (22 September 2011), http://www.state.gov/r/pa/ei/bgn/5439.htm

Biscop, Sven. "As the EU Said at the NATO Summit." *Security Policy Brief*, No. 33. (February 2012), http://www.egmontinstitute.be/papers/12/sec-gov/SPB33.pdf

Castle, Stephen. "With Details Settled, a 2nd Greek Bailout Is Formally Approved." *New York Times* online. (14 March 2012), http://www.nytimes.com/2012/03/15/business/global/greece-gets-formal-approval-for-second-bailout.html

Commission of the European Communities. "Commission Communication to the Council and the European Parliament on Immigration." SEC (91) 1855 final, (23 October 1991), http://aei.pitt.edu/1260/

DAC Members' Net Official Development Assistance in 2009. http://www.oecd.org/document/9/0,3746,en_26

Dempsey, Judy. "For Europe, A Challenge to make Its Voice Resonate." *The New York Times* online. (13 October 2010), www.nytimes.com/2010/10/14/world/europe/14iht-letter.html?pagewanted=2&_r=1&sq=europefinancialcrisis&st=cse&scp=9

European Commission Economic and Financial Affairs official site. www.ec.europa.eu/economy_finance/euro/index_en.htm

—Treaty establishing the European Stability Mechanism (ESM). http://ec.europa.eu/economy_finance/articles/financial_operations/2011–07–11-esm-treaty_en.htm

Fisk, Robert. "The demise of the dollar," (6 October 2009). www.independent.co.uk/news/business/news/thedemise-of-the-dollar.1798175.html

Fowler, Michael Ross and Julie Marie Bunck. *Law, Power, and the Sovereign State: The Evolution and Application of the Concept of Sovereignty.* (University Park, P.A.: The Pennsylvania State University Press, 1995).

Ghani, Ashraf and Clare Lockhard. *Fixing Failed States: A Framework For Rebuilding A Fractured World.* (London: Oxford University Press, 2008).

Ginsberg, Roy H. 2nd edn. *Demystifying the European Union: The Enduring Logic of Regional Integration*. (Lanham, Md.: Rowman & Littlefield Publishers, Inc., 2010).

Gropas, Ruby. "What role for Human Rights in the European Security Strategy?" www.consilium.europa.eu/uedoc&/cm&Upload/78367.pdf

Iraq Coalition Troops. (February 2007), http://www.globalsecurity.org/military/ops/iraq_orbat_coalition.htm

Kagan, Robert. *Of Paradise and Power: America and Europe in the New World Order*. (New York: Vintage Books, 2004).

Kaldor, Mary. *New and Old Wars: Organized Violence in a Global Era*, 2nd edn. (Cambridge: Polity Press, 2006).

Keohane Robert O. "Ironies of Sovereignty: The European Union and the United States." *Journal of Common Market Studies*, Vol. 40, no. 4. (2002).

Kramer, Andrew E. "Before Kyrgyz Uprising, Dose of Russian Soft Power." (18 April 2010), *The New York Times* online, http://www.nytimes.com/2010/04/19/world/asia/19kyrgyz.html?_r=l

Morgenthau, Hans J. "Political Power: A Realist Theory of International Politics," in Vasquez, John A. (ed.) *Classics of International Relations*, 3rd edn. (Upper Saddle River, N.J.: Prentice Hall, 1996).

Mulrine, Anna. "How Petraeus has changed the Afghanistan war." *The Christian Science Monitor*. (31 December 2010), http:www.csmonitor.com/USA/Military/2010/1231/How-Petraeus-has-changed-the-Afghanistan-war.

N. A. "Bailout money witheld from Greece." *BBC News*. (2 November 2011), http://www.bbc.co.uk/news/business–15550422?

—"Dollar stops being Russia's basic reserve currency." (19 May 2009), www.english.pravda.ru/business/finance/19–05–2009/107581-dollar_russia–0/19.05.2009

—German Court Rejects Challenges to Euro Bailouts." *Spiegel* online, http://www.spiegel.de/international/germany/0,1518,druck–784859,00.html

—"G–20 Vows to Avoid Currency War and to Share I.M.F. power." October 23, 2010, www.nytimes.com/2010/10/24business/global/24g20.html?_r=l&hp

—"Libya: Where do NATO countries stand?" *BBC News*. (12 April 2011), http://www.bc.co.uk/news/world-africa–134092451?

—"Markets surge after eurozone summit deal." Agence France-Presse, 27 October 2011, http://www.montrealgazette.com/story_print.html?id=5613972&sponsor=;

—"Sun Tzu and the art of soft power." *The Economist*. (17–30 December 2011), 71,72,74.

—"What the EU lacks is not democracy but popular engagement." See "Beyond the fringe: The rise of populists is a threat both to the euro and to the EU as a whole." *The Economist*. (12 November 2011), http://www.economist.com/node/21536873/

Nowels, Larry. "Foreign Aid: Understanding Data Used to Compare Donors." *Congressional Research Service Report for Congress*, Order Code RS22032.

Nye, Joseph, *Soft Power: The Means to Success in World Politics*. (New York: PublicAffairs, 2004).

Russia and China veto draft Security Council resolution on Syria. UN News Service, http://www.un.org/apps/news/printnews.asp?nid=39935

Schneider, Moritz. "The Crumbling Facade of Europe's Bulwark of Stability-Tunisia's Revolution unmasks the EU's misguided approach in the Southern Backyard." *Europe's World*. (19 January 2011), http://www.europesworld.org/NewEnglish/Home_old/CommunityPosts/tabid/809/PostID/2207/language/en-US/Default.aspx

Sovereign Ratings List for local currencies by Standard & Poors, http://www.standardandpoors.com/ratings/sov (Accessed 4 November 2011).

Stigilitz, Joseph E. *Freefall: America, Free Markets, and the Sinking of the World Economy*. (New York: W. W. Norton & Company, 2010).

Stratton, Allegra. "George Osborne calls on Europe to be decisive over Greece crisis." *The Guardian*. (10 October 2011), http://www.guardian.co.uk/politics/2011/oct/10/george-osborne-europe-greece-crisis

Strauss-Kahn, Dominique. "After the Global Financial Crisis-The Road Ahead for Europe." Address at the Warsaw School of Economics, Warsaw, Poland. (29 March 2010), http://www.imf.org/external/np/speeches/2010/032910.htm

Tocci, Nathalie. "The European Union as a Normative Foreign Policy Actor." *CEPS Working Document No. 281*. (January 2008).

Transatlantic Trends Key Findings 2010. www.flad.pt/documentos/1284748741S1IJ9ablBq18RQ0.pdf

Treanor, Jill and Allen, Katie. "Greek referendum plan causes global stock market panic." *The Guardian*. (1 November 2011), http://www.guardian.co.uk/world/2011/nov/01/greek-referendum-global-stockmarket-panic

Wiesmann, Gerrit; Spiegel, Peter; Wigglesworth,Robin. "S & P Downgrades France and Austria." *Financial Times* online. (14 January 2012), http://www.ft.com/intl/cms/s/0/78bf6fb4–3df6–11e1–91f3–00144feabdc0.html#axzz1qASIwI2D

Wells, Sherrill Brown. *Pioneers of European Integration and Peace 1945–1963: A Brief History with Documents*. (Boston: Bedford/St. Martin's, 2007).

Willis, Andrew. "Merkel Backs European Credit Rating Firm." *Bloomberg BusinessWeek*. (5 May 2010), http:/www.businessweek.com/print/globalbiz/content/may2010/gb2010055_734001.htm

CHAPTER FOUR

Japan and the Emerging Powers: Toward Middle Power Realism?

David Fouse

Introduction

Japan is a country intimately familiar with the role of an emerging power, having ridden its own meteoric rise from the ashes of World War Two to become the second largest global economic power in 1968, with some observers predicting that Japan was on track to surpass the US economy as late as the mid–1990s.[1] During the early postwar period Japanese leadership forged a consensus around a strategy of pursuing rapid economic development while maintaining a low diplomatic and military profile that did not provoke the concerns of its Asian neighbors. This consensus view of Japanese grand strategy during the postwar period, which left Japan heavily dependent on the US for security, came to be known as the Yoshida doctrine (named after early postwar Prime Minister Shigeru Yoshida).

Following the end of the Cold War (and catalyzed by the international criticism levied at Japan for "checkbook diplomacy" during the first Gulf War in 1991), two dominant views emerged regarding how Japan should seek to harmonize its domestic economic interests with the international responsibilities of a major economic power. Japanese progressives offered a vision of Japan as a "global civilian power" that would capitalize on its economic strengths in a new era of low-level intensity threats, focusing its international contributions on such things as overseas development assistance, humanitarian aid, and the promotion of free trade.[2] Conservatives, on the other hand, thought that it was time for the country to forsake the special restrictions placed upon the military by its postwar constitution and become a "normal nation." To what end normalization would eventually lead Japan remained unclear.[3] The common denominator was that both camps were interested in Japan securing its international status as a great power.[4] Progressives wished to see Japan emerge as a new type of great power that continued to eschew military commitments, while conservatives tended to see Japan in more traditional terms of great power status, which included taking a larger role in international security.

Unfortunately for Japan, just as the end of the Cold War brought an opportunity to attempt to lessen its diplomatic and military dependence on the US, the shortcomings of the Yoshida doctrine and Japan's state-driven, export-oriented growth strategy became evident. Japan entered an extended period of economic stagnation without achieving its goal of securing a seat on the United Nations Security Council [UNSC] and prior to firmly establishing its own leadership in Asian regionalism. The rise of China and other emerging powers has in this sense come at a most inopportune time for Japan, raising a broad array of new challenges on a variety of different fronts. Japan's global status has withered with China having emerged as Asia's new economic powerhouse, overtaking Japan as the world's second largest economy in 2010. With the world's most vibrant economy, long-term international status as a permanent member of the UNSC and rapidly expanding military muscle, China presents Japan with more than just a formidable challenge to its regional leadership and international status. Due to conflicting claims over territory and exclusive economic zones, Japan perceives China as a potential threat to its own vital national interests.

The perception of a growing military threat from China and its ally North Korea has bolstered the position of conservatives inside Japan who wish to see the constitution revised and Japan's own military capabilities increased. Even those opposed to Japan moving in this direction have grown cautious with regard to China's long-term intentions and the possible threat that it poses to Japan's own interests and stability in the region.[5] At the same time, continuing economic sluggishness, the onset of demographic decline, and a growing national debt crisis have left Japan constrained in terms of new foreign policy and security options. These factors have led some inside Japan to argue that it is time for the country to abandon any pretensions of becoming a great power and concentrate its resources on multilateral diplomatic efforts that will give the country its most effective means for promoting national welfare and maintaining foreign policy autonomy from the great powers. Those who favor this "middle power" path see no alternative for Japan but to further economic integration with China and Asia more broadly, while sustaining Japan's low military profile under the US-Japan alliance. Though holding much in common with the earlier "global civilian power" schools of thought, leading advocates of this strategy do not think it is truly possible for Japan to compete with either China or the US for leadership in Asia or the world.[6]

In this chapter, I argue that Japan's eroding foundations of national power, in combination with the perception of a rising threat to vital Japanese national interests from China, are pushing Japan toward a new strategic consensus that features both economic integration with China (as an unavoidable economic necessity) and greater efforts to balance against Chinese political influence and military power. Japan's attempts to strengthen relations with emerging powers India, Russia, and Brazil will be discussed in this light, as an attempt toward balancing China's growing power. While hardening Japan's military hedge against possible Chinese aggression, the new strategic consensus that is emerging is more circumspect with regard to Japan's capacity to play a major role in shaping a new world order. The chapter will argue that Japan's emerging strategic consensus, a form of middle power realism, will seek ways to constrain China's growing power and influence while working with other like-minded states to prevent a major shift in the established US-centric order.

The Eroding Foundations of Japan's National Power

Economic Stagnation

Japan's international status in the postwar period has been firmly rooted in its economic power. Japan's economic prestige overshadowed its influence in other spheres, and it has often been ignominiously labeled "an economic giant, but a political pygmy." After the collapse of Japan's asset price bubble in the early 1990s and a prolonged period of stagnation, Japan's international status began to sink along with its vaunted economic miracle. The process of recovery from the bursting of Japan's economic bubble has been a long drawn out process. Not until 2010 did Japan's gross domestic product (GDP) surpass the mark set 15 years earlier in 1995.[7] Over the 15-year span it took Japan to regain the economic output it achieved in 1995, its share of global economic production declined steadily in relationship to China and other emerging powers. Japan's share of global GDP peaked in 1995 at 17.7 percent. At that time Japan's share of global GDP was seven times that of both China and Brazil and nearly 15 times that of India and Russia. Fifteen years later Japan's share of global GDP had been cut in half, while the USA and European Union suffered much more modest declines (1.6 percent and 5 percent respectively) in relationship to the gains being made by China and other emerging powers.[8]

Japan's economic stagnation occurred despite the phenomenal growth of the Asian region as a whole. Between 1995 and 2008 when the global financial crisis hit, the Asian economy grew by an amazing 70 percent.[9] During the same period Japan's share of Asian GDP shrank from 64.9 percent to 35.4 percent, while China's share more than tripled from 9 percent to 31.7 percent and India nearly doubled its share from 4.4 percent to 8.7 percent.[10] While Japan muddled through its so-called "lost decade," intraregional trade in East Asia blossomed. Centered on China's booming economy, intraregional trade within "non-Japan" East Asia actually grew faster (15.2 percent) than the region's external trade from 1987 to 2007.[11] Japan's share of intraregional exports, which peaked in 1995 at 14.4 percent, declined to 8.8 percent in 2007. Over the same period China's share nearly doubled from 6.2 percent to 12.2 percent.[12]

Structural reforms implemented under the Koizumi administration (2001–6) are often credited with jumpstarting Japan's economic recovery, although some observers argued that Koizumi's attempt at reform never really overcame bureaucratic inertia aimed at maintaining the status quo.[13] Government spending remained a large component of GDP growth during the 2002–7 recovery, though attempts were made to scale this back as the recovery stabilized.[14] Corporate restructuring did appear to gain steam during this period, as Japan's growth in economic output surpassed that of the USA on a per-worker basis from 2003–8.[15] However, when the global financial crisis hit, the severity of Japan's recession revealed that many of its structural weaknesses were still intact. Despite Japanese financial institutions largely staying clear of the sub-prime loan problem (losses were less than 4 percent of the global total), Japan ended up suffering the worst decline of any major industrial power, recording negative growth of 6.4 percent in 2008–9. The severity of Japan's downturn demonstrated that it had become even more dependent on overseas exports than prior to economic recovery taking hold (exports rose from 11 percent of GDP in 2000 to 16 percent in 2008).[16] Though corporate profits improved significantly during 2002–7, real wages fell in every year but one. With slumping wages and household income there was no way to create a self-sustaining recovery, leaving Japan vulnerable to lower demand in its major export markets during the financial crisis.[17]

While concerns have risen regarding Japan's growing economic dependence on China, which became Japan's number one trading partner in 2007 (2004 if Hong Kong is included), it was continuing reliance on high value exports to the USA (especially in areas such as automobiles and information related technology) that caused Japan to suffer disproportionately during the 2008–9 financial crisis.[18] Japan's fiscal stimulation of its economy during the 2008–9 recession was eventually successful in creating surprisingly strong GDP growth of 3.9 percent in 2010, but by the time the 11 March 2011 disaster hit Tohoku, Japan's national debt had already ballooned to over 200 percent of GDP, the largest of any country in the world.

Debt and Demographics

Japan's growing debt problem has been a matter of concern for over a decade. The collapse of the asset-price bubble in the early 1990s caused a huge drop in tax revenues that was further exacerbated by the government's economic stimulus measures (especially public works spending) and the costs of assuming the liabilities of failed financial institutions.[19] Moody's, a major international credit rating agency, downgraded Japan's AAA bond rating to AA1 as early as 1998, followed by a Standard and Poor's downgrade in 2002. Renewed economic growth from 2002–7 helped to improve Japan's international standing (Standard and Poor's upgraded Japan's credit rating in 2007), but continuing economic stimulus measures during the recovery and larger stimulus efforts during the 2008–9 financial crisis pushed Japan's national debt to GDP ratio to 211.7 percent in 2011.[20] The actual fiscal crisis Japan is facing today comes into clearer view when one considers that only 44.3 percent of the government's spending in 2011 was funded through tax revenues and 47.9 percent by issuing new government bonds. Outstanding government bonds will reach 668 trillion yen in 2011, corresponding to 16 times the tax revenue collected.[21]

Citing Japan's "lack of a coherent strategy" for tackling its soaring debt problem, Standard and Poor's downgraded Japan's credit rating to three notches below their highest AAA ratings in January 2011.[22] In the aftermath of the March 2011 disaster, two more Western credit rating agencies followed suit, seeing no political will in Tokyo to confront the growing problem and the necessity of a new round of government spending on recovery and reconstruction.[23]

Though Japan will face modest increases in interest rates from foreign lenders because of these downgrades, the impact should be minimal in the short term as Japan continues to fund the vast majority of its public debt (95 percent) domestically, which is unusual in comparison with other major industrialized countries.[24] Japan's large houschold sector savings, channeled through banks, have provided Japan with a buffer from the need for foreign lending. However, rapidly mounting financial liabilities and a declining household savings rate could mean that the domestic market will soon reach the limit of its ability to absorb new bond issues.[25]

All of these issues are complicated by the problem of Japan's rapidly aging population. The Japanese fertility rate moved below the replacement rate in 1974 and has been in steady decline ever since.[26] By 2010 23 percent of Japan's population was aged 65 years old and over, the highest in the world (followed by Germany and Italy at 20.4 percent).[27] Due to its aging population, social security spending has become a major drain on the national budget. From 16.6 percent in 1990, government expenditures on social security rose to 31.1 percent of the national budget in 2011.[28] This growing burden, along with the expanding service payments on the national debt (23.3 percent) and revenue grants for local government (18.2 percent) occupied 72.6 percent of all government expenditures in 2011, severely limiting funds available for discretionary and policy-related spending. Japan's Official Development Assistance (ODA) budget has been in a continuous free-fall since 1997, to the point where outlays had been cut in half by 2010. Military spending has also come under pressure, showing steady declines since 2003.[29] By 2025 more than 30 percent of the Japanese population will be aged 65 and over, increasing social security payments by an estimated 34 percent, and putting steadily increasing pressure on Japan's fiscal stability.[30] A study by the Bank of International Settlements indicated that without significant changes in fiscal policy and social security spending Japan's gross national debt to GDP ratio could rise to as high as 600 percent over the next 30 years.[31]

Because the Japanese population is not only aging, but has begun to shrink as well, there is little likelihood that Japan will be able to offset increases in social security spending by boosting economic growth. Japan's Institute for Population and Social Security Studies recently estimated that the country's population of 128 million will shrink by one-third by 2060, while the number of people 65 or older will nearly double to 40 percent.[32] As the working age population declines, Japan is faced not only with a shrinking tax base from which to fund its growing social security payments, but must also increase productivity substantially or see its economy shrink along with the population. In 2003 the Bank of Japan studied the issue and dismissed such a possibility, arguing that even with a reasonable amount of productivity growth, the contraction of the work force and the declining savings rate caused by the aging population would bring about negative growth rates in the 2020s.[33] Long-term projections from researchers at the IMF give a similarly gloomy prognosis, arguing that Japan's demographic decline will cost it a cumulative 20 percent in GDP growth over the next century.[34]

Japan and the BRICs: Challenges and Opportunities

Japan's economic decline has hastened the relative ascent of the so-called BRIC states, all of which have exceeded expectations since a 2003 Goldman Sachs report predicted that these states as a group would exceed the GDP of the G6 by 2040.[35] In that report, China's GDP (using purchasing power parity) was projected to surpass Japan by 2015, with India surpassing

Japan in 2032. An updated Goldman Sachs report in December of 2009 envisioned all four of the BRICs overtaking Japan by 2037, when Russia is expected to surpass Japan.[36]

While these predictions have not been welcomed in Japan, it has recognized the opportunity as well as the challenge, and is actively seeking ways to benefit from the emergence of new economic powers. Japan's relations with these countries have been deepening, especially in the areas of trade and direct investment. The share of Japan's trade accounted for by the BRICs increased from 7.5 percent to 21.3 percent for exports and from 17.2 percent to 25.6 percent for imports between 2000 and 2009.[37]

The problem for Japan hidden in these numbers is that a very high percentage of the trade growth is with only one BRIC country, namely China. Though the four countries' share of Japan's external trade reached 24.4 percent in 2010, China alone accounted for 20.7 percent.[38] Japan's external trade with the other three countries remains at lower levels, although it is expanding (see Table 1). Given Japan's relatively tense relationship with China in recent times, Japanese leadership has become increasingly anxious with regard to their country becoming asymmetrically dependent upon trade with China. In response the Japan External Trade Organization (JETRO) in 2005 began to urge Japanese corporations to look beyond China and deepen ties with India, Russia, and Brazil.[39] This policy has met with some success, as direct investment in the other three BRIC countries combined has surpassed direct investment in China since 2008.[40] However, obstacles to investing in the other BRIC countries remain high, and Japan can hardly afford to miss out on the much higher expected growth in China given the severity of its macroeconomic problems.

Table 1: Japan's trade with BRICs, 2008–10 (US$ million)

	Exports			Imports		
	2008	2009	2010	2008	2009	2010
China	124,035	109,630	149,086	142,337	122,545	152,801
India	7,850	6,336	9,020	5,215	3,733	5,658
Brazil	5,878	4,236	6,172	9,068	6,369	9,842
Russia	16,374	3,295	8,027	13,281	8,853	16,097

Source: 2011 JETRO Global Trade and Investment Report

China

The growing fiscal crisis caused by Japan's aging and shrinking population leaves Japan little room to maneuver with regard to its deepening dependence on the surging Chinese economy. China no longer represents just a prime location for low cost manufacturing, but is also a rapidly expanding market that Japanese companies can ill afford to ignore. Japan's exports to China surpassed those to the USA in 2009 and are expected to continue to rise substantially over the next decade. Chi Hung Kwan, of the Nomura Institute of Capital Markets Research, estimates that by 2026 China's share of Japan's external trade will rise to 35 percent.[41] Kwan continues to view the Sino-Japan economic relationship as complementary rather than competitive, with Japanese products concentrated in high-tech areas and Chinese products still concentrated in low-tech areas. According to Kwan, competition between the two countries is limited to "mid-tech" products that make up no more than 30 percent of Japanese exports.[42] Though competition is likely to heat up considerably as China expands its high-tech exports, Kwan and many other Japanese economists believe creating a free trade environment with China is Japan's best chance for maintaining economic prosperity.

Japan's major business organizations agree. Dominated by Japan's internationally competitive industries, large business organizations have long been among the strongest advocates for cooperation with China. Anticipating that China's accession to the World Trade Organization (WTO) in 2001 would cause tensions between Japan and China to rise, Nippon Keidanren, the largest business organization in Japan, issued a policy paper which highlighted increasing bilateral economic interdependence between the two countries and argued for deepening mutual trust and broadening economic contacts in order to dampen the growing perception of rivalry between the two countries.[43]

Keidanren has maintained its support for greater economic integration with China, despite continuing deterioration in public sentiment between the two countries over the past decade. In 2003 the organization published another policy paper that argued Japan and China should combine their energies to work for the establishment of an East Asia Free Economic Area, encompassing the Association of South East Asian Nations (ASEAN) countries plus Japan, China, and South Korea (ASEAN + 3).[44] More recently Keidanren has taken part in a series of trilateral business summits along with the China Council for the Promotion of International Trade and the Federation of Korean Industries, working to promote a trilateral free trade agreement between Japan, China, and South Korea.[45] These meetings, which have supported annual trilateral political summits that began in 2008, could, if successful, lay the foundations for wider regional economic integration.

Despite the efforts of the business community, political tensions between Japan and China continue to present obstacles to greater cooperation and integration. Historical animosity related to Japan's invasion and occupation of China (1931–45) that was not specifically addressed when the two countries normalized relations in 1972 continues to plague the relationship and is fueled by disparate historical understandings and ongoing territorial disputes. The end of the Cold War (in which Japan and China both cooperated with the USA in contesting the former Soviet Union) unlocked the geopolitical rivalry and contributed to domestic political changes in both countries that have stoked tensions over the past 20 years.[46] Generational change in Japan has also diluted Japanese war guilt toward China, leading some Japanese leaders to test the old postwar taboos regarding what is permissible in terms of Japan's foreign and security policies, as well as seeking greater freedom at home to demonstrate pride in Japan's heritage. Prime Minister Koizumi's repeated visits from 2001 to 2005 to the Yasukuni Shrine (where the spirits of 14 class A war criminals are enshrined) were in this sense an attempt to put an end to the so-called "postwar era," but they came at the price of inciting a great amount of hostility toward Japan in many countries in Asia and especially in neighboring China, where millions lost their lives during the Japanese occupation from 1931 to 1945. The visits to Yasukuni led to the cessation of high-level summit meetings between Japan and China during this period and contributed to a significant chill in the feelings between the people of the two countries.

Japanese leaders point toward anti-Japanese protests in China that began in the 1990s that have grown more frequent and intense as evidence that the Chinese leadership has been using anti-Japanese sentiment among its public to fortify its own legitimacy.[47] A particularly revealing incident for the Japanese occurred in September 2010, when the Japanese Coast Guard arrested the captain of a Chinese fishing trawler in the waters near the disputed Senkaku (Chinese Diaoyu) islands. The Japanese people perceived as unduly harsh and arrogant the reaction of the Chinese government, which included postponement of high-level visits, energy talks, and joint cultural events, the sudden arrest of four Japanese civilians in China, and demands for compensation and an apology from Japan after the return of the ship's captain. In a survey conducted annually by the prime minister's office on Japan's foreign policy and diplomatic relations, over 88 percent of the respondents felt that Sino-Japanese ties were not good in 2010, the most-ever taking this position since the Treaty of Peace and Friendship was signed with China in 1978.[48]

Events such as the September 2010 fishing boat incident have convinced many policymakers in Tokyo that there are limits to the benefits of growing economic interdependence with China.[49] In fact, a shift away from Japan's traditional engagement policy with China has been long underway. The era of Japan's "friendship diplomacy" toward China may have ended with the Tiananmen massacre in June of 1989, when Japanese views of China began to change substantially.[50] The passage of China's territorial seas law in 1992, that suggested China could use force to assert claims over the disputed Senkaku/Diaoyu Islands, along with a series of nuclear tests in 1995, and Chinese military exercises aimed at intimidation of Taiwan during presidential elections of 1996, all contributed to Japan re-evaluating its policy toward China, although economic engagement accelerated during this period.[51]

China's support for North Korea's totalitarian regime has been another source of concern. North Korea's continued pursuit of nuclear weapons and long range missiles, along with its 2002 admission that it had kidnapped Japanese citizens during the 1970s and 1980s, alarmed Japanese citizens and has contributed to what Michael Green has termed Japan's new "reluctant realism."[52] China's decision to begin to drill for oil and natural gas in an area closely adjacent to Japan's claimed exclusive economic zone (EEZ) should also be added to the list of irritants in the relationship. Increasing Chinese naval activity in and around this area has been a major factor causing Japan to question China's peaceful intentions. Japan gradually phased out its ODA for China, who had been the top recipient of Japanese aid for many years. Growing apprehensions motivated Japan to list both North Korea and China as security concerns for the first time ever in the National Defense Program Guidelines (NDPG) of 2004.[53] In order to hedge against what it believes to be a heightening threat from China and North Korea, Japan has taken gradual steps to strengthen its alliance with the USA and incrementally increase its own defense capabilities from the late 1990s.[54]

In 2007, Michael Mochizuki characterized the developing "clusters" of Japanese political debate (1996–2006) about how to respond to a rising China under four strategic options: (1) cooperative engagement with a soft hedge, (2) competitive engagement with a hard edge, (3) balancing and containment, and (4) strategic containment.[55] The analysis indicated that options one and two were the most strongly supported, and that, " 'cooperative engagement with a soft hedge' became the mainstream successor to the 'friendship diplomacy' paradigm and 'competitive engagement with a hard edge' the leading alternative contender."[56] Mochizuki's analysis also carefully pointed out that the weighting between cooperative and competitive behavior in Japan's policy prescriptions toward China would in the future depend greatly on Chinese behavior, and could shift toward the latter should the Chinese continue its tough posture on the disputed EEZ issue and military activities in the East China Sea.[57] More recent events, including increasing Chinese assertiveness with regard to its territorial claims in both the South and East China Seas, accompanied by an ongoing naval build-up and increasing Chinese naval activity in these areas have combined to forge a strategic consensus in Japan on the need to further harden its military hedge toward China.[58] The NDPG announced in December 2010 introduced a number of significant changes in security policy aimed specifically at increasing Japan's capacity to defend its southern island chain and surrounding waters, and warns that, "China is stepping up and expanding maritime activities in the region's surrounding waters, and these activities, coupled with the lack of transparency shrouding China's military and security aims are of concern to the regional and global community."[59]

Though bilateral Sino-Japanese diplomacy resumed following Prime Minister Koizumi's departure from office in 2006, Japan's wider diplomacy has aimed at limiting China's growing influence both regionally and globally.[60] The harbinger of this competition came in 2001, when ASEAN endorsed Chinese Premier Zhu Rongji's proposal to develop a China-ASEAN Free Trade Area by 2010.[61] Prime Minister Junichiro Koizumi responded with a proposal for a Japan-ASEAN Closer Economic Partnership but appeared to be playing "catch-up" with China in an area that had long been a foreign policy stronghold for Japan.

With its shrinking ODA budgets and economic clout, Japan has shifted toward a more assertive approach in its diplomacy.[62] Japan's policy toward the region has undergone a significant transformation, taking on, as Yoshimatsu and Trinidad have argued, a much more strategic orientation with the goal of balancing China's growing influence in the region.[63] This includes the full spectrum of Japan's engagement, including its support for ASEAN integration, its disbursement of aid, the forging of bilateral and regional free trade agreements and economic partnerships with ASEAN, and recent initiatives related to Mekong regional development.[64] Japan has promoted a more "open" approach to regionalism, along with a focus on functional issues, universal values (democracy and human rights), and conformity to international regimes in an attempt to differentiate itself from China.[65] This shift has moved Japanese foreign policy closer in line with the United States, supplementing the stronger security ties mentioned above.

Sino-Japanese regional competition came to a head prior to the inaugural East Asia Summit in 2005, when Japan insisted upon the inclusion of India, Australia, and New Zealand as a means of diluting China's influence in the newly formed body.[66] In 2007 Japan proposed its own 16-country Comprehensive Economic Partnership Agreement (CEPA) for East Asia that further complicated the picture for regional integration. This facet of Japan's developing strategy toward China, in Christopher Hughes' words, "is thus to create a near-surfeit of regional frameworks in order to dilute its rival's rising power and to deny it clear or overall leadership in Asia."[67]

Japan has also attempted to build new strategic partnerships in order to counter China's influence. In areas such as Central Asia, the Middle East, and Africa, where it competes with China (and other emerging powers such as India) for energy and other natural resources, Japan has attempted to build on the foundations laid by its long-term economic assistance to play a more dynamic role in economic and political development. In doing so, Japan faces many challenges that will only grow with its dwindling ODA budget and economic stature. China's linkages to Central Asian countries through the Shanghai Cooperation Organization, the lack of conditionality to its rapidly expanding aid and investment in Africa, and its willingness to ignore international sanctions placed on Iran in the Middle East have given it a significant advantage in resource competition with Japan.[68] Because of Japan's relatively late start and China's growing advantages, many observers believe that this competition is China's game to win.[69]

India

If China represents the largest foreign policy challenge to Japan among the BRICs, India is perceived as the country with the most potential for helping Japan to cope with that challenge. By the 2030s India is expected to have the world's largest population and possibly the third largest economy behind China and the United States.[70] As a large democratic country in Asia registering annual average GDP growth rates of 6.6 percent between 1990 and 2010, India has grown increasingly attractive to Japanese policymakers as it attempts to confront China's growing influence in the region. The two countries share a mutual concern about China's rising power in Asia and have both moved to strengthen relations with the USA, though both countries also seek ways of preserving autonomy as they navigate between these two great powers.

Japan-India relations began to evolve following the end of the Cold War, especially as India began its economic reforms in the early 1990s. India's nuclear tests in May 1998 brought relations to a relative standstill for three years, but the relationship was revived when Japanese Prime Minister Yoshiro Mori visited New Delhi in August 2000 and signed an agreement for a bilateral "global partnership in a new Asian era."[71] Little follow-up to this agreement occurred until 2005, when Prime Minister Koizumi visited India to sign a new agreement with Indian Prime Minister Manmohan Singh for a "Japan-India partnership in a new Asian era." The Koizumi visit coincided with a shift in US policy toward India, signified in July of 2005 when US President George W. Bush and Prime Minister Singh issued a joint statement to begin negotiations on a peaceful nuclear cooperation agreement that would not require India to join the nuclear Non-Proliferation Treaty (NPT).[72] Japan's renewed efforts at strengthening its relationship with India during this period were also explicitly linked to its new "value oriented" diplomacy, which aimed at creating an "Arc of Freedom and Prosperity" across the outer rim of the Eurasian continent.[73]

The Koizumi-Singh meeting of 2005 laid the groundwork for annual summit meetings between the two countries. An exchange of visits by

Prime Minister Shinzo Abe and Prime Minister Singh in December 2006 and August 2007 led to the establishment of a "Japan-India global and strategic partnership," including the decision to launch negotiations for the conclusion of a bilateral CEPA. Japan also stepped up its ODA for India, with investments primarily focused on infrastructure development such as the Delhi-Mumbai industrial corridor (DMIC) and the Dedicated Freight Corridor (DFC) projects. These ODA investments have laid the groundwork for increased investment by Japanese corporations, which rose dramatically from 29.8 billion yen in 2005 to 542.9 billion yen in 2008.[74]

With the economic dimension of the new strategic partnership beginning to pay dividends, Prime Minister Singh went to Tokyo in October 2008 to sign the "Joint Declaration on Security Cooperation between Japan and India." The declaration indicated a broad array of common security interests, including protecting the sea lanes of communication and similar perceptions of "the evolving environment and world at large."[75] The document also indicated the intent to establish a variety of mechanisms for carrying out bilateral cooperation through ministerial and sub-ministerial level strategic dialogues between foreign affairs and defense officials. An implementation plan for the joint declaration was established when newly elected Prime Minister Yukio Hatoyama of the Democratic Party of Japan (DPJ) visited India on 29 December 2009 and signed the "Joint Statement on the New Stage of Japan and India Strategic Partnership." The action plan established "two plus two" foreign and defense ministerial meetings modeled on the Security Consultative Committee of the US-Japan Security Treaty. Hatoyama's early decision to follow through on the Liberal Democratic Party's policy by showing support for the Japan-India strategic partnership, despite his intent to build closer ties with China and enhance Japan's autonomy within the US-Japan alliance, reflected the overwhelming "geostrategic logic and momentum" gathering behind the relationship.[76]

Though Japan's economic relations with China continue to dwarf those between Japan and India, and actual security cooperation between the two countries remains limited, Japan appears to view the relationship with an eye to the future. Despite a relative stalemate in terms of resolving issues related to peaceful nuclear cooperation, the two countries managed to sign a CEPA agreement in February 2011 which then came into force in August of 2011. Japan's decision to exempt India from reductions in its ODA program following the March 2011 disasters further signified the strategic value it places on the relationship, as did announcements during Prime Minister Yoshiko Noda's December 2011 visit to India that Japan would contribute an additional 4.5 billion dollars for the DMIC project and expand an existing currency swap agreement from three to 15 billion dollars.

Russia

Unlike Japan's long-term cordial relations with India, geopolitical competition between Japan and Russia has marred their relationship for over a century. The negative legacy of the Russo-Japanese war of 1904–5, World War Two and Japan's alignment with the USA during the Cold War has undermined the efforts of these countries to develop stronger relations amidst mutual concerns with regard to Chinese influence in the region.[77] Though Japan and Russia normalized relations in 1956, they have yet to sign a peace treaty in order to formally end their brief hostilities during the final days of World War Two. The major sticking point in concluding a peace treaty and expanding bilateral relations has been a dispute over four islands off the northern tip of Hokkaido seized by the Soviet Union at the end of the war.

A number of attempts to resolve the dispute have been made, with each attempt ending in failure and resulting in renewed mistrust between the people of the two countries. In bilateral negotiations Japan has traditionally prioritized its demand for the return of all four islands, which it refers to as the Northern Territories. Russia has, on the other hand, emphasized the need to strengthen the bilateral relationship through cooperation and trade prior to a final resolution of the territorial problem. Russia is particularly concerned with gaining Japanese cooperation in developing the sparsely populated Russian Far East, which it fears may become economically dependent upon China to the south.[78] Lured by the promise of lessening its energy dependence on the Middle East and the prospect of establishing the basis for a future resolution of the territorial issue, Japan has pursued a more comprehensive approach to the relationship along the lines suggested by the Russians over the past decade. In May 2003 Prime Minister Koizumi initiated a Japan-Russia Action Plan, which was supplemented in 2007 by Japan's "Initiative for Strengthening Japan-Russia Cooperation in the Russian Far East and Eastern Siberia." The Action Plan promotes cooperation in a number of areas, including economics, defense exchanges, and especially energy cooperation.[79]

Under the Action Plan trade, between Japan and Russia expanded rapidly, from less than US$6 billion in 2003 to almost 30 billion in 2008, prior to declining during the global financial crisis. Japan has exported primarily automobiles and machinery, while imports have been heavily weighted in favor of energy and minerals.[80] Japan and Russia have extended their energy cooperation in a number of areas, including Japan's involvement in the Sakhalin 1 and Sakhalin 2 energy projects, several joint development projects between Russian energy companies, and Japan's Oil, Gas and Metals National Corporation (JOGMEC), and an agreement on cooperation in the peaceful use of nuclear energy that was signed by the two governments in May of 2009. Russia's share of Japan's oil imports increased from 0.7 percent in 2005 to 6.1 percent by the first half of 2010, making it the largest supplier of oil to Japan outside the Middle East.[81]

This increase in trade and energy cooperation has, however, not yielded Japan's desired result in terms of improving the strategic relationship or moving toward the return of the four islands which Japan claims as its own. Despite the increases in trade and energy cooperation, the bilateral relationship as a whole appears to have worsened over the past few years. The Russian stance toward the disputed islands appears to have only stiffened, with President Dmitry Medvedev making an unprecedented visit to the island of Kunashiri in November 2010. Public criticism of the event by Japanese leadership set off a more intense nationalistic response in Russia and the announcement in February 2011 that the island's military contingent would be fortified. Japan's National Institute for Defense Studies, which is closely affiliated with the Japanese Ministry of Defense, characterized Russia's stance on the Northern Territories as "increasingly belligerent" in 2011, noting not only the above actions but also military exercises that have recently included the disputed territories.[82]

Brazil

Brazil plays a much less significant role in Japan's foreign policy than the other BRIC nations, despite close social connections that developed as a result of Japanese immigration that began in the early 1900s. There are currently about 1.5 million people of Japanese descent living in Brazil, representing approximately 60 percent of the Japanese diaspora worldwide. A good number of the Nikkei (as the Japanese refer to them) began to migrate "back" to Japan in the 1980s when the economy was booming. In 2009 the Nikkei population in Japan was approximately 267,500, making them the third largest immigrant population behind the Chinese and Korean populations.[83]

Economic relations between Japan and Brazil languished throughout the 1980s and 1990s as first Brazil and then Japan suffered through long periods of economic recession and stagnation. Bilateral relations received a shot in the arm when Prime Minister Koizumi visited Brazil in September 2004 to discuss his "Vision for a New Japan-Latin America and Caribbean Partnership." Koizumi's talks with President Luiz Inacio Lula da Silva of Brazil focused on reinvigorating economic relations, coordinating the two countries bid with India and Germany to become permanent members of the UN Security Council, and established 2008 as the year of "Japan-Brazil Exchange." Koizumi's efforts in 2004 also laid the groundwork for Japan's free trade agreement with MERCOSUL (Common Market of the South) in 2007.[84]

Japan's move to rebuild its relationship with Brazil coincided with China's efforts to increase its presence in Latin America. In 2004, an exchange of state visits between Brazilian President Lula da Silva and Chinese President Hu Jintao led to the signing of an agreement to establish a bilateral mechanism of high-level strategic dialogue to address bilateral, regional and global issues of concern. China's interest, much like Japan's, has been to acquire Brazilian natural resources such as oil, iron-ore, and food stuffs. China's trade with Brazil grew from US$2.3 billion in 2000 to US39.9 billion in 2009, when it became Brazil's number one trade partner.[85] Meanwhile, Japan-Brazil trade expanded from US$2.5 billion in 2000 to only US$6.2 billion by 2010.[86] The Japanese government's attempt to foster greater investment in Brazil by Japanese corporations has similarly been overshadowed by Chinese efforts in the past few years. Chinese State Owned Enterprises (SOEs), flush with cheap government loans, flooded Brazil with some 17.4 billion of FDI in 2010.[87]

Recently there has been some blowback from Chinese investments in the politically sensitive area of farmlands, causing Brazilian leaders to reflect on the strategic partnership that they have formed with China.[88] China is also on the wrong side of Brazil's attempt to gain a permanent UN Security Council seat along with Japan, India, and Germany. Still, it is Chinese trade and investment, much more than Japan's, which has driven Brazil's rise and provided hope for millions of Brazilian people. Despite Japan's deep historical roots in Brazil and a common interest in UN Security Council reform, China's influence in Brazil is likely to continue to grow.

Relations with the EU and US

In attempting to counter China's growing influence and reinforce its own international stature Japan has moved to strengthen relations with the European Union (EU), emphasizing the need to broaden the strategic relationship beyond traditional economic matters to encompass political and security issues of common concerns. The EU recognized Japan as one of its strategic partners in 2003, but thus far the relationship has been hamstrung by a number of differences on trade-related issues and a close operational partnership to deal with common concerns related to climate change and other transnational problems has not been achieved. Japan's diplomatic efforts toward the EU were catalyzed during 2004–5, when the EU began considering lifting the ban on arms sales to China that was instituted after the Tiananmen incident in 1989. China has made getting the arms ban lifted and obtaining market economy status under the WTO two of its major objectives in its own diplomatic efforts toward the EU. In support of these goals China has increased its investment in EU countries and begun purchasing debt bonds from individual EU countries attempting to cope with severe fiscal crises, along with purchasing bonds from the EFSF.[89] Japan has made its own purchases of EFSF bonds, but will need to deal effectively with longstanding complaints regarding nontariff trade barriers if it intends to forge a more dynamic economic relationship with the EU, which like Japan faces severe macroeconomic problems and is competing fiercely to broaden its position in the China market. In May 2011 Japanese Prime Minister Naoto Kan agreed with EU Council President Herman Van Rompuy and European Commission President Jose Manuel Barroso to start "the process for negotiations" on a free-trade pact, which will include discussions to decide the areas that such a deal would cover.[90] Though formal negotiations for a free trade pact have not begun, both sides have emphasized the need to develop the strategic relationship based on a shared commitment to fundamental values and principles, including democracy, the rule of law and human rights, market-based economies and sustainable development.

While the security dimension plays a relatively small part in Japan's relations with the EU, a security alliance with the USA forms the cornerstone of Japanese foreign policy. Japan's security alliance with the USA provides extended leverage in hedging against Chinese adventurism and enhances its position relative to other East Asian states interested in keeping the USA credible in regional deterrence.[91] Many of the incremental steps Japan has taken over the past 20 years to enhance its role in international security, including its support for international peacekeeping activities, broadening the scope of its logistical support to US forces, and participating in joint development of missile defense technology, have been implemented as part of a strategy to demonstrate the ongoing value of the alliance to the United States. Japan's support for US military bases in its territory, though controversial domestically, has also allowed Japan to maintain a much lower military profile in Asia than would have been necessary otherwise. However, as China increases its military strength and influence the demands on Japan to keep the alliance relevant to the USA have grown accordingly. To meet these demands Japan will need to not only increase its own defense capacity, but also develop the political will to find solutions to long-standing irritants in the US-Japan relationship, including trade issues and issues related to the relocation of US military bases in Okinawa. Resolutions to these issues will provide the relationship with new impetus for confronting the many challenges of a changing world order.

Conclusion: Japan's Role in the Emerging World Order

While destined to decline amongst the world's economic powers, Japan has a number of strengths that will continue to provide it with leverage as a new order emerges. Japan's population is highly educated and its high-tech industries remain competitive, though many are losing ground to South Korea, China, and Taiwan.[92] The World Economic Forum ranked Japan ninth in overall competiveness in its 2011–12 Global Competitiveness Report, down from sixth a year earlier.[93] The report indicates that Japan continues to retain a major competitive edge in business sophistication and innovation, ranking first and fourth in these areas respectively. Spending on research and development is another Japanese strength, as it ranks second highest in terms of the number of new patents filed per capita. Japan's overall competitiveness, however, continues to be dragged down by its "severe macroeconomic weaknesses."[94]

Without drastic policy shifts to deal with these macroeconomic weaknesses Japan's descent from the world stage could be a precipitous one. The dramatic victory of the DPJ in August 2009 raised hopes among some observers that the Japanese electorate had finally "spoken" with regard to the economic and social failures of the past, demanding change that would confront vested interests and take bold steps toward the many problems facing the Japanese political economy.[95] The DPJ offered new policies aimed at making it easier for families to bear the costs of raising children and attempted early on to confront the entrenched powers of the bureaucracy. The March 2011 earthquake, tsunami, and nuclear disasters have since drawn resources and political inertia away from these efforts, without inspiring the Japanese to pull together for the sake of the nation's long-term benefit. Political factionalism, vested interests, and stagnation continue to rule the day. Nor has the public shown much awareness that change is desperately needed. Current Japanese Prime Minister Yoshihiko Noda, intent upon doubling the sales tax from 5 to 10 percent, faces strong opposition not only from the public (53 percent) and opposition parties, but from many inside the DPJ itself.[96] This lack of support for what many observers believe to be an insufficient remedy comes despite the fact that Japan's tax burden remains among the lowest in the industrialized world.[97]

This fundamental complacency and lack of political will to tackle Japan's domestic problems leave the country very few options with regard to confronting the challenges it faces with the rise of China and other emerging powers. With dwindling economic resources, Japan has turned toward a more strategic and ideological approach to foreign policy over the past decade, promoting the universal values championed by its alliance partner while attempting to undermine China's growing influence in the region and the world. This ideological shift in Japanese foreign policy initiated by conservative nationalists was initially criticized by many liberals and has been toned down in recent years. Yet as the public has grown increasingly wary of a China threat, even more liberal minded Japanese strategists have begun to support policies which emphasize stronger defense capabilities and building security cooperation with "like-minded" countries in the region.[98]

Many conservative strategists have meanwhile begun to demonstrate cognizance of Japan's limitations with regard to confronting China. A recent policy proposal led by the conservative Tokyo Foundation on Japan's security strategy toward China clearly recognizes Japan's eclipse by Asia's new giant and recommends integrating with China bilaterally, regionally, and globally, while at the same time balancing China diplomatically and upgrading Japan's deterrence capabilities.[99] The fear of Japanese strategists is no longer that Japan will lose its top status in Asia, but that China will soon be powerful enough to achieve equilibrium with the United States. As Ken Jimbo and his fellow project members at the Tokyo Foundation write:

> As the US-China power relationship changes progressively in the direction of parity with the USA, the possibility that China's national power or influence could be shaped by one country or one-sidedly becomes increasingly remote for a small and medium-sized country that is deepening its mutual interdependence with China. In fact, that possibility is already remote even for Japan and the USA acting together.[100]

Japanese perceive a deep divide between China's official pronouncements regarding its willingness to support the established liberal international order and an unyielding pursuit of its national interests in foreign relations. Japan views its future international role as both complex and limited, aimed at sustaining the US-centered liberal international order while building pathways to integrate China. Whereas only two decades ago Japan was exploring paths to establish its own global leadership, today its focus is primarily on ways of staying relevant.

Endnotes

1 Eamonn Fingleton, *Blindside: Why Japan is still on track to overtake the U.S. by the year 2000.* (Tokyo: Kodansha International, 1995).

2 Yoichi Funabashi, "Japan and the New World Order," *Foreign Affairs.* (Winter, 1991/1992), 58–74.

3 What is meant by a "normal nation" varies significantly among proponents of this idea. The notion centers around removing the abnormal limitations

imposed on Japan by its postwar constitution, in particular Article 9, which renounces war as a sovereign right and formally bans Japan from maintaining military forces. The seminal statement of this position is found in Ichiro Ozawa, *Nihon Kaizo Keikaku* (Tokyo: Kodansha International, 1993); published in English as *Blueprint for a New Japan: Rethinking of a Nation*, translated by Louisa Rubenfien (Tokyo: Kodansha International, 1994). For a discussion of various conservative views on normalizing Japan see Cheol Hee Park, "Conservative Conceptions of Japan as a 'Normal Country': Comparing Ozawa, Nakasone, and Ishihara," in Yoshihide Soeya, Masayuki Tadokoro, and David A. Welch eds., *Japan as a Normal Country? A Nation in Search of its Place in the World.* (Toronto: University of Toronto Press, 2011).

4 See Gilbert Rozman's discussion in, "Japan's Quest for Great Power Identity," *Orbis* 46, no. 1. (Winter 2002), 73–91.

5 See for example Yoichi Funabashi, "Japan-China Relations Stand at Ground Zero," *Asahi Shimbun.* (9 October 2010).

6 Yoshihide Soeya, *Nihon no "Midoru Pawaa" Gaiko: Sengo Nihon no Sentaku to Kōsō* [Japan's Middle Power Diplomacy: Postwar Japan's Choices and Conceptions]. (Tokyo: Chikuma Shinsho, 2005).

7 World Bank, World Development Indicators, 2011, http://data.worldbank. org/data-catalog/world-development-indicators

8 Ibid.

9 Yasuhiro Goto, "Asian Economy at a Glance: Development and Challenges," presentation for The 15th International Conference on the Future of Asia. (Tokyo, 21 May 2009).

10 Ibid.

11 Douglas H. Brooks and Susan F. Stone, "Accelerating Regional Integration: Issues at the Border," ADBI Working Paper 200, Asian Development Bank Institute (February 2010), http://www.adbi.org/working-paper/2010/02/25/ 3587.accelerating.regional.integration/

12 Ibid., 4.

13 For a positive evaluation of Koizumi's economic reforms see Yoshihiro Sakai, "Japan's Economy in the Post Reform Era," Center for Strategic and International Studies. (26 April 2006), http://csis.org/files/media/csis/ pubs/060426_jcp.pdf For a critical view see Aurelia George Mulgan, *Japan's Failed Revolution: Koizumi and the Politics of Economic Reform.* (Canberra: Asia Pacific press, 2002).

14 William W. Grimes, "Japan, the Global Financial Crisis, and the Stability of East Asia" in Ashley J. Tellis, Andrew Marble, and Travis Tanner (eds), *Strategic Asia 2009–2010: Economic Meltdown and Geopolitical Stability.* (Seattle and Washington D.C.: The National Bureau of Asian Research, 2009), 107.

15 Peter Tasker, "Reflating Japan," in Clay Chandler, Heang Chhor, and Brian Salsberg executive (eds), *Reimagining Japan: The Quest for a Future That Works.* (San Francisco: Mckinsey & Company, 2011).

16 Akira Kojima, "Japan's Economy and the Global Financial Crisis," *Asia-Pacific Review*, 16, no. 2. (2009), 15–25.

17 William W. Grimes, "Japan, the Global Financial Crisis, and the Stability of East Asia," *Strategic Asia 2009–2010: Economic Meltdown and Geopolitical Stability*, National Bureau of Asian Research. (September 2009), 105–7.

18 Akira Kojima, "Japan's Economy and the Global Financial Crisis," 18–20, "Japan unable to fend for itself," *The Economist* (24 January 2008), http://www.economist.com/node/10567586 and Martin Sommer, "Why has Japan been hit so hard by the Global Recession" IMF Staff Position Note, International Monetary Fund (18 March 2009): http://www.imf.org/external/pubs/ft/spn/2009/spn0905.pdf

19 Martin Mühleisen and Harmid Faruqee, "Japan Population Aging and the Fiscal Challenge," *Finance and Development*, 38, no. 1, International Monetary Fund (March 2001), http://www.imf.org/external/pubs/ft/fandd/2001/03/muhleise.htm

20 OECD "Economic Outlook 90," (December 2011), http://www.oecd.org/document/18/0,3746,en_2649_33733_20347538_1_1_1_1,00.html

21 Japanese Ministry of Finance, "Highlights of the Budget for 2011," December 2010, http://www.mof.go.jp/english/budget/budget/fy2011/e20101224a.pdf

22 Lindsay Whipp and Mure Dickie, "S&P downgrades Japan on debt worries," *Financial Times*. (27 January 2011), http://www.ft.com/cms/s/0/095efb70-29f3-11e0-997c-00144feab49a.html#axzz1dY1Xkq3Y

23 Graeme Wearden, "Japan credit rating downgraded over ballooning deficit," *The Guardian*. (24 August 2011), http://www.guardian.co.uk/business/2011/aug/24/japan-credit-rating-downgraded

24 International Monetary Fund, "Addressing Fiscal Challenges to Reduce Economic Risks," *Fiscal Monitor*. (September 2011), http://www.imf.org/external/pubs/ft/fm/2011/02/pdf/fm1102.pdf

25 See Narai Osamu, "The Sorry State of Japan's Public Finances," (3 October 2011), http://nippon.com/en/in-depth/a00103/

26 Michael Sutton, "Lowest-Low Fertility in Japan: Consequences for a Once-Great Nation," *Bulletin of Geography*, Socio-Economic Series 12 (2009), 61–72.

27 Statistics Bureau of Japan, "2010 Japan Census," (26 October 2011), http://www.stat.go.jp/english/data/kokusei/2010/basic1/pdf/summary.pdf

28 Japanese Ministry of Finance, "Highlights of the Budget for FY2011," (December 2010), http://www.mof.go.jp/english/budget/budget/fy2011/e20101224a.pdf

29 Japanese Ministry of Foreign Affairs, "Japan's Official Development Assistance White Paper 2010," http://www.mofa.go.jp/policy/oda/white/2010/index.html

30 See Osamu Nariai, "The Sorry State of Japan's Public Finances," (3 October 2011), http://nippon.com/en/in-depth/a00103/

31 Stephen G. Cecchetti, M.S. Mohanty and Fabrizio Zampolli, "The Future of Public Debt: Prospects and implications," *BIS Working Papers*, Bank for International Settlements (March 2010), http://www.bis.org/publ/work300.pdf

32 National Institute of Population and Social Security Research, "Population Projection for Japan 2011–2060," (30 January 2012), http://www.ipss.go.jp/syoushika/tohkei/newest04/gh2401.pdf

33 The Bank of Japan, "The Effects of Demographics in Japan on the Macro-Economy" cited in Kazumasa Oguro, "Japan's Looming Financial Collapse," *Asia-Pacific Review* 17, no. 2 (2010): 126–7. Similar projections are provided in Robert L. Clark, Naohiro Ogawa, Makoto Kondo and Rikiya Matsukura, "Population Decline, Labor Force Stability and the Future of the Japanese Economy," *European Journal of Population* 26. (2010), 207–27.

34 Martin Mühleisen and Harmid Faruqee, "Japan Population Aging and the Fiscal Challenge," *Finance and Development*, International Monetary Fund. (March 2001), http://www.imf.org/external/pubs/ft/fandd/2001/03/muhleise.htm

35 Dominic Wilson and Roopa Purushothaman, "Dreaming with the BRICs: The Path to 2050," Goldman Sachs, Global Economics Paper 99. (1 October 2003). The "G6" refers to the USA, Japan, Germany, France, Italy and the United Kingdom.

36 Jim O'Neill and Anna Stupnytska, "The Long-Term Outlook for the BRICs and N-11 Post Crisis," Goldman Sachs, Global Economics Paper 192. (4 December 2009).

37 Research Institute of Economy, Trade and Industry, "China as the Central Player of the BRICs: Driving the world and the Japanese economy," RIETI (accessed 10 October 2011), http://www.rieti.go.jp/en/china/10082701.html

38 Research Institute of Economy, Trade and Industry, "Emerging-Nation Effect or "China Effect," RIETI. (accessed 10 October 2011), http://www.rieti.go.jp/en/china/11031501.html

39 2005 JETRO White Paper on Trade and Foreign Direct Investment (Tokyo: Japan External Trade Organization, 2005), 29–33.

40 Research Institute of Economy, Trade and Industry, "Emerging-Nation Effect," 2.

41 Chi Hung Kwan, quoted at a professional luncheon on August 24, 2010 in Tyler Deffebach, "Japan as Number Three," The Foreign Correspondent's Club of Japan, http://www.fccj.or.jp/node/6028 (accessed 3 November 2011).

42 Ibid.

43 Nippon Keidanren, "Japan-China Relations in the 21st Century: Recommendations for Building a Relationship of Trust and Expanding Economic Exchanges between Japan and China," (Tokyo, 20 February 2001), http://www.keidanren.or.jp/english/policy/2001/006.html

44 Nippon Keidanren, "Recommendations for Expanding Economic and Trade Ties with China Following Its Accession to the World Trade Organization,"

(Tokyo, 20 May 2003), http://www.keidanren.or.jp/english/policy/2003/045/part1.html#s1

45 Nippon Keidanren, "The Third Japan-China-Korea Business Summit Joint Statement," (Tokyo, 22 May 2011), http://www.keidanren.or.jp/english/policy/2011/052.html

46 Christopher W. Hughes, "Japan's policy towards China: domestic structural change, globalization, history and nationalism," in Christopher M. Dent ed., *China, Japan and regional Leadership in East Asia.* (Cheltenham and Northampton, M.A.: Edward Elgar, 2008), 37–51.

47 Michael Yahuda, "Sino-Japanese relations: partners and rivals?" *Korean Journal of Defense Analysis*, 21, no. 4. (December 2009), 371.

48 Japanese Cabinet Office, "2010 Gaiko ni suru Yoron Chōsa," [2010 Foreign Relations Poll], http://www8.cao.go.jp/survey/h22/h22-gaiko/zh/z10.html

49 For discussion of the limits of economic interdependence in Sino-Japanese relations see Michael Yahuda, "The Limits of Economic Interdependence: Sino-Japanese Relations," in Alastair Iain Johnson and Robert S. Ross eds., *New Directions in the Study of China's Foreign Policy.* (Stanford: Stanford University Press, 2006), 162–85 and Denny Roy, "The Sources and Limits of Sino-Japanese Tensions," Survival 47 (Summer 2005), 191–214.

50 Mike M. Mochizuki, "Japan's Shifting Strategy toward the Rise of China," *The Journal of Strategic Studies* 30, no. 4–5. (August-October 2007), 739–76.

51 Yahuda, "Sino-Japanese relations: partners and rivals?," 371 and David Fouse, "History as a Mirror, the Future as a Window: Japan's China Debate," in Satu Limaye ed., Asia's China Debate. (Honolulu: Asia-Pacific Center for Security Studies, December 2003).

52 Michael J. Green, Japan's *Reluctant Realism: Foreign Policy Challenges in an Era of Uncertain Power.* (New York: Palgrave Macmillan, 2001).

53 David Fouse, "Japan's FY 2005 National Defense Program Outline: New Concepts, Old Compromises," Asia-Pacific Center for Security Studies, 4, no. 3. (March 2005).

54 For detailed discussion see Christopher W. Hughes, *Japan's Remilitarization* (London: Routledge, 2009) and Richard J. Samuels, *Securing Japan: Tokyo's Grand Strategy and the Future of East Asia* (Ithaca and London: Cornell University Press, 2007).

55 Mike M. Mochizuki, "Japan's Shifting Strategy," 758.

56 Ibid., 767.

57 Ibid., 771–3.

58 David Fouse, "Japan's New Defense Policy for 2010: Hardening the Hedge," *Korean Journal of Defense Analysis* 23, no. 4. (December 2011), 489–501.

59 Japanese Ministry of Defense, "National Defense Program Guidelines for FY 2011 and beyond," (December 2010), http://www.mod.go.jp/e/d_act/d_policy/pdf/guidelinesFY2011.pdf

60 Christopher W. Hughes, "Japan's response to China's rise: regional engagement, global containment, dangers of collision," *International Affairs* 85, no. 4. (2009), 837–56.

61 Michael Weasley, "Jealous suitors: Sino-Japanese competitive regionalism and the future of East Asia," in Michael Heazle and Nick Knight eds., *China-Japan Relations in the Twenty-first Century: Creating a Future Past?* (Cheltenham and Northampton, M.A., Edward Elgar, 2007), 216–217.

62 Ibid., 210.

63 Hidetaka Yoshimatsu and Dennis D. Trinidad, "Development Assistance, Strategic Interests, and the China Factor in Japan's Role in ASEAN Integration," *Japanese Journal of Political Science* 11, no. 2. (2010), 199–219.

64 Ibid., 236.

65 Hughes, "Japan's response to China," 847.

66 Mohan Malik, "China and the East Asia Summit: More Discord than Accord," Asia-Pacific Center for Security Studies (February 2006).

67 Hughes, "Japan's response to China," 847.

68 Ibid., 848–55.

69 See for example, Jacob Townsend and Amy King, "Sino-Japanese Competition for Central Asian Energy: China's Game to Win," *China and Eurasia Forum Quarterly*, 5, no. 4. (2007), 23–45.

70 Jim O'Neill and Anna Stupnytska, "The Long-Term Outlook for the BRICs," 23.

71 Satu Limaye, "Japan and India after the Cold War," in Yoichiro Sato and Satu Limaye eds., *Japan in a Dynamic Asia: Coping with the New Security Challenges.* (Lanham, M.D.: Lexington, 2006), 225–9.

72 Michael Green, "Japan, India, and the Strategic Triangle with China," in Ashley J. Tellis, Travis Tanner, and Jessica Keough, eds., *Strategic Asia 2011–12: Asia Responds to Its Rising Powers – China and India.* (National Bureau of Asian Research, 2011), 137.

73 Speech by Mr. Taro Aso, Minister for Foreign Affairs, on the Occasion of the Japan Institute of International Affairs Seminar, "Arc of Freedom and Prosperity: Japan's Expanding Diplomatic Horizons." (30 November 2006), http://www.mofa.go.jp/announce/fm/aso/speech0611.html

74 Japanese Ministry of Foreign Affairs, "Japan-India Relations," http://www.mofa.go.jp/region/asia-paci/india/index.html

75 Japanese Ministry of Foreign Affairs, "Joint Declaration on Security Cooperation between Japan and India," (22 October 2008), http://www.mofa.go.jp/region/asia-paci/india/pmv0810/joint_d.html

76 Green, "Japan, India, and the Strategic Triangle with China," 142.

77 For Russia's interest in strengthening relations with Japan in order to hedge against China see Leszek Buszynski, "Overshadowed by China: The

Russia-China Strategic Partnership in the Asia-Pacific Region" in James Bellacqua (ed.), *The Future of China-Russia Relations.* (Lexington: University of Kentucky Press, 2010), 266–89.

78 Eric Pardo Sauvageot, "Northern Territories and Japan-Russia Relations: Latest Developments under Prime Minister Taro," UNISCI Discussion Papers 20 (May 2009).

79 Hughes, "Japan's response to China," 848.

80 Japanese Ministry of Foreign Affairs, "Trends in Japan-USSR and Japan-Russia Trade Volume (1991–2010) and "Structure of Japan-Russia Trade 2010," http://www.mofa.go.jp/region/europe/russia/economy/index.html

81 World Politics Review, "Russia-Japan Energy Cooperation," (31 January 2011), http://www.worldpoliticsreview.com/trend-lines/7730/global-insider-russia-japan-energy-cooperation

82 National Institute for Defense Studies, *East Asian Strategic Review 2011.* (Tokyo: The Japan Times, 2011).

83 Japanese Ministry of Foreign Affairs, "Japan-Brazil Relations," http://www.mofa.go.jp/region/latin/brazil/index.html

84 Japanese Ministry of Foreign Affairs, "Visit by Prime Minister Junichiro Koizumi to Latin America (Overview, Evaluation and Specific Results)," (September 2009), http://www.mofa.go.jp/region/latin/pmv0409/overview.html

85 Carlos Pereira and Joao Augusto de Castro Neves, "Brazil and China: South-South Partnership or North-South Competition?" Brookings Institution, Policy Paper 26. (March 2011), http://www.brookings.edu/papers/2011/03_brazil_china_pereira.aspx

86 World Trade Organization, *International Trade Statistics 2011*, http://www.wto.org/english/res_e/statis_e/its2011_e/its11_toc_e.htm

87 Alexander Kliment, "Brazil's Official Tally of Chinese investment, *Financial Times.* (15 September 2011), http://tilt.ft.com/#!posts/2011–09/30246/brazils-official-tally-of-chinese-investment

88 Alexei Barrionuevo, "China's Interest in Farmland Makes Brazil Uneasy," *New York Times.* (26 May 2011), http://www.nytimes.com/2011/05/27/world/americas/27brazil.html?pagewanted=all

89 Alicia Sorroza, "Is the Eurozone Crisis Changing EU-China Relations?" Real Instituto Elcano. (4 December 2011), http://www.realinstitutoelcano.org/wps/portal/rielcano_eng/Print?WCM_GLOBAL_CONTEXT=/wps/wcm/connect/elcano/Elcano_in/Zonas_in/ARI154–2011

90 Japanese Ministry of Foreign Affairs, "20th EU-Japan Summit," Joint Press Statement. (28 May 2011), http://www.mofa.go.jp/region/europe/eu/joint1105.html

91 Evelyn Goh, "How Japan matters in the evolving East Asian security order," *International Affairs* 87, no. 4. (2011), 887–902.

92 The Economist, "Japan's Technology Champions: Invisible but Indispensable," (5 November 2009), http://www.economist.com/node/14793432

93 World Economic Forum, "Global Competitiveness Report for 2011–2012," http://www3.weforum.org/docs/WEF_GCR_Report_2011–12.pdf

94 Ibid., 24.

95 J.A.A. Stockwin, "Political Earthquake in Japan: How Much of a Difference Will it Make?" in Purnendra Jain and Brad Williams (eds), *Japan in Decline: Fact or Fiction?* (Folkstone: Global Oriental, 2011), 18–34.

96 Yuko Kobota, "Japan PM eyes election if tax bills don't pass: report," Reuters. (2 January 2012), http://www.reuters.com/article/2012/01/03/us-japan-politics-idUSTRE80203520120103

97 Japanese Ministry of Finance, "Budget for FY 2012: Appendix," http://www.mof.go.jp/english/budget/budget/fy2012/e20111224c.pdf

98 Results of an AP-GFK poll carried out by Roper July 20–August 10, 2011 in Japan indicated that 73 percent of the Japanese public thinks that China poses a threat to peace in the world. For discussion of liberal strategists supporting upgrading defense measures aimed at China and increasing security cooperation with like-minded countries in the region see David Fouse, "Japan's New Defense Policy for 2010," 491–2.

99 Ken Jimbo et al., "Japan's Strategy Toward China: Integration, Balancing and Deterrence in an Era of Power Shift," (The Tokyo Foundation, October 2011), http://www.tokyofoundation.org/en/additional_info/security_strategy_toward_china.pdf

100 Ibid, 32.

Bibliography

Aso, Taro. "Arc of Freedom and Prosperity: Japan's Expanding Diplomatic Horizons," (30 November 2006), http://www.mofa.go.jp/announce/fm/aso/speech0611.html

Barrionuevo, Alexei. "China's Interest in Farmland Makes Brazil Uneasy," *The New York Times*. (26 May 2011), http://www.nytimes.com/2011/05/27/world/americas/27brazil.html?pagewanted=all

Bellacqua, James (ed.). *The Future of China-Russia Relations*. (Lexington: University of Kentucky Press, 2010).

Brooks, Douglas H. and Susan F. Stone. "Accelerating Regional Integration: Issues at the Border," ADBI Working Paper 200, *Asian Development Bank Institute*. (February 2010), http://www.adbi.org/working-paper/2010/02/25/3587.accelerating.regional.integration/

Buszynski, Leszek. "Overshadowed by China: The Russia-China Strategic Partnership in the Asia-Pacific Region," in James Bellacqua (ed.), *The Future of China-Russia Relations*. (Lexington: University of Kentucky Press, 2010).

Cecchetti, Stephen G., M. S. Mohanty and Fabrizio Zampolli. "The Future of Public Debt: Prospects and Implications," BIS Working Papers, Bank for International Settlements. (March 2010), http://www.bis.org/publ/work300.pdf

Chandler, Clay, Heang Chhor, and Brian Salsberg (eds), *Reimagining Japan: The Quest for a Future That Works*. (San Francisco: Mckinsey & Company, 2011).

Clark, Robert L., Naohiro Ogawa, Makoto Kondo and Rikiya Matsukura. "Population Decline, Labor Force Stability and the Future of the Japanese Economy," *European Journal of Population* 26 (2010), 207–27.

Dent, Christopher M. (ed.). *China, Japan and regional Leadership in East Asia.* (Cheltenham and Northampton, M.A., Edward Elgar, 2008), 37–51.

Economist, "Japan's Technology Champions: Invisible but Indispensable," (5 November 2009), http://www.economist.com/node/14793432

Fingleton, Eamonn. *Blindside: Why Japan is still on track to overtake the U.S. by the year 2000.* (Tokyo: Kodansha International, 1995).

Fouse, David. "History as a Mirror, the Future as a Window: Japan's China Debate," in Satu Limaye (ed.), *Asia's China Debate.* (Honolulu: Asia-Pacific Center for Security Studies, December 2003).

—"Japan's FY 2005 National Defense Program Outline: New Concepts, Old Compromises," Asia-Pacific Center for Security Studies, 4, no. 3. (March 2005).

—"Japan's New Defense Policy for 2010: Hardening the Hedge," *Korean Journal of Defense Analysis* 23, no. 4. (December 2011), 489–501.

Funabashi, Yoichi. "Japan and the New World Order," *Foreign Affairs* (Winter, 1991/1992), 58–74.

Funabashi, Yoichi. "Japan-China Relations Stand at Ground Zero," *Asahi Shimbun.* (9 October 2010).

George Mulgan, Aurelia. *Japan's Failed Revolution: Koizumi and the Politics of Economic Reform.* (Canberra: Asia Pacific Press, 2002).

Goh, Evelyn. "How Japan matters in the evolving East Asian security order," *International Affairs* 87, no. 4. (2011), 887–902.

Goto, Yasuhiro. "Asian Economy at a Glance: Development and Challenges," The 15th International Conference on the Future of Asia. (Tokyo, 21 May 2009).

Green, Michael J. "Japan, India, and the Strategic Triangle with China," in Ashley J. Tellis, Travis Tanner, and Jessica Keough (eds). *Strategic Asia 2011–12: Asia Responds to Its Rising Powers – China and India.* (National Bureau of Asian Research, 2011), 137.

—*Japan's Reluctant Realism: Foreign Policy Challenges in an Era of Uncertain Power.* (New York: Palgrave Macmillan, 2001).

Grimes, William W. "Japan, the Global Financial Crisis, and the Stability of East Asia," *Strategic Asia 2009–2010: Economic Meltdown and Geopolitical Stability*, The National Bureau of Asian Research. (September 2009), 105–7.

Heazle, Michael, and Nick Knight (eds), *China-Japan Relations in the Twenty-first Century: Creating a Future Past?* (Cheltenham and Northampton, M.A., Edward Elgar, 2007), 216–17.

Hughes, Christopher W. "Japan's policy towards China: domestic structural change, globalization, history and nationalism," in Christopher M. Dent (ed.), *China, Japan and regional Leadership in East Asia.* (Cheltenham and Northampton, M.A.: Edward Elgar, 2008), 37–51.

—"Japan's response to China's rise: regional engagement, global containment, dangers of collision," *International Affairs.* 85:4 (2009), 837–56.

—*Japan's Remilitarization* (London: Routledge, 2009).

International Monetary Fund, "Addressing Fiscal Challenges to Reduce Economic Risks," Fiscal Monitor. (September 2011), http://www.imf.org/external/pubs/ft/fm/2011/02/pdf/fm1102.pdf

Jain, Purnendra and Brad Williams (eds). *Japan in Decline: Fact or Fiction?* (Folkstone: Global Oriental, 2011), 18–34.

Japan External Trade Organization. "2005 JETRO White Paper on International Trade and Foreign Direct Investment," http://www.jetro.go.jp/en/reports/white_paper/2005.pdf

—"2011 JETRO Global Trade and Investment Report," http://www.jetro.go.jp/en/reports/white_paper/trade_invest_2011.pdf

Japanese Ministry of Defense. "National Defense Program Guidelines for FY 2011 and Beyond," (December 2011), http://www.mod.go.jp/e/d_act/d_policy/pdf/guidelinesFY2011.pdf

Japanese Ministry of Finance. "Budget for FY 2012: Appendix," http://www.mof.go.jp/english/budget/budget/fy2012/e20111224c.pdf

—"Highlights of the Budget for 2011," (December 2010), http://www.mof.go.jp/english/budget/budget/fy2011/e20101224a.pdf

Japanese Ministry of Foreign Affairs. "20th EU-Japan Summit," Joint Press Statement. (28 May 2011), http://www.mofa.go.jp/region/europe/eu/joint1105.html

—"Japan-Brazil Relations," http://www.mofa.go.jp/region/latin/brazil/index.html

—"Japan-India Relations," http://www.mofa.go.jp/region/asia-paci/india/index.html

—"Joint Declaration on Security Cooperation between Japan and India," (22 October 2008), http://www.mofa.go.jp/region/asia-paci/india/pmv0810/joint_d.html

—"Trends in Japan-USSR and Japan-Russia Trade Volume (1991–2010)," and "Structure of Japan-Russia Trade 2010," http://www.mofa.go.jp/region/europe/russia/economy/index.html

—"Visit by Prime Minister Junichiro Koizumi to Latin America (Overview, Evaluation and Specific Results)," (September 2009), http://www.mofa.go.jp/region/latin/pmv0409/overview.html

Jimbo, Ken, Ryo Sahashi, Sugio Takahashi, Yasuyo Sakata, Masayuki Masuda, Takeshi Yuzawa. "Japan's Strategy Toward China: Integration, Balancing and Deterrence in an Era of Power Shift," The Tokyo Foundation. (October 2011), http://www.tokyofoundation.org/en/additional_info/security_strategy_toward_china.pdf

Johnson, Alastair Iain, and Robert S. Ross (eds). *New Directions in the Study of China's Foreign Policy.* (Stanford: Stanford University Press, 2006), 162–85.

Keidanren. "Japan-China Relations in the 21st Century: Recommendations for Building a Relationship of Trust and Expanding Economic Exchanges between Japan and China," Tokyo. (20 February 2001), http://www.keidanren.or.jp/english/policy/2001/006.html

—"Recommendations for Expanding Economic and Trade Ties with China Following Its Accession to the World Trade Organization," (Tokyo, 20 May 2003), http://www.keidanren.or.jp/english/policy/2003/045/part1.html#s1

—"The Third Japan-China-Korea Business Summit Joint Statement," (Tokyo, 22 May 2011), http://www.keidanren.or.jp/english/policy/2011/052.html

Kliment, Alexander. "Brazil's Official Tally of Chinese investment," *Financial Times*. (15 September 2011), http://tilt.ft.com/#!posts/2011–09/30246/brazils-official-tally-of-chinese-investment

Kobota, Yuko. "Japan PM eyes election if tax bills don't pass: report," *Reuters*. (2 January 2012), http://www.reuters.com/article/2012/01/03/us-japan-politics-idUSTRE80203520120103

Kojima, Akira. "Japan's Economy and the Global Financial Crisis," *Asia-Pacific Review*, 16, no. 2. (2009), 15–25.

Kwan, Chi Hung. "Japan as Number Three," The Foreign Correspondent's Club of Japan, http://www.fccj.or.jp/node/6028 (accessed 3 November 2011).

Limaye, Satu (ed.), *Asia's China Debate*. (Honolulu: Asia-Pacific Center for Security Studies, December 2003).

—"Japan and India after the Cold War," in Yoichiro Sato and Satu Limaye (eds), *Japan in a Dynamic Asia: Coping with the New Security Challenges*. (Lanham, M.D.: Lexington, 2006), 225–9.

Malik, Mohan. "China and the East Asia Summit: More Discord than Accord," Asia-Pacific Center for Security Studies (February 2006).

Mochizuki, Mike M. "Japan's Shifting Strategy toward the Rise of China," *The Journal of Strategic Studies* 30, no. 4–5 (August–October 2007), 739–76.

Mühleisen, Martin, and Harmid Faruqee. "Japan Population Aging and the Fiscal Challenge," *Finance and Development*, 38, no. 1, International Monetary Fund. (March 2001), http://www.imf.org/external/pubs/ft/fandd/2001/03/muhleise.htm

Nariai, Osamu. "The Sorry State of Japan's Public Finances," (3 October 2011), http://nippon.com/en/in-depth/a00103/

National Institute for Defense Studies, *East Asian Strategic Review 2011* (Tokyo: The Japan Times, 2011).

O'Neill, Jim, and Anna Stupnytska. "The Long-Term Outlook for the BRICs and N–11 Post Crisis," Goldman Sachs, Global Economics Paper 192. (4 December 2009).

Oguro, Kazumasa. "Japan's Looming Financial Collapse," *Asia-Pacific Review* 17, no. 2. (2010), 126–7.

Ozawa, Ichiro. *Nihon Kaizo Keikau* (Tokyo: Kodansha International, 1993), published in English as *Blueprint for a New Japan: Rethinking of a Nation*, translated by Louisa Rubenfien (Tokyo: Kodansha International, 1994).

Park, Cheol Hee. "Conservative Conceptions of Japan as a 'Normal Country': Comparing Ozawa, Nakasone, and Ishihara," in Yoshihide Soeya, Masayuki Tadokoro, and David A. Welch (eds), Japan as a Normal Country? A Nation in Search of its Place in the World (Toronto: University of Toronto Press, 2011).

Pereira, Carlos and Joao Augusto de Castro Neves. "Brazil and China: South-South Partnership or North-South Competition?" Brookings Institution, Policy Paper 26. (March 2011), http://www.brookings.edu/papers/2011/03_brazil_china_pereira.aspx

Research Institute of Economy, Trade and Industry, "China as the Central Player of the BRICs: Driving the world and the Japanese economy," RIETI, http://www.rieti.go.jp/en/china/10082701.html (accessed 10 October 2011).

—"Emerging-Nation Effect or "China Effect," RIETI, http://www.rieti.go.jp/en/china/11031501.html (accessed 10 October 2011).

Roy, Denny. "The Sources and Limits of Sino-Japanese Tensions," *Survival* 47 (Summer 2005), 191–214.

Rozman, Gilbert. "Japan's Quest for Great Power Identity," *Orbis* 46:1 (Winter 2002), 73–91.

Sakai, Yoshihiro. "Japan's Economy in the Post Reform Era," Center for Strategic and International Studies. (26 April 2006), http://csis.org/files/media/csis/pubs/060426_jcp.pdf

Samuels, Richard J. *Securing Japan: Tokyo's Grand Strategy and the Future of East Asia* (Ithaca and London: Cornell University Press, 2007).

Sato, Yoichiro and Satu Limaye (eds). *Japan in a Dynamic Asia: Coping with the New Security Challenges* (Lanham, M.D.: Lexington, 2006), 225–9.

Sauvageot, Eric Pardo. "Northern Territories and Japan-Russia Relations: Latest Developments under Prime Minister Taro," UNISCI Discussion Papers 20 (May 2009).

Soeya, Yoshihide, Masayuki Tadokoro, and David A Welch (eds). *Japan as a Normal Country? A Nation in Search of its Place in the World.* (Toronto: University of Toronto Press, 2011).

Soeya, Yoshihide. Nihon no "Midoru Pawaa" Gaiko: Sengo Nihon no Sentaku to Kōsō [Japan's Middle Power Diplomacy: Postwar Japan's Choices and Conceptions] (Tokyo: Chikuma Shinsho, 2005).

Sommer, Martin. "Why has Japan been hit so hard by the Global Recession," IMF Staff Position Note, International Monetary Fund. (18 March 2009): http://www.imf.org/external/pubs/ft/spn/2009/spn0905.pdf

Statistics Bureau of Japan, "2010 Japan Census," (26 October 2011), http://www.stat.go.jp/english/data/kokusei/2010/basic1/pdf/summary.pdf

Stockwin, J. A. A. "Political Earthquake in Japan: How Much of a Difference Will it Make?" in Purnendra Jain and Brad Williams (eds), *Japan in Decline: Fact or Fiction?* (Folkstone: Global Oriental, 2011), 18–34.

Sutton, Michael. "Lowest-Low Fertility in Japan: Consequences for a Once-Great Nation," Bulletin of Geography, Socio-Economic Series 12 (2009), 61–72.

Tasker, Peter. "Reflating Japan," in Clay Chandler, Heang Chhor, and Brian Salsberg executive (eds), *Reimagining Japan: The Quest for a Future That Works.* (San Francisco: Mckinsey & Company, 2011).

Tellis, Ashley J., Andrew Marble, and Travis Tanner (eds), *Strategic Asia 2009–2010: Economic Meltdown and Geopolitical Stability.* (Seattle and Washington D.C.: The National Bureau of Asian Research, 2009), 107.

Tellis, Ashley J., Travis Tanner, and Jessica Keough (eds). *Strategic Asia 2011–12: Asia Responds to Its Rising Powers – China and India.* (National Bureau of Asian Research, 2011), 137.

Townsend, Jacob, and Amy King, "Sino-Japanese Competition for Central Asian Energy: China's Game to Win," China and Eurasia Forum Quarterly, 5:4 (2007), 23–45.

Wearden, Graeme. "Japan credit rating downgraded over ballooning deficit," *The Guardian.* (24 August 2011), http://www.guardian.co.uk/business/2011/aug/24/japan-credit-rating-downgraded

Weasley, Michael. "Jealous suitors: Sino-Japanese competitive regionalism and the future of East Asia," in Michael Heazle and Nick Knight (eds), *China-Japan Relations in the Twenty-first Century: Creating a Future Past?* (Cheltenham and Northampton, M.A.: Edward Elgar, 2007), 216–17.

Whipp, Lindsay, and Mure Dickie. "S&P downgrades Japan on debt worries," *Financial Times.* (27 January 2011), http://www.ft.com/cms/s/0/095efb70-29f3-11e0-997c-00144feab49a.html#axzz1dY1Xkq3Y

Wilson, Dominic, and Roopa Purushothaman. "Dreaming with the BRICs: The Path to 2050," Goldman Sachs, Global Economics Paper 99. (1 October 2003).

World Economic Forum, "Global Competitiveness Report for 2011–2012," http://www3.weforum.org/docs/WEF_GCR_Report_2011–12.pdf

World Politics Review, "Russia-Japan Energy Cooperation," 31 January 2011, http://www.worldpoliticsreview.com/trend-lines/7730/global-insider-russia-japan-energy-cooperation

Yahuda, Michael. "Sino-Japanese relations: partners and rivals?" *Korean Journal of Defense Analysis*, 21, no. 4. (December 2009), 371.

—"The Limits of Economic Interdependence: Sino-Japanese Relations," in Alastair Iain Johnson and Robert S. Ross (eds), *New Directions in the Study of China's Foreign Policy.* (Stanford: Stanford University Press, 2006), 162–85

Yoshimatsu, Hidetaka and Dennis D. Trinidad. "Development Assistance, Strategic Interests, and the China Factor in Japan's Role in ASEAN Integration," *Japanese Journal of Political Science* 11, no. 2. (2010), 199–219.

CHAPTER FIVE

China: A Reluctant Global Power in the Search for its Rightful Place

Suisheng Zhao

China's phenomenal rise has raised high expectations among some Western policymakers for China to take a global leadership role and international responsibility as a great power in confronting problems such as climate change, genocide, and nuclear proliferation. China, however, has been reluctant to meet these expectations as it is still in the search for its rightful place in the twenty-first century world. For many years after the end of the Cold War, aware that its circumscribed national strength did not allow it to exert big enough clout, China followed the *taoguangyanghui* policy—hiding its capabilities, focusing on its national strength-building, and biding its time—set by Deng Xiaoping in the early 1990s and kept its head low and avoided confronting the USA and other Western powers.[1] After rapid economic growth over the past three decades, China weathered the global economic slowdown in 2008–10 better than many Western countries. While major Western powers saw their economies plummet and their financial institutions close to ruin, Chinese financial institutions, considered insolvent only a few years ago, boasted positive balance sheets and market capitalization, China's state-owned companies were buying companies and resources all over the world, China surpassed Germany as the world's largest exporter in 2009 and overtook Japan as the world's second-largest economy in 2010.

This increase in China's national strength was accompanied by a change in China's foreign policy behavior. In response to US President Obama's meeting with the Dalai Lama in early 2010, instead of following the low profile dictum, China reminded the West of the tough statement that Deng once made: "no one should expect China to swallow the bitter fruit that hurts its interest."² Many Western observers were astonished by what they perceived as China's "increasingly muscular position" during the global downturn, such as "berating American officials for the global economic crisis, stage-managing President Obama's visit to China in November, refusing to back a tougher climate change agreement in Copenhagen and standing fast against American demands for tough new Security Council sanctions against Iran."³ This development led to the suggestion that China emerged "sooner and more assertively than had been expected before the wrenching global financial crisis."⁴ A Western scholar even went so far to argue that "Beijing now asserts its interests—and its willingness to prevail, even at the expense of appearing the villain."⁵ Another Western observer believed that China was "moving gingerly beyond the paradigm of developmental modesty."⁶

Has the Chinese leadership abandoned Deng's low profile diplomacy and reoriented Chinese foreign policy in a more assertive direction supported by its new quotient of wealth and power? Is China prepared to play the role of a great power in the twenty-first century? In seeking an answer to this question, this chapter focuses on China's foreign policy behavior during the global downturn in 2008–10 and finds that most of China's foreign policy decisions were made through the lens of the issues that were of importance only to China, rather than on the basis of broader regional or global economic and security concerns. While China has built its national strength to effectively defend its state sovereignty and wield significant global influence, it is still obsessed by its immediate or so-called core interests in response to the daunting internal and external challenges to its regime survival, economic development, and territorial integrity. Beijing's assertiveness in defending its core interests, therefore, is not joined with a broader vision as a rising global power, making China often reluctant to shoulder greater international responsibilities. This chapter starts with an analysis of China's pursuit of its core interests during the global downturn and goes on to explain its driving forces. The third section examines the implications of China's new assertiveness in pursuance of its core interests.

Pursuance of the Core interests during the Global Downturn

China's low-profile policy had been a response to China's vulnerability in the wake of the Western sanctions after the Tiananmen protests in 1989.

Conditioned by China's limited strength and geostrategic position, Beijing had to make pragmatic accommodations to the USA by "learning to live with the hegemon," i.e. making adaptation and policy adjustments to accord with the reality of US dominance in the international system and because the USA held the key to China's continuing modernization efforts.[7] China's perception of Western powers in general and the US in particular, however, began to change after the financial meltdown in 2008. With Western economies floundering and Chinese economic and diplomatic clout rising, a perception of the USA in heavy debt to China but still attempting to leverage its superiority to keep China down made Chinese leaders less willing to continue with adaptation and more ready to challenge the USA in defending core Chinese interests. At the first China-US Strategic & Economic Dialogue in Washington, D.C. in July 2009, State Councilor Dai Binguo told his American interlocutors that China's number one core interest is to maintain its fundamental system and state security, followed by state sovereignty and territorial integrity and finally, the continued stable development of its economy and society.[8]

These are narrowly defined interests having more to do with the preoccupation of Chinese leaders with regime survival and national security than with China's great power aspirations. The survival of the Chinese Communist Party (CCP) regime is the first core interest because, given the authoritarian nature of the Chinese political system, the CCP always worries about challenges to its regime legitimacy. A combination of foreign forces with domestic discontents could seriously threaten the CCP regime.[9] The second core interest of state sovereignty and territorial integration refers almost exclusively to the Taiwan and Tibet issues and has become increasingly sensitive in the context of rising nationalist sentiment among the Chinese people. Continued economic development and social stability becomes the third core interest because it is the foundation of the CCP's performance legitimacy to justify its continued rule in China.

China was indeed more willing to assert its core interests during the global downturn. For example, President Obama's town hall meeting with young Chinese in Shanghai was not broadcast live nationwide. At his joint press conference with President Hu Jintao during President Obama's first official visit to China in November 2009, no questions were allowed from the audience and although President Obama urged China to revalue its currency, President Hu avoided mentioning the currency issue and instead emphasized the need to avoid trade protectionism, which referred to China's irritation over the US announcement of punitive tariffs on Chinese-made tires in September 2009. China retaliated by imposing penalties on American chicken imports. A Chinese scholar, Sun Zhe, suggested that "Hu's silence on the currency may stem in part from reluctance by China to be seen as making concessions under foreign pressure" on China's core interests.[10]

China then confronted the USA and other developed countries at the Copenhagen climate change summit in December 2009. To avoid making new promises about its future emission targets and having international inspections of its performance, China unusually picked up the banner of leader of developing countries by proposing the principle of "common but differentiated responsibilities" and strongly supported exemptions for developing nations against the developed countries' rallying call underscoring the common responsibilities of all mankind to curb climate change. Pressing developed countries hard to detail deep quantified carbon reduction commitments as well as their financial pledges to poorer nations, China dispatched a Vice Foreign Minister to represent Premier Wen Jiabao at an event for the heads of state. Sitting across from President Obama, he fought strenuously against fixed targets for emission cuts in the developing world. President Obama later had to track down Wen, appearing at the doorway of a conference room where Wen was at a meeting with the leaders of Brazil, South Africa, and India. For many years, while China claimed to be a member of the bloc of developing countries, it tried to avoid taking a lead in confronting Western powers. Beijing's position at the summit astonished many China watchers. As an observer commented, "When China was seeking to join the World Trade Organization a decade ago, it accepted compromises to US and European demands. At climate talks in Copenhagen, however, China blocked a comprehensive deal and refused to go beyond its earlier promises."[11]

Following the Copenhagen fiasco came the standoff over Google's threat to leave China in protest against Chinese internet censorship and cyber attacks in January 2010. While the Chinese government at first tried to downplay the case as just a commercial dispute, its stance became unusually tough after US Secretary of State Hillary Clinton made a speech on 22 January criticizing China, among other countries, for disrupting information freedom and calling on Chinese authorities to conduct a thorough review of the cyber-intrusions. Seeing the US government's high-profile reaction as a threat to China's political system, a core interest issue, the Chinese government became very truculent. Refusing to investigate the alleged hacking of Google and other foreign companies, it held that "behind the US so-called information freedom is a naked political attempt to employing cyber warfare against its enemies."[12] James Fallows, known for his positive view of China, sadly found that the Google case signified "an inversion of recent Chinese and US roles. In the switch from George W. Bush to Barack Obama, the US went from a president much of the world saw as deliberately antagonizing them to a president whose Nobel Prize reflected (perhaps desperate) gratitude at his efforts at conciliation. China, by contrast, seems to be entering its Bush-Cheney era."[13]

In the midst of the tussle between Google and Beijing, China ratcheted up the rhetoric in its dire-sounding warnings about the consequences of arms sales to Taiwan as a serious challenge to China's core interest. As influential foreign and security policy analysts such as Rear-Admiral Yang Yi openly stated that it was time for China to sanction US defense firms behind the sales to "reshape the policy choices of the US"[14] While China raised the stakes with regard to the routine and predictable arms sales, the Obama administration still notified Congress of the US$6.4 billion arms sale to Taiwan on 29 January. The decision was met with unprecedented Chinese objections. In addition to what China did in the past to immediately announce the suspension of some military exchanges with the USA and unleash a storm of bluster by various relevant government and military agencies, the Chinese Foreign Ministry spokesman for the first time officially threatened to impose sanctions on American companies involved in the arms sales.[15]

During the global downturn, China's assertiveness vis-à-vis Europe on issues involving its core interests was even more apparent. Regularly punishing European countries when their leaders met the Dalai Lama in an official setting, China denounced German Chancellor Angela Merkel over her meeting with the Tibetan spiritual leader. China also suspended ties with Denmark after its prime minister met the Dalai Lama and resumed them only after the Danish government issued a statement saying it would oppose Tibetan independence and consider Beijing's reaction before inviting him again. After French President Nicolas Sarkozy met with the Dalai Lama in his capacity as the President of the EU, Beijing abruptly canceled the scheduled EU summit in December 2008 to show that, even amid the global economic crisis, it was ready to confront the leaders of its biggest trading partner.

China also ignored British protests over China's execution in December 2009 of Akmail Shaikh, a British national with an alleged history of mental illness who was arrested in 2007 for smuggling heroin. While Shaikh's family and friends claimed he was duped by Eastern European criminals into unwittingly smuggling drugs into China, Britain Prime Minister Gordon Brown personally sought clemency for Shaikh. The Rights group Reprieve also mounted a web campaign, claiming that the Chinese justice system brushed aside requests that Shaikh be given a psychiatric evaluation.[16] The British plea to China on humanitarian grounds yielded nothing, just as the concern abroad about the fate of Charter 08 dissident Liu Xiaobo did nothing to prevent him from receiving a stiff prison sentence of 11 years on Christmas Day in 2009. Beijing felt it had to act harshly on these cases that directly challenged regime legitimacy.

China's toughness also played out in the renewed dispute with India over what India claims as its northeastern state of Arunachal Pradesh and China claims as its territory of southern Tibet. During the 1962 Sino-Indian border war, China had advanced deep into this region and withdrawn after a brief occupation. Although Arunachal Pradesh achieved statehood in

1987, China has continued to lay claim to this territory and objected to any Indian assertion of sovereignty over the area, expressing this in increasingly strident language in recent years. In summer 2009, for instance, China blocked the Asian Development Bank from making a US$60 million multi-year loan because the loan was for infrastructure improvements in the state.[17] India then moved to fund the projects itself, prompting China to send more troops to the border. A trip by the Dalai Lama in November 2009 to the state led Sino-Indian relations to deteriorate even further. Beijing was angered because the Dalai Lama did not just visit Itanagar, the state capital, but Tawang, which is the main bone of contention between India and China and was described by Indian officials involved in the border negotiations with China as "the piece of Indian real estate that China covets the most in the border dispute."[18] In Indian eyes China became increasingly provocative over their long-running territorial disputes in the Himalayas. As tensions intensified, India was awash with predictions about China's impending attack by 2012.[19]

Sources of China's New Assertiveness

There are many factors that help explain China's new assertiveness. One is that because the Chinese economy rebounded quickly and strongly from the global downturn, Chinese leaders became increasingly confident in their ability to deal with the West and more willing proactively to shape the external environment rather than passively react to it and forcefully to safeguard China's core interests. The second factor is China's frustration over perceived anti-China forces trying to prevent China's rise to its rightful place. This frustration sustained a nationalist sentiment to assert China's core interests and prevail. The third factor is that the possible slowdown of China's economic growth during the global downturn and the ongoing leadership transition brought uneasiness among Chinese leaders who had to meet any perceived threat to regime legitimacy with an unusually harsh reaction. It is a combination of confidence, frustration, and uncertainty that resulted in China's new assertiveness.

Confidence

China's confidence derived mostly from its relative success in shrugging off the global financial crisis and maintaining a strong growth trajectory. China's financial system and its banks were relatively well shielded from the problems that led to economic chaos in the USA and other Western countries because they were less involved in highly sophisticated but dubious financial transactions. Attributing the financial meltdown entirely to "inappropriate macroeconomic policies" of Western countries and "their unsustainable model of development,"[20] Premier Wen Jiabao at a news conference in March called on the USA to "maintain its good credit, to honor its promises and to guarantee the safety of China's assets" because as the lender of vast sums of money to the US, "we are concerned about the safety of our assets."[21] For many years, the Chinese were on the receiving end of patronizing lectures from Western leaders about the superiority of their brand of capitalism. Now the tables were turned. At the April 2009 Boao Asia Forum, an annual high level gathering of political and business leaders from Asia-Pacific countries on China's Hainan Island, a Western journalist reported that "there seemed scarcely a moment when a top Chinese official wasn't ridiculing the world's financial institutions, demanding major concessions from the USA, proposing new Asia-centric international architecture or threatening to turn off the taps of Chinese capital which the rest of the world so desperately needs."[22]

Indeed, the power transition from President George W. Bush to President Barack Obama and political gridlock in Congress delayed adoption of a stimulus bill until February 2009, shortly after President Obama took office, too late to prevent the deep economic contraction. In comparison, the Chinese government was much more effective in deploying its enormous state capacity to ward off the economic recession. After Lehman Brothers fell in September 2008, a two-day CCP Politburo meeting in early October 2008 was devoted to battling the global economic tsunami.[23] After the meeting, the State Council announced a four-trillion-yuan (US$586 billion) economic stimulus package on 9 November. Thereafter, state-run banks were busy pumping money throughout the economy. This huge fiscal stimulus package and expansion of state-owned bank lending pushed China's economy out of the downturn quickly. For the first time in history, Chinese spending, rather than the US consumers, became the key to a global recovery. Even an article in *The Washington Times*, known for its critical position on China, admitted that "the Asian giant's massive US$586 billion stimulus package—implemented with speed in November just as the world economy was crashing—is credited with helping to stabilize world markets and contribute to a budding recovery in Asia, Europe and the USA, where the stimulus package came too late to prevent the worst recession in modern times."[24]

With an annual growth rate of 8.7 percent and fourth-quarter growth reaching 10.7 percent in 2009, many Chinese were convinced that a China model that could strike a balance between economic growth and political stability and between a market-oriented economy and an authoritarian state worked better for China than the Western model of modernization. Indeed, China's economic success made the China model an alternative to the liberal model of modernization by default.[25] In parts of Asia, Africa and Latin America, the China model or "Beijing consensus" became more popular than the previously dominant "Washington consensus." As many developing countries looked for a recipe for faster growth and greater stability than that offered by the neo liberal prescriptions of open markets and free elections, the China model became an intellectual symbol of national pride in China.

For some Chinese, the global financial crisis also confirmed the relative decline of the West: the fiscal situation in the USA was out of control, its banking system discredited, its military stretched by two protracted wars, and its moral high ground lost. In contrast, China's economic ascent was mind-boggling with a prime position as critical creditor to the USA. It is from this perspective that a Chinese scholar claimed that "the global financial crisis damaged the USA's financial position. US economic recovery depends on rapid economic growth in China and cooperation from Beijing. US interests in China have increased as a result and Beijing's crisis management skills which have earned Beijing credibility in the eyes of Washington."[26]

With the West in financial turmoil and its leaders seemingly desperate for cash-rich China to come to its aid, the Chinese became confident that China was finally resuming its role as one of the great powers after two centuries of exploitation by the West. During the global downturn, this confidence was demonstrated by a greater-than-ever readiness to display its rapidly modernized military forces, increasingly capable of power projection. China held a grand naval display, including the debut of China's nuclear submarines to mark the 60th anniversary of the founding of the PLA Navy in April 2009. Senior naval officers from 29 countries were invited, "the first large multilateral military exchange of its kind in the history of the People's Republic of China."[27] The intercontinental ballistic missiles that rumbled down Beijing's Eternal Peace Avenue and the tanker planes that lumbered overhead at the military parade to mark the 60th anniversary of the founding of the People's Republic of China on 1 October 2009 sent a powerful message to the world that China finally had become a military power able to project beyond its shores.

Becoming confident in the balance of power tilting in its favor and trying to determine how much power and influence China generated over the USA and by extension the international system, China pressed harder than ever for concessions from the USA and other powers on its core interest issues.

Frustration

China was frustrated by what it perceived as anti-China forces seeking to prevent China from rising to its rightful place. A Mid-Kingdom for centuries, China began a steady decline in the late nineteenth century after it suffered defeats and humiliation at the hands of foreign imperial powers and plunged into chaos with war, famine, isolation, and revolution. Struggling for national independence and modernization, China was now rising to regain the glorious position it enjoyed about two centuries ago. This great power aspiration, however, was met with suspicion and resistance by perceived anti-China forces in the West, serving as an uncomfortable reminder of the historical humiliation when China was weak. Committing to overcome humiliation and restore its great power status, "the Chinese have sometimes used the term international status as if it were their only foreign policy goal"[28] and were therefore frustrated by at least the following three perceived barriers to China's achievement of international status.

The first is the so-called structural conflict between China as a rising power and the USA as the sole superpower in the post-Cold War world. Beijing was therefore convinced that the USA would never give up the policy of containing China. As a Chinese foreign policy analyst stated, "With China's rapid rise, the nature of the (China-US) bilateral ties may evolve from the 'sole superpower against one of multiple other great powers' into 'Number One and Number Two powers,' and this may lead to a rise in tensions and conflicts."[29]

Obama's presidency at a deep financial meltdown provided an opportunity to test this thesis. Many Chinese assumed that a weakened USA heavily in debt to China would have to make more concessions on China's core interests. This assumption seemed to be confirmed by the first overseas trip in late February 2009 of a duly penitent US Secretary of State Hillary Clinton who once boasted about how strongly she had emphasized human rights during her 1995 visit to Beijing but now suggested that China's human rights record should not get in the way of cooperation on the financial crisis and security issues. As a Chinese scholar indicated, after this visit, many Chinese thought that the USA "should respond nicely to China" because China did "favours for the US on a couple of fronts—like investing in its bonds and jointly stimulating the world economy." These Chinese were, therefore, frustrated at the end of the year by "the rigid US position" that "does not reflect the nature of the new Sino-US symbiosis and fails to recognize Beijing's growing international clout."[30] For these Chinese, the troubled relationship with the Obama administration once again confirmed that due to the structural conflict thesis, the US engagement policy is simply another face to cover its hidden agenda of preventing China from rising as a peer power. Although many Americans blamed China's illiberal political system as one of the main points of friction and pressed China on the issues of human rights and democracy, the Chinese have wondered whether or not conflict would remain and grow starker even if China became democratic, as the USA would not want to see China, democratic or not, to be richer and stronger.

Second, many Chinese policy makers were frustrated by what they perceived as a Western conspiracy to slow down China's rise by blocking

China's global search for natural resources and acquisition of foreign assets. China's rapid economic growth brought about an unprecedented resource vulnerability. China overtook Japan as the second largest oil consumer next to the USA in 2003 and overtook the USA as the world's biggest consumer of grain, meat, coal and steel in 2004. China, therefore, had to search for resources overseas to sustain its rise. Chinese policy makers, however, were frustrated by the perceived attempts by the USA and other Western countries to block China in its global search for resources.

One of the most often cited example is the failure of China National Offshore Oil Corporation (CNOOC)'s US$18.5 billion business takeover bid for California-based oil firm Unocal Corp in early 2005 because of unusual political intervention from the US Congress, which considered that, as a state-run entity, the CNOOC takeover of Unocal would constitute a threat to US national security. As a result, Chevron Corporation, the second largest US petroleum company, acquired Unocal for US$17 billion, US$1.5 billion less than CNOOC's offer.[31] This setback, perceived as ignominious by the Chinese leadership, was repeated in 2009 when Anglo-Australian mining giant Rio Tinto walked away from a tentative agreement reached in 2008 with China Aluminum Corp (Chinalco), which had offered to pay US$19.5 billion to increase its stake in the global mining giant. The deal would have ranked as the largest-ever foreign corporate investment by a Chinese company. But to Beijing's frustration, Rio Tinto rejected the deal citing fierce shareholder opposition and the skepticism of Australian regulators because "there are lots of Aussies in high political places who don't want ... land and resources sold to China."[32] The rejection was "a blow to China's ambitions to buy access to raw materials crucial for its economic growth."[33]

The third frustration was that China's rise led to intensified international scrutiny of many of China's awkward domestic and external challenges, such as human rights, media freedom, Tibet, Taiwan, pollution, and relationships with some third world allies whom the West considered questionable. For example, when China was celebrating its success in preparing the showcase of the Beijing Olympics Games, the Chinese government was caught by surprise when angry Tibetans burned non-Tibetan businesses and attacked Han migrants in March 2008. Seeing the riot as organized by foreign forces featherbedding China on human rights, including ethnic minority rights in Tibet to embarrass China ahead of the Olympics, Beijing dispatched a large number of troops to suppress the protests. The suppression spotlighted China's human rights and ethnic problems and led not only to wide Western media condemnation but also to demonstrations by international human rights groups and Tibetan exile communities that plagued the Olympic torch relay in London, Paris, and San Francisco. The perception that much of the foreign media took a clear anti-China stance on the issue not only frustrated but also angered the Chinese government and the Chinese people.

The Chinese leaders were also embarrassed by the announcement of Hollywood director Steven Spielberg to quit as an artistic consultant to the Olympic Games to protest Beijing's Sudan policy. This was followed by nine Nobel Peace Prize laureates who signed a letter to President Hu, urging China to uphold Olympic ideals by pressing Sudan to stop atrocities in Darfur. The international scrutiny of China's Sudan policy was related to the rising expectation of China's responsible behavior in relations with many of its third world friends. Many Western countries criticized China for undermining their efforts to promote transparency and human rights as China vied for energy resources in some of the most unstable parts of the world. They were particularly critical of China for pursuing deals with countries such as Iran and Sudan that were off-limits to Western companies because of sanctions, security concerns, or the threat of bad publicity. To respond to Western concerns, China joined the USA and voted to impose and tighten sanctions on Iran, supported the deployment of an UN-African Union force in Darfur and even sent its own military engineers to join the force in 2007. But Beijing was increasingly frustrated over whether China could match the heightened Western expectations because positive responses could invite greater demands upon China to follow Western expectations that China could not or should not meet. In an angry response to the intensified international scrutiny, Vice-President Xi Jinping, the heir-apparent to President Hu Jintao, used extraordinarily strong language at a meeting with representatives of the Chinese community during a visit to Mexico City in February 2009 to accuse "well-fed foreigners with nothing better to do but keep pointing fingers at China although China was not exporting revolution or poverty or hunger or making trouble for other countries. So what else is there to say?"[34]

This peculiar sense of frustration sustained a popular nationalist sentiment, which the Chinese government also exploited to compensate for the declining appeal of communism. Chinese popular nationalism was more vocal than the state in its criticism of the perceived Western intention to prevent China's rise. Popular nationalism ran particularly high when the global economy sputtered in 2008–9 because a battered West presented a gratifying target for pent-up contempt. A popular book, *China is Not Happy* tapped into what the authors believed to be a widespread public feeling of disgruntlement with the West, claiming that the financial crisis could result in an envious West doing whatever it could to keep China down. Relations between the West and China, they argued, had reached a critical point, whereby a showdown was imminent. The authors cited both the Tibetan issue and the disputes over energy resources in Africa as expressions of these conflicts and urged China to assert itself militarily, diplomatically, and in every other way to grasp its great power place in history.[35] The boiling Chinese nationalist rhetoric was suffused with a sense of China as victim yearning for redress. Seeking status, acceptance, and respect on the world stage and holding high expectations for the government to fulfill its promise of safeguarding China's national interests, popular nationalists often charged the Chinese government as too soft in dealing with Western powers.

The pressures, therefore, were built upon the Chinese government to flex its muscles in defending its core interests.[36] Although China's authoritarian political system gives the state immense power to drive foreign policy, its power became more and more conditional on its ability to defend China's national interests. Chinese foreign policy makers had to occasionally but increasingly refer to the constraints that the surging popular nationalism in the form of "public opinion" placed upon them to resist foreign entreaties and make their own policy positions more credible.[37] Part of the legitimacy of the CCP lies in the notion that it ousted foreign powers from China and tried to restore the lost territories during the century of humiliation. China's quick economic comeback during the global economic crisis and the positive developments in relations with the Obama administration in early 2009 raised the expectation that China's rising power position brought the state not only greater international respect, but also the ability to alter the USA position on Taiwan and Tibet. "China's leaders face pressure to meet those expectations, or risk seeing their authority eroded."[38] In this case, when the USA proceeded with arms sales to Taiwan and President Obama met the Dalai Lama in early 2010, the US was seen not only as directly harming China's core interests of sovereignty and territorial integrity but also delivering an insult to China's national pride. Chinese leaders were left with almost no room but to make unusually strong response even at the danger of overplaying nationalism.

Uncertainty

While China's assertiveness was driven mostly by growing confidence and frustration, the economic and political uncertainties at home also played an important part. Although China was a relative bright spot in the global downturn, rapid economic growth in the recent decade not only created huge social, economic, and political tensions but also raised expectations of the Chinese people for the performance of the government. The state faced serious challenges from growing public demands related to the government's policies on economic and social inequality, endemic corruption, epidemic pollution, inadequate health care, shredded social services, entrenched industrial overcapacity, and swiftly aging population, ethnic conflict, etc. "The Party leadership is terrified of their outsized expectations. People under age 40, the progeny of the one-child policy, didn't live through Maoist poverty and upheaval. They are pampered, impatient and demanding. They consider exponential growth as a basic benchmark of life, and access to information to be a civil right."[39] While few Chinese people would want Western-style democracy at the moment, the leaders knew that their legitimacy depended on their ability to meet the various demands from the society.

When the global financial turmoil started, the Chinese leaders were not sure if it would batter China's economy and produce unrest in society. Their concern was not unfounded because, in addition to the high-profile riots in Tibet in 2008 and the Muslim region of Xinjiang in 2009 that caught them by surprise, they had to deal routinely with tens of thousands of civil and ethnic protests from those robbed of their land for development and laid-off workers to those suffering from the side-effects of environmental despoliation. As the financial meltdown swept all over the globe, they did not know what would happen to the millions of migrant workers who lost their jobs as labor-intensive industries churning out cheap products for export put up their shutters and the many white-collar workers who were laid off or had their bonuses and wages cut. By attributing the financial meltdown entirely to "economic mismanagement" of Western countries, the Chinese government, in deploying its enormous state capacity to pull its economic out of the downturn, was able to avoid criticism if its policy was a failure but could also receive praise if it was effective.

The leadership transition in the run-up to the 2012 Party Congress also brought political uncertainty. The current leaders, President Hu Jintao and Premier Wen Jiabao, were white-knuckling their way through their final two years in office before handing over the baton to the next generation of leaders. As the succession process geared up, hard-line nationalist policies were popular because they could become springboards to power for ambitious and unscrupulous leaders during an uncertain period. Nationalism had always been a double-edged sword for the state: both a means for the state to legitimize its rule and a means for the Chinese people to judge the performance of the state. During normal times, while the Chinese leadership often encouraged nationalist expression for certain political and foreign policy objectives, they were very cautious to prevent nationalist sentiment from getting out of hand because they would be vulnerable to nationalistic criticism if they could not deliver on their nationalist promises.

However, facing rumblings of discontent from those who saw the global downturn as a chance for China to assert itself more stridently, the Chinese leaders did not make serious effort to control the extreme popular nationalist demands. Senior military officers were allowed to openly put pressure on the government to shove back against the USA over trade, Tibet, and arms sales to Taiwan. Colonel Dai Xu's popular book in late 2009 and his provocative speeches that were among the most popular videos on China's internet claimed that China was encircled in a C-shape by hostile or wary countries beholden to the USA and could not escape the calamity of war in the not-too-distant future. Because the USA, figuratively, put a fire in China's backyard, he called for the Chinese leaders to light a fire in the US backyard.[40] Senior Colonel Liu Mingfu's 2010 book, *The China Dream*, stood out for its boldness in the chorus of popular nationalist expressions. Reflecting China's swelling nationalist ambitions, the book called for China to abandon its modest foreign policy and build the world's strongest military to deter a wary USA from challenging China's rise while the West was still mired in an economic slowdown. If China were powerful, the USA would not dare and not be able to intervene in military conflict in the Taiwan Strait.[41]

Under these circumstances, political leaders pushing a nationalist line on sensitive issues would not only stir up disgruntled youth but also boost support among government officials and military officers. There was not any strongman like Mao Zedong or Deng Xiaoping in the Chinese leadership who could make a major policy initiative without worrying about challenges from his colleagues or buttressing the power of entrenched interests. While this development is in a way healthy, it could result in inflexibility and stop the give-and-take that China often did well, as no Chinese leader could afford to be seen as too dovish or appear weak to the Chinese people. This "could trigger a power struggle whereby hawks, accusing the leaders of being spineless weaklings, could try to topple them and change the overall political system, endangering the political stability of the whole country."[42] Political leaders understood that mishandling sensitive issues could not only lead to social instability but also provide political competitors an avenue by which to undermine their political standing. This created a vague sense of "boundary of permissible,"[43] which led to the match of who was tougher on the issues that defined the game for political gains or at least not to lose any ground.

Core Interests versus Global Power Responsibility

Vigorously pursuing its core interests, China is not ready to take on the role of the global leadership. There is no doubt that a more powerful China has been more willing to leverage its growing capabilities to shift the global power balance in its favor. Beijing has also made positive and important contributions to regional and global security, stability and governance by taking a more active role in international institutions at both the regional and global levels, not only accepting but also becoming an active advocate to common security and cooperative development as a non-zero sum game in the process of globalization.[44]

For a long time in the PRC history, China felt more comfortable with bilateralism and was reluctant to participate in international institutions because of the concern over possible erosion of state sovereignty. A contradiction between multilateralism and bilateralism, therefore, has constantly tested China's foreign policy makers.[45] The post-Cold War era has witnessed rise of multilateralism in international politics, which is creating more and more pressure on China's traditional diplomacy. In response, while China still feels more comfortable with bilateralism, it has sought memberships and actively participated in more and more multilateral institutions at both global and regional levels. In the Asia-Pacific, China has not only expressed particular enthusiasm to participate in regional institutions such as Asia Pacific Economic Cooperation (APEC), ASEAN Regional Forum (ARF), ASEAN +3, and East Asia Summit but also launched the Shanghai Cooperation Organization (SCO) and hosted the Six Party Talks to resolve the North Korean nuclear crisis. Becoming an important player in global organizations such as the World Bank, IMF, WTO, and G20, China has also engaged emerging powers such as India, Brazil, South Africa, and Russia through its active participation in the annual BRIC summits. This is an adaptation behavior, reflecting China's increasing involvement in an increasingly interdependent world and signifying its growing commitment to a rule-based and norm-driven international order. China's turn to multilateralism is also based on a strategic calculation in shaping the distribution of power to China's favor. Frustrated by what it sees a structural conflict between China as a rising power and the USA as the sole superpower in the post-Cold War world, China has adopted a soft balancing strategy against US preponderance, relying on participation in international institutions and other diplomatic maneuvering. International institutions, therefore, become instrumental in China's strategic maneuvering.[46] In this context, although China has often been accused of supporting a string of despots and genocidal regimes, "Beijing has been quietly overhauling its policies toward pariah states... willing to condition its diplomatic protection of pariah countries, forcing them to become more acceptable to the international community" in the recent years.[47] Instead of simply defending its third world allies against Western interference, China now often stands together with the Western powers to promote their responsible behavior.

However, China has not made a commensurate commitment to the call for China to assume more international responsibilities as a rising global power. Most notably, former US Deputy Secretary of State Robert Zoellick urged China to become "a responsible stakeholder" in the international system that has enabled its success.[48] While the Chinese leadership generally welcomed the "responsible stakeholder" call because, as a *China Daily* commentary suggested, it was an indication of the US government to see China as a "strategic partner,"[49] concentrating mostly on its core interests in a fairly narrow sense, China is still reluctant and very selective in taking on the global and regional responsibilities. One observer in China even suggested that the Western call for China to take greater responsibility was to dictate China's international performance, which was another version of the "China threat" view.[50] In this case, China's participation in international affairs is not simply to meet the expectation of its rising great power responsibility in an increasingly interdependent world but most often in light of the calculation of its core interests. Thus, one scholar criticized China's approach toward international regime as guided by the "maxi-mini-principle—maximization of rights and minimization of responsibilities."[51] Another observer believed that "China has been a reluctant follower not a leader."[52] Yet another observer even suggested that China's policies reflected a "me first" notion.[53]

One Chinese scholar rebutted the Western criticism as a distortion of China's international responsibility, which, according to him, follows two principles. One is making commitment according to its ability (*liangli erxing*) and the other is the combination of China's interests with the common interests of the international society.[54] An official *Outlook Weekly* article, "Hu Jintao's Viewpoints about the Times," proposed a concept of "shared responsibility," which sets two important parameters of Beijing's international responsibility with regard to many sensitive global and regional issues. First, China's contributions to the global commonwealth cannot adversely affect China's core interests. Second, China's international commitments are conditional upon the inputs of other states, especially developed countries and regions such as the USA and the EU.[55] Based upon this logic, China opposed mandatory emission reductions for developing countries while pressing developed countries for deep carbon reduction commitments as well as their financial assistance to poorer nations at the Copenhagen Climate Change Summit. By the same token, China set conditions for its participation in the global efforts to bail out debt-ridden European countries in 2012. One of the conditions was that "the efforts are multilateral, not just bilateral."[56] On international peace and security, China was also often reluctant to step up proactively in response to the call for Beijing to take more responsibility in solving key global issues in troubled countries such as North Korea, Iran, Afghanistan, Sudan, and Pakistan when China's interests in these hot spots were different from those of the Western countries.

On North Korea, for example, while China played a leading role in the Six-Party talks to rein in Pyongyang's nuclear program and even joined the USA in imposing UN sanctions after Pyongyang launched a long-range missile, withdrew from the six-party talks, and tested its second nuclear device in early 2009, Beijing continues to shield North Korea from more punitive measures and is hesitant to threaten the shut off of Chinese oil and food that keeps the regime alive because the proximity of North Korea to China makes Beijing's calculations of interest different from those of the USA While a nuclear-free North Korea is a security interest of China, China's overriding interest is stability on the peninsula as the collapse of

North Korea would not only unleash a flood of North Korean refugees across the border but also place US forces at China's northeast frontier.

On the Iran issue, although China shares Western concerns over regional instability and nuclear proliferation and could play a critical role in the effort to pressure Tehran over its nuclear program, China has resisted tougher sanctions against Iran because Iran is its second-largest oil supplier. It is revealing to see that while China signaled its willingness to join the negotiation on a UN resolution to curb Tehran's nuclear program after President Hu answered a phone call from President Obama on 2 April 2010, China's official news report on the phone conversation only mentioned that Hu stressed China's core interests, i.e. "the appropriate handling of Taiwan and Tibet issues were key to stable development of the Sino-US ties and the two nations should resolve trade disputes through negotiations."[57] Hu's answer to Obama's appeal for the two countries to work together to ensure that Iran lives up to its obligations was not reported. The report was presented as if Obama had to listen to Hu's boilerplate complaints about US arms sales to Taiwan and the meeting with the Dalai Lama although the phone conversation was solely focused on China's position on the Iran sanctions.

On the Pakistan and Afghanistan issues, although China has an important stake in the success of the international efforts to destroy Al Qaeda and the Taliban and bring stability and security to Afghanistan and the Pakistani border region, China views the US presence as part of an American strategy to encroach upon China's neighborhood and secure a long-term role in Central Asia, the Indian Ocean, and Persian Gulf. Moreover, fearing that a backlash in Xinjiang and the wider Muslim world could make China a first-order target for transnational terrorist groups, Beijing is hesitant to place itself on the front lines against the terrorist threat and lend support to "NATO's war." In spite of repeated calls from the USA and other NATO members for China to contribute more through investments and assistance of various kinds—and China exploits a large copper mine south of Kabul—China has not contributed significantly to hard infrastructure building, schools, and public health clinics, or domestic security in Afghanistan. An official Xinhua news report admitted that China offered only about US$131 million in assistance to Afghanistan between 2002 and 2010, far behind India, which gave more than US$1.2 billion between 2001 and 2010.[58]

These examples demonstrate that China has not taken on a broad international responsibility to be the visionary and magnanimous global player looking beyond its own often desperate and narrowly-focused core interests. From this perspective, one Western observer accused China of being a "global free rider" because "Beijing remains highly reluctant to take on more burdens—whether economic, political, or military."[59] It was indeed revealing that at the G20 summit in April 2009 "the only thing China cared about was keeping Hong Kong off the list of offshore tax havens being scrutinized. Beijing's coffers may be bulging with US$2.1 trillion in foreign-currency reserves, but it is not exactly offering to spend that cash on common crises. Besides calling for a new international reserve currency, China has remained mostly silent on how to reform the global financial system."[60] Whether a free rider or not, juggling its emerging great power status with its parochially defined core interests, "the Chinese appeared torn between seizing their moment in the geopolitical spotlight and shying from it."[61] On the one hand, cherishing China's rising power status, Chinese Vice-Minister of Foreign Affairs Wu Dawei said that "the Hu leadership has engaged more actively in world affairs in response to growing international calls for it to take up greater global responsibility and taken part more in affairs that affected global development and stability."[62] On the other hand, focusing mostly on its immediate interests and emphasizing "shared responsibility," the Chinese government has tried to avoid heightened international expectations.

In this case, Chinese scholars and policy makers have expressed at least three views in the debate on China's changing international role. One view urged the government to abandon the passive "*taoguangyanghui*" policy and take a "great power" (*daguo*) responsibility to ensure a "just" world order. The second view calls for a modified *taoguangyanghui* policy to give more emphasis to "*youshuo zuowei*" (striking some points/successes) and take a more active or even a leadership role in pursing certain foreign policy objectives, particularly in China's core interest issue areas. The third view is to continue the low-key policy and avoid taking a leadership position on most issues. The first view has received the most attention in the Western media and is also popular among the Chinese people but is not the official position of the Chinese government, which has taken the third view—although the second view is the actual policy practice. Clearly, Chinese leaders at least in public have not abandoned the low profile policy, evident in Premier Wen Jiabao's statement that "Precisely by not raising our banner or taking the lead internationally we've been able to expand our room for maneuver in international affairs." Therefore, "there is no reason whatsoever to alter this policy."[63] During a visit to Europe in early 2009, when some sensitive Western reporters pricked up their ears at Wen's statement that China would be a peaceful and cooperative great power and asked for clarification of the phrase "great power," the government news agency, Xinhua, released an English translation of the word as "country" instead. At the same time, after the remarks caused a sensation in the international media, Chinese government censors deleted from Chinese news reports and official websites the unguarded remarks of Chinese Vice-President Xi Jinping in Mexico that foreign powers had eaten their fill and had nothing better to do, messing around and pointing their fingers at China's affairs. The domestic media were banned from reporting his comments.[64]

This ambivalent behavior is a reflection of a confusing dual-identity of China as a rising power and a developing country. One example is that, delighting in the notion that China was recognized as a global power, many Chinese were initially flattered by the G2 idea, which saw the world as a bipolar affair with America and China as the only two powers that mattered. They, however, quickly criticized the notion as "a potential trap for China that could expose it on the world stage."[65] Wrapping its great power aspirations in modesty and pointing out that China is still a developing country with only one-tenth of the per capita GDP of the US, Premier Wen Jiabao firmly rejected the G2 idea as "not appropriate," "baseless and wrong," and reiterated that "China remains a developing country despite remarkable achievements and its modernization will take a long time and the efforts of several generations."[66] Wen's statement was not simply an expression of modesty to soothe Western worries about the China threat. As Minxin Pei indicated, "It's far more likely that China's leaders are actually telling the truth."[67] Although China pulled off the world's most impressive recovery earlier than many Western countries, it still faces numerous internal social, economic, environmental, demographic, and political challenges that could significantly overshadow China's long-term economic growth. China also faces severe geopolitical challenges. Even in its neighboring Asia-Pacific region, the reach of China's power is checked by the presence and influence of the USA and the strength of dynamic and vigilant regional powers, such as India, Japan, Vietnam, and Russia. As a result, "China will be unable to become hegemony in Asia—a power with complete dominance over its regional rivals. By definition, a country cannot become a global superpower unless it is also a regional hegemony, such as the USA … China must constantly watch its back while trying to project power and influence on the global stage."[68]

In this case, the world is not bipolar because the *USA as the world's biggest economy and military power has the capacity to shape the environment* in which China makes its policy choices by strengthening cooperation with its allies in Asia as well as in other parts of the world, working with other countries in the UN Security Council and broadening engagement across the board to bring China along. While the Chinese leaders have faced nationalist pressures at home to defend its core interests, US politicians have faced similar domestic pressures to roll back China's assertiveness. After all, political survival at home always is the top priority and foreign policies are usually more expendable in this regard for political leaders, Chinese and Americans alike. China's assertiveness during the global slowdown made "demonizing China" popular in the US media and clearly hardened US positions on some issues that China defined as its core interests and to an extent increased at least some hostility in the US Congress towards China. Thus, when China reacted very strongly to the US arms sale to Taiwan in early 2010, Joseph Nye warned that "China has miscalculated by violating the wisdom of Deng Xiaoping, who advised that China should proceed cautiously and keep its light under a basket."[69]

Coming to the realization that "they had let their rhetoric get ahead of their interests, and were looking for a way to climb down,"[70] at the height of China's confrontation with the USA over its core interests, two experienced Chinese diplomats, former Ambassador to Germany Lu Qiutian and former Ambassador to Russia Li Fenglin, held a web chat with Chinese netizens in their official capacity as advisory members of the Chinese Ministry of Foreign Affairs on 20 March 2010. They reminded their online audience that China was still a few generations away from being a true great power and cautioned them to have a realistic attitude toward the view that "China will replace the USA to become the dominant power in the world." Therefore, China's *taoguangyanghui* strategy would continue for a long time.[71] It is interesting to note that, while the Chinese suspended part of the military exchange with the USA after the arms sale to Taiwan, it allowed the USS Nimitz aircraft carrier battle group to visit Hong Kong on 7 February, one day before President Obama's meeting with the Dalai Lama.[72] In spite of angry words and a threat to sanction US companies involved in the arms sales, China has not taken action on that threat so far. President Hu participated in the Nuclear Security Summit in April 2010 although, according to a Chinese scholar, "quite a significant number of Chinese officials objected to Hu's attendance" because they thought that "Hu's appearance was a one-sided concession to the ruthless undermining of Chinese national dignity." This scholar revealed that "Given the bitter debate within China on how to react in the wake of the US violation of core interests and the divisions among Chinese elites," Hu's decision to go to Washington represented "a new consensus and the punctuation of domestic debates in China. By persistently broadening converging interests with the US and strengthening cooperation on transnational issues, Beijing's pragmatism prevails once again."[73]

Conclusion

Four conclusions may be drawn from this study. First, keeping its head low for many years, China raised its head during the global economic downturn in 2008–9 when the Western countries' obvious weakness propelled the Chinese to rethink China's relations with the Western powers.[74] This shows that China's growing national strength could alter and perhaps has already altered its foreign policy behavior. A Chinese scholar indicated a fundamental foreign policy transformation in the mid–2000s, characterized by "the change of China from an ordinary state diplomacy to great power diplomacy, from weak-posture diplomacy to strong-posture diplomacy, and from a passive diplomacy to a proactive diplomacy."[75] Another Chinese scholar points out specifically that "in comparison with the past years, Chinese foreign policy in 2009 witnessed an important change" as "China no longer bends to the Western pressures and heeds about what the Western would think of its behavior (*bumai xigang de zhang*) in the pursuit of its interests."[76]

Second, China softened its tone and sent President Hu to Washington in April 2010 because of the realization that the confidence among many Chinese during the global economic downturn was based on a miscalculation of China's strength and interests. Rising as a great power but still trailing far behind the US to dislodge America from its position of global dominance, China still could not afford to jeopardize ties with the USA.

Third, reflecting China's growing confidence in its increasing power and influence, its frustration as a rising power in the world stage, and the regime's fear of many social, economic, and political uncertainties at home, China's new assertiveness has, however, focused on pursing its immediate interests and Beijing is still hesitant to use its rising power status to bolster the global common welfare. It is, therefore, too soon "to expect China to play a broader role, taking on responsibilities for global order and making concessions for broader interests."[77] It is from this perspective, one observer suggested that "China has not been psychologically prepared to play a full 'great power' leadership role in confronting problems such as climate change, genocide, civil war, nuclear proliferation, much less abusive governments. Its rigid notion of sovereign rights has made leaders reluctant to publicly criticize or overtly intrude into the internal affairs of other countries. This reluctance has only been reinforced by China's view of itself as a victim of hegemonic predation by colonialist and imperialist stronger powers over the past century and a half."[78]

Fourth, one defining tension in China's foreign policy agenda is still to find a balance between taking a broad great power responsibility and focusing on its narrowly defined core interests to play down its pretense of being a global power. As an expression of this delicate position, Chinese foreign minister Yang Jiechi in a policy speech emphasized the importance of holding on the low-profile axiom while called to "act as a responsible big country (power)."[79] Two Chinese scholars elaborated this position, arguing that "[f]ollowing Deng's low-profile policy, China has been "modest and realistic in assessing China's strengths and weakness and kept a sober mind on and even rejected occasional temptations to overestimate its power and influence in the world. But this does not mean that the Chinese should shake off their international obligations."[80] The continuing growth of China's national strength may eventually eliminate this contradiction when the Chinese leaders would come to "view their country less as a poor nation and more as a great power."[81] Until then, Chinese foreign policy is still in a transitional stage from a reluctant rising power to a true great power.

Endnotes

1 Den Qirong, *Gaige kaifang yilai de zhongguo waijiao*. (Chinese Diplomacy since the Reform and Opening Up), (Beijing: Shijie Zhishi Chuban She, 2009), 18.

2 "Press conference of the PRC State Council Information Office for contacts between Central Government and Dalai Lama," *Xinhua*. (11 February 2010), http://news.xinhuanet.com/english2010/china/2010–02/11/c_13172224.htm

3 Helene Cooper, "U.S. Starts to Push Back Against China in Growing Rift," *New York Times*. (31 January 2010), http://www.nytimes.com/2010/02/01/world/asia/01china.html?hp

4 Katrin Bennhold, "As China Rises, Conflict With West Rises Too," *The New York Times*. (27 January 2010).

5 Andrew Small, "Dealing with a More Assertive China," *GMF blog*. (2 February 2010), http://blog.gmfus.org/2010/02/08/dealing-with-a-more-assertive-china/

6 Timothy Garton Ash, "China arrives as a world power today – and we should welcome it," *The Guardian*. (2 April 2009).

7 Jia Qingguo, "Learning to Live with the Hegemon: Evolution of China's Policy toward the U.S. since the End of the Cold War," *Journal of Contemporary China*, Vol. 14, No. 44. (2005).

8 "首轮中美经济对话：除上月球外主要问题均已谈," 中新社, (28 July 2009), http://www.chinanews.com.cn/gn/news/2009/07-29/1794984.shtml

9 Feiling Wang, "Preservation, Prosperity and Power, What Motivates China's Foreign Policy," *Journal of Contemporary China*, 14, no. 45. (2005).

10 Caren Bohan and Patricia Zengerle, "Obama prods China on yuan, but Hu silent on issue," *Reuters*. (18 November 2009).

11 Katrin Bennhold, "As China Rises, Conflict With West Rises Too," *The New York Times*. (27 January 2010).

12 Wang Xiaoyang, "qiekan meiguo de xinxi ziyou" (Looking at the US information freedom), *Renmin Ribao*. (24 January 2010), 3.

13 James Fallows, "The Google news: China enters its Bush-Cheney era," *Atlantic*. (12 January 2010), http://jamesfallows.theatlantic.com/archives/2010/01/first_reactions_on_google_and.php

14 "China yesterday urged the USA to cancel a massive arms deal to Taiwan, warning of severe consequences if it does not heed the call," *China Daily*. (8 January 2010).

15 "Chinese threats to sanction Boeing are more sound than fury," *Chinese Economic Review*. (February 3, 2010), http://www.chinaeconomicreview.com/today-in-china/2010_02_03/Dont_worry_about_Boeing.html

16 "The World from Berlin, Execution Underscores 'China's Contempt for the West'" *Spiegel Online*. (30 December 2009), http://www.spiegel.de/international/europe/0,1518,669573,00.html#ref=nlint

17 Amy Kazmin, "China bar on border road angers India," *Financial Times*. (30 November 2009), http://www.ft.com/cms/s/0/3f11bbb6-ddd4–11de-b8e2–00144feabdc0,dwp_uuid=9c33700c-4c86-11da-89df-0000779e2340.html

18 Sudha Ramachandran, "Dalai Lama caught in Sino-Indian dispute," *The Asia Times*. (18 September 2009), http://www.atimes.com/atimes/South_Asia/KI18Df02.html

19 Harsh V. Pant, "China's challenge moves India to expect the worst," *The Japan Times*. (28 September 2009), http://search.japantimes.co.jp/cgi-bin/eo20090928a1.html

20 "Full text of Chinese premier's speech at World Economic Forum Annual Meeting 2009," *Xinhua*. (28 January 2009), http://news.xinhuanet.com/english/2009-01/29/content_10731877.htm

21 "Premier Wen meets Press," *Xinhua*. (13 March 2009), http://news.xinhuanet.com/english/2009–03/13/content_11002970.htm

22 John Garnaut, "China's money mandarins take the hard line," *Sydney Morning Herald*. (20 April 2009).

23 "China opens top economic work meeting with focus on stable growth," *Xinhua*. (9 December 2008), http://www.xinhuanet.com/fortune/08zygzhy/

24 Patrice Hill, "China's stimulus powers world economies," *The Washington Times*. (8 September 2009).

25 Suisheng Zhao, "The China Model: Can it replace the Western Model of Modernization," *Journal of Contemporary China*, Vol. 19, No. 65. (2010), 433.

26 Jin Canrong, "Reason for optimism in Sino-American relations," *East Asia Forum*. (14 February 2010), http://www.eastasiaforum.org/2010/02/14/reason-for-optimism-in-sino-american-relations

27 "China invites foreign delegates to navy ships to boost military openness, cooperaiton," *Xinhua*. (22 April 2009).

28 Yong Deng, *China's Struggle for Status: the Realignment of International Relations*. (Cambridge, Cambridge University Press, 2008), 10, 12.

29 Yuan Peng, "China's Strategic Choices," *Contemporary International Relations*. Vol. 20, No. 1. (2010), 30.

30 Zhu Feng, "A return of Chinese Pragmatism," *PacNet*, #16. (5 April 2010).

31 Justin Blum, "Shareholders Vote in Favor Of Unocal Acquisition," *The Washington Post*. (11 August 2005), http://www.washingtonpost.com/wp-dyn/content/article/2005/08/10/AR2005081000986.html

32 Myra P. Saefong and Simon Kennedy, "Rio Tinto rejects Chinalco deal, to sell stock," The *Wall Street Journal*. (5 June 2009), http://www.marketwatch.com/story/rio-tinto-hints–195-bln-chinalco-deal-may-fail

33 Dana Cimilluca, Shai Oster and Amy Or, "Rio Tinto Scuttles Its Deal with Chinalco," *The Wall Street Journal*. (5 June 2009).

34 Xi Jinping: "外国人不要无视中国贡献，吃饱没事干" (Foreigners shouldn't overlook China's contribution, well fed and with nothing to

do), 球场'评论员的博客, (21 February 2009), http://blog.sina.com.cn/s/blog_5d769d690100cy3x.html~type=v5_one&label=rela_nextarticle

35 Song Xiaojun, Wang Xiaodong, Huang Jisu, Song Qiang, etc, *Zhongguo Bugaoxing* (China is Not Happy). (Nanjing: Jiangsu Renmin Chuban She, 2009).

36 Wang Yizhou, "China's Diplomacy: Ten Features," *Contemporary International Relations*, Vol. 19, No. 1. (2009), 46.

37 Joseph Fewsmith and Stanley Rosen, "The Domestic Context of Chinese Foreign Policy: Does Public Opinion Matter?" in David M. Lampton, *The Making of Chinese Foreign and Security Policy*. (Stanford, C.A.: Stanford University Press, 2001), 151–90.

38 Chris Buckley, "Changing China tied to rough ride with U.S.," *Reuters*. (4 February 2010), http://www.reuters.com/article/idUSTRE6130IP20100204

39 James McGregor, "The China Fix," Time, 1 February 2010.

40 戴旭 (Dai Xu), C形包围——内忧外患下的中国突围 (C shape encircle, China's Breakthrough with the internal concerns and external dangers), (Beijing: Wenhui Chubanshe, 2009).

41 刘明福 (Liu Mingfu), 中国梦 (The China Dream), (Beijing: Youyi Chuban Gongshi, 2010).

42 Francesco Sisci, "The peace imperative," *AsiaTime Online*. (8 January 2010), http://www.atimes.com/atimes/China/LA08Ad02.html

43 David M. Lampton, "China's Foreign and National Security Policy-Making Process: Is It Changing and does It Matter?" in David M. Lampton, ed. *The Making of Chinese Foreign and Security Policy*. (Stanford, C.A. Stanford University Press, 2001), 14.

44 Jian Xu, "Comparing Security Concepts of China and the USA," in Suisheng Zhao, (ed.) *China-US Relations Transformed: Perspectives and Strategic Interactions*. (London: Routledge, 2008), 76–8.

45 Wu Xinbo, "Four Contradictions Constraining China's Foreign Policy Behavior," *Journal of Contemporary China*, vol. 10, no. 27. (May 2001), 293–302.

46 Suisheng Zhao, "Adaptation and Strategic Calculation: China's Participation in International Regimes and Institutions," in Peter Kien-hong Yu, W. Emily Chow, and Shawn S. F. Kao, (eds), *International Governance, Regimes, and Globalization*. (Lanham, M.D., Lexington Books, 2010), 69–70.

47 Stephanie Kleine-Ahlbrandt and Andrew Small, "China's New Dictatorship Diplomacy," *Foreign Affairs*. (January/February 2008), 38–9.

48 Robert B. Zoellick, "Whither China: From Membership to Responsibility?" *NBR Analysis*, 16, no. 4. (2005), 7.

49 Xue Fukang, "Hedging Strategy Won't Do Relationship Good," *China Daily*. (21 November 2005), 4.

50 Liu Haibing, "Pingxi Zhongguo Zheren Lun" (On the argument of China Responsibility), in Pan Zhongqi, (ed.), *Guoji Zheren yu Daguo zhanlue*

(International Responsibility and Great Power Strategy), (Shanghai: Shanghai Renmin Chuban She, 2008), 95.

51 Elizabeth Economy, "The Impact of International Regimes on Chinese Foreign Policy Making: Broadening Perspectives and Policies… But only to a point," in David M. Lampton, (ed.) *The Making of Chinese Foreign and Security Policy.* (Stanford, C.A.: Stanford University Press, 2001), 230–53.

52 John Garnaut, "Battle for Shanghai takes centre stage in Hu's strategy," *Sydney Morning Herald.* (1 February 2010).

53 Robert J. Samuelson, "The danger behind China's 'me first' worldview," *Washington Post.* (15 February 2010), A17.

54 Guo Zhengyuan, "21 shiji de erge shinian zhongguo de guoji diwei he zuoyong" (China's International status and role in the second decade of the twenty-first century), *Zhongguo pinglun* (China Review), no. 137. (2010), 11.

55 "重大理论创新:瞭望载文阐述胡锦涛时代观五大主张" (Important Theoretical Innovation: *Outlook Weekly* on Hu Jintao's Five Pointviews of the Time), *RenminNet.* (24 November 2009), http://politics.people.com.cn/GB/1024/10438064.html

56 Fu Jing, "China willing to aid bailout: EU leaders," *People's Daily.* (28 January 2012), http://www.cdeclips.com/en/world/fullstory.html?id=71713

57 Qin Jize, "Hu, Obama vow more cooperation," *China Daily.* (3 April 2010), http://www.cdeclips.com/en/world/fullstory.html?id=42114

58 Zhang Haizhou, "US seeks bigger role for China in Afghanistan," *Xinhua.* (5 May 2010), http://www.cdeclips.com/en/world/fullstory.html?id=43780

59 Stephanie T. Kleine-Ahlbrandt, "Beijing, Global Free-Rider," *Foreign Policy.* (12 November 2009), http://www.foreignpolicy.com/articles/2009/11/12/beijing_global_free_rider

60 Minxin Pei, "Why China Won't Rule the World,"*Newsweek.* (7 December 2009), http://www.newsweek.com/id/225627

61 Michael Wines and Edward Wong, "An Unsure China Steps onto the Global Stage," *The New York Times.* (2 April 2009).

62 Chow Chung-yan, "Beijing heeds call to play big role on world stage Official unveils major shift in foreign policy," *South China Morning Post.* (11 March 2008), 6.

63 Wen Jiabao, "Our Historical Tasks at the Primary Stage of Socialism and Several Issues Concerning China's Foreign Policy," *People's Daily.* (27 February 2007).

64 James Miles, "China and the West, A time for muscle-flexing," *The Economist.* (19 March 2009).

65 Jonas Parello-Plesner, "The G 2: no good for China and for world governance," *PacNet* #31A. (30 April 2009).

66 "Wen rejects allegation of China, U.S. monopolizing world affairs in future," *Xinhua.* (21 May 2009).

67 Minxin Pei, "Why China Won't Rule the World," *Newsweek.* (7 December 2009), http://www.newsweek.com/id/225627

68 Minxin Pei, "China is Not a Superpower," *The Diplomat*. (29 December 2009), http://www.carnegieendowment.org/publications/index.cfm?fa=view&id=24404

69 Nye also believed that "If Deng were in charge today, he would lead China back to the cooperative relations with the U.S. that marked early 2009." Joseph S. Nye. Jr., "China's Bad Bet against America," *PacNet* #14. (25 March 2010).

70 Douglas H. Paal, "Beijing's Attitude Adjustment," National Interest, (5 April 2010), http://www.nationalinterest.org/Article.aspx?id=23140

71 "外交部外交政策咨询委员会卢秋田和李凤林委员 就"世界如何看中国"话题与公众在线交流答问实录," (online exchange transcript between MOFA foreign policy advisory members, Lu Qiutian and Li Fenglin, and the pubilc on "how the world sees China"), http://bbs.fmprc.gov.cn/detail.jsp?id=347534

72 Kristine Kwok and Minnie Chan, "Surprise consent for U.S. ship visit," *South China Morning Post*. (11 February 2010), http://www.scmp.com/portal/site/SCMP/menuitem.2af62ecb329d3d7733492d9253a0a0a0/?vgnextoid=dec1331c158b6210VgnVCM100000360a0a0aRCRD&ss=China&s=News

73 Zhu Feng, "A Return of Chinese Pragmatism," *Pacnet* #16. (5 April 2010).

74 Jin Canrong, Liu Shiqiang, "Guoji xinshi de shengke biandong jiqi dui zhongguo de yingxiang" (The Significant Change in International Situation and its Impacts on China), *Xiandai guoji guanxi* (Contemporary International Relations). (1 December 2009).

75 Liu Shengxiang, "Zhongguo waijiao zhouqi yu waijiao zhuanxin" (China's Diplomatic Cycles and Diplomatic Transformation), *Xiandai Guoji Guanxi* (Contemporary International Relations), No. 1. (2010), 49.

76 Wang Xiaodong, "Wo kanhao zhongguo" (I look good at China), *Zhongguo Gaige Wang* (China Reform Net). (12 February 2010), http://www.chinareform.net/2010/0212/12486.html

77 Fareed Zakaria, "U.S.-China growing pains," *The Economist*. (8 February 2010), A15.

78 Orville Schell, "China Reluctant to lead," *YaleGlobal*. (11 March 2009).

79 Yang Jiechi, "China's Diplomacy since the Beginning of Reform and Opening up," *Foregin Affairs Journal*. (Winter 2008), 15.

80 Wang Jisi and Zheng Wingmin, "New Thinking in China's Diplomacy since the Inception of Reform and Opening Up," *Foregin Affairs Journal*. (Winter 2008), 21.

81 Bonnie S. Glaser, "Discussion of Four Contradictions Constraining China's Foreign Policy Behavior," *Journal of Contemporary China*. Vol. 10, No. 27. (2001).

Bibliography

Ash, Timothy G. "China arrves as a world power today – and we should welcome it." *The Guardian*. (2 April 2009).

Bennhold, Katrin, "As China Rises, Conflict With West Rises Too." *The New York Times*. (27 January 2010).

Blum, Justin. "Shareholders Vote in Favor of Unocal Acquisition." *The Washington Post*. (11 August 2005). www.washingtonpost.com/wpdyn/content/article/2005/08/10/AR2005081000986.html

Bohan, Caren and P. Zengerle. "Obama prods China on yuan, but Hu silent on issue." *Reuters*. (18 November 2009).

Buckley, Chris. "Changing China tied to rough ride with U.S." *Reuters*. (4 February 2010). www.reuters.com/article/idUSTRE6130IP20100204

"China invites foreign delegates to navy ships to boost military openness, cooperation." *Xinhua*. (22 April 2009).

"China opens top economic work meeting with focus on stable growth." *Xinhua*. (9 December 2008). www.xinhuanet.com/fortune/08zygzhy/

"China yesterday urged the United States to cancel a massive arms deal to Taiwan, warning of severe consequences if it does not heed the call." *China Daily*. (8 January 2010).

"Chinese threats to sanction Boeing are more sound than fury" (2010), *Chinese Economic Review*. (3 February 2010). www.chinaeconomicreview.com/today-in-china/2010_02_03/Dont_worry_about_Boeing.html

Chow, Chung-yan. "Beijing heeds call to play big role on world stage Official unveils major shift in foreign policy." *South China Morning Post*. (11 March 2008), 6.

Cimilluca, Dana, S. Oster and A. Or. "Rio Tinto Scuttles Its Deal with Chinalco." *The Wall Street Journal*. (5 June 2009).

Cooper, Helene. "U.S. Starts to Push Back Against China in Growing Rift." *The New York Times*. (31 January 2010). http://www.nytimes.com/2010/02/01/world/asia/01china.html?hp

Dai, Xu. C形包围——内忧外患下的中国突围 (C shape encircle, China's Breakthrough with the internal concerns and external dangers). (Beijing: Wenhui Chubanshe, 2009).

Deng, Qirong. Gaige kaifang yilai de zhongguo waijiao (Chinese Diplomacy since the Reform and Opening Up). (Beijing: Shijie Zhishi Chuban She, 2009).

Economy, Elizabeth. "The Impact of International Regimes on Chinese Foreign Policy Making: Broadening Perspectives and Policies... But only to a point," in David M. Lampton (ed.), The Making of Chinese Foreign and Security Policy. (Stanford, C.A.: Stanford University Press, 2001), 230–53.

Fallows, James. "The Google news: China enters its Bush-Cheney era." *Atlantic*, 12 January 2010. jamesfallows.theatlantic.com/archives/2010/01/first_reactions_on_google_and.php.

Fewsmith, Joseph and S. Rosen (2001), "The Domestic Context of Chinese Foreign Policy: Does Public Opinion Matter?" in David M. Lampton (ed.), *The Making of Chinese Foreign and Security Policy*. (Stanford, C.A.: Stanford University Press, 2001), 151–90.

"Full text of Chinese premier's speech at World Economic Forum Annual Meeting 2009." *Xinhua*. (28 January 2009). http://news.xinhuanet.com/english/2009–01/29/content_10731877.htm

Garnaut, John. "China's money mandarins take the hard line." *Sydney Morning Herald*. (20 April 2009).

—"Battle for Shanghai takes centre stage in Hu's strategy." *Sydney Morning Herald*. (1 February 2010).

Glaser, Bonnie S. "Discussion of Four Contradictions Constraining China's Foreign Policy Behavior." *Journal of Contemporary China*, Vol. 10, No. 27. (2001).

Guo, Zhengyuan. "21 shiji de erge shinian zhongguo de guoji diwei he zuoyong (China's internaitonal status and role in the second decade of the 21st century)." *Zhongguo pinglun (China Review)*, No. 137. (2010), 11.

Hill, Patrice. "China's stimulus powers world economies." *The Washington Times*. (8 September 2009).

Jia, Qingguo. "Learning to Live with the Hegemon: Evolution of China's Policy toward the U.S. since the End of the Cold War." *Journal of Contemporary China*, Vol. 14, No. 44. (2005), 395–407.

Jian, Xu. "Comparing Security Concepts of China and the USA," in Suisheng Zhao (ed.), *China-US Relations Transformed: Perspectives and Strategic Interactions*. (London: Routledge, 2008), 76–8.

Jin, Canrong. "Reason for optimism in Sino-American relations." *East Asia Forum*. (14 February 2010), www.eastasiaforum.org/2010/02/14/reason-for-optimism-in-sino-american-relations/

Jin, Canrong and S. Liu. "Guoji xinshi de shengke biandong jiqi dui zhongguo de yingxiang" (The Significant Change in International Situation and its Impacts on China) in *Xiandai guoji guanxi* (Contemporary International Relations). (December 2009), 1.

Kazmin, Amy. "China bar on border road angers India." *Financial Times*. (30 November 2009), http://www.ft.com/cms/s/0/3f11bbb6-ddd4-11de-b8e2-00144feabdc0,dwp_uuid=9c33700c-4c86-11da-89df-0000779e2340.html

Kleine-Ahlbrandt, Stephanie T. "Beijing, Global Free-Rider." *Foreign Policy*. (12 November 2009), www.foreignpolicy.com/articles/2009/11/12/beijing_global_free_rider

Kleine-Ahlbrandt, Stephanie T. and A. Small (2008), "China's New Dictatorship Diplomacy," *Foregin Affairs*, Vol. 87, No. 1. (January/February 2008), 38–9.

Kwok, Kristine and M. Chan. "Surprise consent for U.S. ship visit." *South China Morning Post*. (11 February 2010), www.scmp.com/portal/site/SCMP/menuite m.2af62ecb329d3d7733492d9253a0a0a0/?vgnextoid=dec1331c158b6210Vgn VCM100000360a0a0aRCRD&ss=China&s=News

Lampton, David M. "China's Foreign and National Security Policy-Making Process: Is It Changing and does It Matter?" in David M. Lampton (ed.), *The Making of Chinese Foreign and Security Policy*. (Stanford, C.A.: Stanford University Press, 2001).

Liu, Haibing. "Pingxi Zhongguo Zeren Lun (On the argument of China Responsibility)" in Pan Zhongqi, (ed.), *Guoji Zeren yu Daguo zhanlue* (*International Responsibility and Great Power Strategy*). (Shanghai: Shanghai Renmin Chubanshe, 2008), 95.

Liu, Mingfu. 中国梦 (*The China Dream*), (Beijing: Youyi Chuban Gongsi, 2010).

Liu, Shengxiang. "Zhongguo waijiao zhouqi yu waijiao zhuanxin" (China's Diplomatic Cycles and Diplomatic Transformation). *Xiandai Guoji Guanxi* (Contemporary International Relations), No. (1 January 2010), 49.

McGregor, James. "The China Fix." *Time*. (1 February 2010).

Mikes, James. "China and the West, A time for Muscle-flexing." *The Economist*. (19 March 2009).

Nye, Joseph S. Jr. "China's Bad Bet against America." *PacNet*, No. 14. (25 March 2010).

Paal, Douglas H. "Beijing's Attitude Adjustment." National Interest, (5 April 2010), www.nationalinterest.org/Article.aspx?id=23140

Parello-Plesner, Jonas. "The G 2: no good for China and for world governance." *PacNet* No. 31A. (30 April 2009).

Pant, Harsh V. "China's challenge moves India to expect the worst." *The Japan Times*. (28 September 2009), http://search.japantimes.co.jp/cgi-bin/eo20090928a1.html

Pei, Minxin. "Why China Won't Rule the World." *Newsweek*. (7 December 2009), www.newsweek.com/id/225627

—"China is Not a Superpower." *The Diplomat*. (December 2009), http://www.carnegieendowment.org/publications/index.cfm?fa=view&id=24404

"Premier Wen meets Press," *Xinhua*. (13 March 2009), http://news.xinhuanet.com/english/2009–03/13/content_11002970.htm

"Press conference of the PRC State Council Information Office for contacts between Central Government and Dalai Lama," *Xinhua*. (11 February 2010), http://news.xinhuanet.com/english2010/china/2010–02/11/c_13172224.htm

Qin, Jize. "Hu, Obama vow more cooperation." *China Daily*. (3 April 2010), www.cdeclips.com/en/world/fullstory.html?id=42114

Ramachandra, Sudha. "Dalai Lama caught in Sino-Indian dispute." *The Asia Times*. (18 September 2009), http://www.atimes.com/atimes/South_Asia/KI18Df02.html

Saefong, Myra P. and S. Kennedy. "Rio Tinto rejects Chinalco deal, to sell stock." *The Wall Street Journal*. (5 June 2009), http://www.marketwatch.com/story/rio-tinto-hints–195-bln-chinalco-deal-may-fail

Samuelson, Robert J. "The danger behind China's 'me first' worldview." *The Washington Post*. (15 February 2009), A17.

Shell, Orville. "China Reluctant to lead." *YaleGlobal*. (11 March), 2009.

Sisci, Francesco. "The peace imperative." *AsiaTimes Online*. (8 January 2010), http://www.atimes.com/atimes/China/LA08Ad02.html

Small, Andrew. "Dealing with a More Assertive China." *GMF blog*. (2 February 2010), http://blog.gmfus.org/2010/02/08/dealing-with-a-more-assertive-china

Song, Xiaojun, X. Wang, J. Huang, Q. Song, et al. *Zhongguo Bugaoxing (China is Not Happy)*. (Nanjing: Jiangsu Renmin Chubanshe, 2009).

"The World from Berlin, Execution Underscores 'China's Contempt for the West'" *Spiegel Online*. (30 December 2009), www.spiegel.de/international/europe/0,1518,669573,00.html#ref=nlint

Wang, Feiling. "Preservation, Prosperity and Power, What Motivates China's Foreign Policy." *Journal of Contemporary China*, Vol. 14, No. 45. (2005), 669–94.

Wang, Jisi and W. Zheng. "New Thinking in China's Diplomacy since the Inception of Reform and Opening Up." *Foregin Affairs Journal*, No. 4. (Winter 2008), 17–23.

Wang, Xiaodong. "Wo kanhao zhongguo (I look good at China)." *Zhongguo Gaige Wang* (China Reform Net). (12 February 2010), http://www.chinareform.net/2010/0212/12486.html

Wang, Xiaoyang. "Qiekan meiguo de xinxi ziyou (Looking at the U.S. information freedom)" *Renmin Ribao*. (24 January 2010), 3.

Wang, Yizhou. "China's Diplomacy: Ten Features." *Contemporary International Relations*, Vol. 19, No. 1. (2009), 45–64.

Wen, Jiabao. "Our Historical Tasks at the Primary Stage of Socialism and Several Issues Concerning China's Foreign Policy." *People's Daily*. (27 February 2007).

"Wen rejects allegation of China, U.S. monopolizing world affairs in future." *Xinhua*, 21 May 2009.

Wines, Michael and E. Wong "An Unsure China Steps onto the Global Stage." *The New York Times*. (2 April 2009).

Xi, Jinping. "外国人不要无视中国贡献，吃饱没事干(Foreigners shouldn't overlook China's contribution, well fed and with nothing to do)." 球场'评论员的博客, (21 February 2009), blog.sina.com.cn/s/blog_5d769d690100cy3x.html~type=v5_one&label=rela_nextarticle.

Xue, Fukang. "Hedging Strategy Won't Do Relationship Good." *China Daily*. (21 November 2005), 4.

Yang, Jiechi. "China's Diplomacy since the Beginning of Reform and Opening up." *Foregin Affairs Journal*, No. 4. (Winter 2008), 1–16.

Yong, Deng. *China's Struggle for Status: the Realignemnt of International Relations*. (Cambridge: Cambridge University Press, 2010).

Yuan, Peng. "China's Strategic Choices." *Contemporary International Relations*, Vol. 20, No. 1. (2010), 17–32.

Zakaria, Fareed. "U.S.-China growing pains." *The Economist*. (8 February 2010), A15.

Zhang, Haizhou. "US seeks bigger role for China in Afghanistan." *Xinhua*. (5 May 2010), www.cdeclips.com/en/world/fullstory.html?id=43780

Zhao, Suisheng (2010), "Adaptation and Strategic Calculation: China's Participation in International Regimes and Institutions," in Peter Kien-hong Yu, W. Emily Chow, and Shawn S. F. Kao (ed.). *International Governance, Regimes, and Globalization*. (Lanham, M.D.: Lexington Books, 2010), 69–93.

—(2010), "The China Model: Can it replace the Western Model of Modernization," Journal of Contemporary China, Vol. 19, No. 65, 419–36.

Zhu, Feng. "A return of Chinese Pragmatism." *PacNet*, No. 16. (5 April 2010).

Zoellick, Robert B. "Whither China: From Membership to Responsibility?" *NBR Analysis*, 16 (4) (2005), 5–14.

"首轮中美经济对话:除上月球外主要问题均已谈" *China News Service*. (28 July 2009). www.chinanews.com.cn/gn/news/2009/07-29/1794984.shtml

"外交部外交政策咨询委员会卢秋田和李凤林委员　就"世界如何看中国"话题与公众在线交流答问实录(online exchange transcript between MOFA foreign policy advisory members, Lu Qiutian and Li Fenglin, and the pubilc on 'how the world sees China')," bbs.fmprc.gov.cn/detail.jsp?id=347534.

"重大理论创新:瞭望载文阐述胡锦涛时代观五大主张(Important Theoretical Innovation: *Outlook Weekly* on Hu Jintao's Five Pointviews of the Time)." *RenminNet*. (24 November 2009), politics.people.com.cn/GB/1024/10438064.html

CHAPTER SIX

India—An Aspiring Global Power

Vidya Nadkarni

Since the turn of the twenty-first century, India's leaders have articulated an ambitious vision for the country as an emerging global power. Speaking in Paris on 5 May 2011, India's Foreign Secretary Nirupama Rao asserted that India, "buoyed by its rapid and sustainable growth," sought to "play a role commensurate with its size and destiny." She remarked that size, population, a strong economy, a vibrant democratic culture, and a strategic location gave Indian leaders a "keen sense" of the country's "potential to be a great power." But she also noted that India would play a greater role on the global stage without sacrificing its prized "strategic autonomy." As a consequence, New Delhi, she added, has pursued and successfully forged "well-rounded strategic relationships and partnerships with all major powers."[1]

Engagement with all centers of power has been the strategy that India has pointedly adopted in its twenty-first century quest for wealth, power, and status.[2] Along with deepening its links with the EU and Japan, forging a strong partnership with the USA, and renewing traditionally friendly ties with Russia, India has also made important strides in establishing a pragmatic relationship with its long-time rival, China.[3] On its home continent, India's "extended neighborhood" policy has proposed active engagement with countries in East Asia (Look East policy), Central Asia, and West Asia.[4] As part and parcel of this overall strategy, New Delhi has also reached out to countries in Africa and Latin America and has sought to carve out a greater role and voice for the country in major multilateral forums of global and regional scope.

The obverse of this picture of an India moving inexorably toward great power status is that of a country facing enormous obstacles in the path of achieving this vision. Domestic insurgencies, vast income inequalities, a huge population with rising expectations, fractious relations with smaller sub-continental neighbors, and the promise and perils of a globalizing world represent the many challenges that compound New Delhi's development vs. security and energy vs. environment conundrums and often undercut the attainment of more expansive status goals. This chapter critically examines the challenges and opportunities in the path of India's quest for global power.

A Long Journey

By virtue of its sub-continental size and civilizational heritage, Indian leaders since independence in 1947 have envisioned their country as a great power. Only with the turn of the century, however, has India's potential as an emerging global power received validation from other large states in the international system. The complex dynamics of India's checkered rise cannot be divorced from larger regional and global historical processes. Over the course of the latter half of the twentieth century, system- and state-level factors severely curtailed India's ability to project power beyond the sub-continent.[5] Factors such as the sub-regional effects of Cold War divisions, India's rivalries with China and Pakistan, as well as domestic vulnerabilities and the lack of hard capabilities served to limit India's regional and global imprint.

In the 1950s, New Delhi's global leadership role was largely symbolic. India, under its first post-independence Prime Minister Jawaharlal Nehru, was a self-styled global leader and purveyor of an international order that rejected rigid Cold War ideological divisions and the military alliances they had spawned and decried the use of force as an instrument of statecraft. This self-image contributed to the articulation of an independent course in global affairs immediately after independence in 1945—a decision that cast India in the role of a reformist state in an ideologically polarized world.[6] As a recently decolonized state, India's leadership was anti-imperialist. Under the stewardship of Nehru, India's foreign policy was defined by a posture of ideological non-alignment that sought to avoid entanglement in divisive Cold War confrontations. At home, guided by the goals of poverty alleviation and income redistribution, Nehru embraced economic self-reliance, adopting a mixed-economy model that relied on planning, state control over key industries, and a heavily regulated private sector.

This mix of foreign and domestic policy choices was viewed with suspicion and distrust by the USA because they frontally opposed the primary US global objective of containing Soviet communism. What for Nehru constituted reformist ideas in the liberal mold was interpreted by

US leaders as revisionism and as a clear attempt to challenge American preferences. India's unwillingness to join the US-sponsored anti-Soviet bloc led American leaders to work actively to frustrate India's regional and global ambitions. In the 1950s and 1960s, America's regional containment strategy in South Asia targeted India by forging an alliance with Pakistan in 1954 and supplying that country with modern armaments. In the 1970s, the Sino-US rapprochement, which was aimed primarily against the Soviet Union, also isolated India—an objective that was favored by both the USA and China.[7]

Nehru had entertained high hopes that the decolonized Asian states would inaugurate a new era of international cooperation predicated on the non-violent resolution of conflicts. Even before India's formal independence, Nehru had waded into international waters, convening an Asian Relations Conference in New Delhi in March-April 1947 where he declared:

We have no designs against anybody; ours is the great design of promoting peace and progress all over the world. For too long, we of Asia have been petitioners in Western courts and chancelleries. That story must now belong to the past.... There is today conflict in many countries, and all of us in Asia are full of our troubles. Nevertheless, the whole spirit and outlook of Asia are peaceful, and the emergence of Asia in world affairs will be a powerful influence for world peace.[8]

But Nehru's idealistic call for "One World" found little support from the new communist leaders in China after their successful revolution in 1949. The subsequent forcible Chinese take-over of Tibet in 1950 shook both Nehru's liberal faith and put paid to his dreams of Asian solidarity. By the time of the 1955 Asian-African Conference in Bandung, Nehru's prestige had waned considerably. Even so, Nehru championed the wisdom of non-alignment at the1961 Belgrade conference at which the Non-Aligned Movement (NAM) was officially established.

Nehru's stance during the 1950s was not unlike that adopted by the USA in the post-revolutionary period when American leaders displayed a strong distaste for foreign (European) entanglements and promoted an "isolationism" carefully tailored to protect American national interests. Isolationism in the US view precluded neither international commerce nor an assertive regional internationalism underwritten by the Monroe Doctrine and coupled with relentless westward territorial expansion on the North American continent even when it entailed military clashes with European imperial powers. American exceptionalism, not unlike Nehru's ideas, projected an image of the USA as an exemplary democracy that had jettisoned the diplomatic chicanery of the Old World. But whereas the USA successfully mounted such a challenge to the European international order both because of its favorable geographical location and the security afforded by the British Navy, India's post-independence geopolitical position was far more vulnerable.

By the 1960s, Nehru's ideas were losing traction. His foreign policy vis-à-vis China represented a signal diplomatic and military failure. Seeing China through the prism of a historical fellow traveler, albeit one that had experienced indirect colonialism, Nehru had cherished the hope that the two countries would journey hand-in-hand to usher in a new world order where conflicts would be resolved through diplomacy and non-violence. Nehru's neglect of India's military defenses left the country woefully unprepared in the war with China in 1962, which ensued after Indian leaders discovered and challenged the legality of a Chinese-built road through the Aksai Chin area in the north-eastern portion of the state of Kashmir.[9] While the Sino-Indian confrontation led to a closer relationship with the USA, which was eager to contain communist China, the thaw in US-Indian relations proved temporary.

India's defeat at the hands of China unmasked the wide discrepancy between New Delhi's projected global role and actual capabilities and sparked a major shift in defense and strategic thinking. Following this debacle, Nehru belatedly started a program of military enhancement, which was continued under Prime Minister Lal Bahadur Shastri (1964–6) and his successor Indira Gandhi (1966–77; 1980–4).[10] This defense build-up allowed India to prevail in a war with Pakistan in 1965 over Kashmir. India's 1971 war with Pakistan led to the creation of Bangladesh.[11] In December 1971, faced with Chinese and American support for Pakistan and President Nixon's decision to normalize relations with Beijing, Indira Gandhi sought to avoid diplomatic isolation by signing a friendship treaty with the Soviet Union before intervening militarily in the war in support of secessionist forces in East Pakistan. This action, defying both the USA and China and relying on the diplomatic support of the Soviet Union, helped to establish India as the pre-eminent regional power in South Asia.

During the ensuing decades, India focused on building up its domestic capabilities and enhancing its standing in the South Asian sub-region, while not entirely abandoning its participation in the non-aligned movement, despite the tilt toward the Soviet Union. In the wake of the 1973 Arab oil embargo and the ensuing oil crisis, India also joined other developing countries in the Group of 77 (G77) in 1974 in calling for a new international economic order (NIEO) to replace the liberal international economic order (LIEO) as represented by the Bretton Woods system inaugurated by the USA after World War Two. Positioning itself as a leader in subaltern diplomacy, India championed the causes of states outside hegemonic power structures but was constrained by its limited economic capabilities in successfully challenging the prevailing liberal international economic order. Apart from these occasional forays in global diplomacy, the scope of India's foreign policy during this period was largely regional.

Moving away from the Nehruvian global posturing of the 1950s, the Indian leadership under Indira Gandhi focused on consolidating India's status as a sub-continental power. To augment India's hard power credentials in the wake of the 1971 India-Pakistan War, Indira Gandhi proceeded with a latent nuclear weapons program that culminated in a successful nuclear test in 1974. The Indian government, seeking to signal benign intent, referred to this test as a "peaceful nuclear explosion" (PNE). While refraining from building nuclear weapons, Mrs. Gandhi kept open the country's future nuclear options.

The 1974 PNE set the stage for the 1998 nuclear tests after which then Prime Minister Atal Behari Vajpayee declared that India had joined the ranks of nuclear weapons powers. With this action, India took a significant step in issuing an open and direct challenge to the Non-Proliferation Treaty (NPT) regime of which, as a non-signatory, it had never been a part.[12] India's decision to pursue a nuclear weapons program came from status and security considerations. However, Pakistan's simultaneous entry into the ranks of nuclear weapons states undercut the Indian military advantage. Islamabad undertook riskier strategies of aiding and abetting proxy wars in the form of terrorist assaults against India launched from Pakistani soil and engaging in brinkmanship, as for instance when Pakistan initiated a limited war against India in 1999 in the Kargil sector of Kashmir.[13]

Twin developments in the early 1990s served as a catalyst in the re-orientation of India's world view from a limited to a more expansive vision of its global role. The first development was the Indian government's involuntary embrace of a drastic economic liberalization program in July 1991 when faced with the prospect of a near default on international debt payments and vanishing hard currency reserves. The IMF had prepared a bailout package for India conditional on the adoption of stringent liberal reforms.[14] The second development stemmed from the late 1991 collapse of the Soviet Union and the attendant challenge of revamping a strategic posture that had relied on unstinting Soviet support of India's interests in the region. The special relationship that India and the USSR had enjoyed since 1971 when the two countries had signed a defensive treaty was dormant for the next few years during which Russia was preoccupied with managing the consequences of the Soviet break-up.

Economic liberalization brought immediate economic benefits to India, manifested by a return to macroeconomic stability and, more importantly, by robust rates of economic growth. The end of the Cold War, which preceded the Soviet collapse, set into motion a radical realignment of US-India ties. During the Cold War, the US-India relationship had been fraught with tension and conflict as the USA worked to neutralize India's role as an independent ("non-aligned") third force. Relations had deteriorated further when New Delhi felt compelled to move toward "alignment" with the Soviet Union after the US-China rapprochement that was inaugurated with then National Security Adviser Henry Kissinger's secret trip to Beijing in July 1971. The collapse of the Soviet Union and the rise of China as a global power altered the strategic dynamic regionally and globally. Beginning with a thaw in bilateral ties during the Clinton presidency, the US-India nexus grew steadily stronger. The USA moved gradually from a Cold War policy of secondary containment of India to one of active accommodation of India's rise as a global power.

Path to Great Power: The Mechanics of India's Rise

The concept of *national role conception* serves as a useful analytical tool in gauging the aspirations and policies of any given state.[15] National roles derive both from a process of self-definition and externally generated expectations. Roles serve as a source for the definition of foreign policy goals and the articulation of foreign policy interests. Roles, in turn, are reinforced or readjusted in accordance with the level of a state's success in achieving those goals, which is, in no small measure, dependent upon a state's capabilities and the receptivity of powerful states toward accommodation of the ambitions of would-be great powers. When India's self-defined role expectations of global leadership in the 1950s could not be sustained in the face of opposition from the USA and China, Indian leaders were forced to recognize the untenability of lofty aspirations that were not underpinned by hard capabilities and were unsupported by the system-wide distribution of power. The geopolitical realignments that ensued with the end of the Cold War in the late 1980s and the collapse of the Soviet Union in 1991, coupled with the emergence of a range of transnational challenges and the impact of globalization processes, created a more hospitable external environment for India's gradual rise, which was also aided by high rates of economic growth and, more significantly, by the decision of the USA to support India's status goals. These developments served to kindle India's twenty-first century great power aspirations.

In the 1990s, American unipolarity was resisted, though not directly challenged, by several secondary powers: China, as a rising global power; Brazil and India, as emerging powers; and Russia, as a declining state seeking to reprise its earlier status as a major power. Likewise, European countries, particularly Germany and France, and Japan resisted the sharply unilateralist turn in US policy during the presidency of George W. Bush but eschewed open confrontation. By the turn of the century, China's emergence as America's nearest peer competitor and India's emerging global role have set the stage for a protracted period of "power shift" from the West to Asia. Even as the predominant power (USA) and its allies in Europe and Japan together with the rising and emerging powers (China, India,

Russia, and Brazil) have continued to cooperate in the fight against security threats from transnational terrorism and other global challenges, China's increasing global profile and towering presence in Asia have changed the calculus of the US-India relationship from suspicion during the Cold War to growing cooperation in the twenty-first century.

Common strategic interests have brought the two erstwhile "estranged democracies" to view each other as "natural allies."[16] From a position of hostility to India's regional and global aspirations, the USA has moved to a posture of accommodation, indeed active support, of India's status goals. American recognition of India's potential as a global power has made possible the country's "negotiated rise."[17] The singular achievement of this partnership was the implicit legitimization of India's nuclear weapons status under President George W. Bush when the USA and India signed the civilian nuclear cooperation agreement in 2005.

Despite his administration's prioritization of the Sino-US relationship, President Obama has continued to maintain strong ties with India, although some analysts maintain that the momentum behind the partnership has stalled.[18] But there have been symbolic gestures, such as in an address to Indian parliamentarians during his visit to India in November 2010, when President Obama publicly offered support of India's bid for a permanent seat in the United Nations Security Council.[19] During the same visit, in a speech in Mumbai, President Obama stated:

> The USA does not just believe, as some people say, that India is a rising power; we believe that India has already risen. India is taking its rightful place in Asia and on the global stage. *And we see India's emergence as good for the USA and good for the world.*[20]

In July 2009, India and the USA agreed to establish a ministerial-level strategic dialogue in several key areas: strategic cooperation, energy and climate change, education and development, trade and agriculture, science and technology, and health and innovation. The inaugural India-US dialogue co-chaired by Indian Minister of External Affairs S. M. Krishna and US Secretary of State Hillary Clinton was held in Washington, D.C. in June 2010, followed by a second session in New Delhi in April 2011.[21] In a speech in Chennai, Secretary Clinton lauded India's growing leadership role in Southeast Asia and Central and South Asia, noting that the USA hoped to join with India in establishing a regional architecture based on "international norms on security, trade, rule of law, human rights, and accountable governance."[22]

American endorsement of New Delhi's rising global role has been an important factor in catapulting India into the tier of great powers. But the two countries have several areas of disagreement on issues relating to trade, market access, climate change, and Indian unwillingness to support

American positions on isolating Iran and Burma—countries with which India maintains diplomatic ties. While largely rooted in several common geopolitical objectives, strong people-to-people ties and a common faith in democratic values underpin the US-India partnership.

Indices of Power and Influence—Growing Capabilities, Rising Status

India's diplomats are active around the world, and a visit to New Delhi has become *de rigueur* for the world's political elite. A 2011 report of the US Congressional Research Service noted:

> Expanded [global] engagement is evident through the huge increase in the number of bilateral defense arrangements the Indian government has made in the past decade, more than tripling from 7 in 2000 to at least 26 today [2010]. During the latter half of 2010, every major leader paid a visit to India, including those from all five permanent UN Security Council members. Much of the international attention on India is due to the country's vast market potential—the retail sector alone is worth an estimated US$450 billion.[23]

India's growing global profile is supported by an upward trajectory in military power, economic strength, and cultural attractiveness.

Military Power

According to the *Annual Report 2010–11* issued by the Indian Ministry of Defence (MoD), India's "robust and autonomous" defense strategy is being shaped in a fluid security environment, which includes "non-traditional and asymmetric threats."[24] Based on geo-strategic as well as economic and social imperatives, such a strategy encompasses strengthening India's defenses as well as "engaging with and contributing to regional and global efforts to promote peace and stability."[25] Besides providing for the country's security along its land and maritime boundaries, India seeks a power projection capability commensurate with its aspirations to global power. To this end, Indian military planners have outlined an ambitious program of military modernization and the goal of achieving significant self-reliance in weapons manufacturing. The shopping list for military modernization runs the gamut from fighter aircraft, armored vehicles, radars and missiles to ships. India's leaders have sought to indigenize the arms design and development process but this vision is a long way from reaching fruition.

According to India's Defence Minister A. K. Anthony, fully 70 percent of India's military arsenal in 2010–11 was imported.[26] Between 2006 and 2010, India was the largest purchaser of conventional armaments in the world, reflecting the pace of the military modernization drive while also revealing the inability of the indigenous arms industry to meet the demands of military modernization.

Historically, Indian defense expenditures as a percentage of gross domestic product (GDP) had stagnated at around 1.8 percent in the 1950s. Nehru, as India expert Stephen P. Cohen has noted, had a singular "distaste for armed forces and things military"—a predilection that was reinforced by the unfortunate experience of civilian governments in Pakistan, which regularly fell prey to military coups.[27] Nehru was satisfied with the capability of the Indian Army to repel military incursions from Pakistan, as it did in 1948. Anxious neither to allow defense expenditures to undercut his domestic policy agenda nor to create a strong military that might overturn civilian rule, Nehru kept defense budgets low. More important from a security perspective, however, defense planning was "virtually non-existent" and India was utterly unprepared to fight the coming 1962 war with China.[28]

After India's defeat in the 1962 Sino-Indian War, New Delhi embarked upon a program of military modernization. Defense expenditures were stepped up, peaking in 1963–4 to 4.5 percent of GDP but falling to 3.3 percent in the latter half of the 1960s.[29] More significantly, the military was given a voice in the formulation of military policy with the reversal of the decision to protect foreign policy from the influence of the defense establishment. Defense strategists began to plan seriously for a two-front war and to acquire credible forces to underwrite this objective. The Indian government approved the creation of a million-man army that was to include mountain infantry forces with the capacity for high-altitude warfare, an increase in the number of air force squadrons, and greater attention to expanding the navy.

Military outlays averaged 2.74 percent of GDP in the 1970s and 2.95 percent in the 1980s.[30] In the 1990s, expenditures averaged 2.86 percent.[31] Thereafter, the percentage share of military expenditures began to decline and the decade of the 2000s has seen a drop to 2.18 percent.[32] According to data from the Stockholm International Peace Research Institute (SIPRI), defense outlays for 2010 registered a 2.8 percent decline over the previous year but were 54 percent higher than in 2001. This downward "rebalancing" reflects high economic growth rates that have allowed absolute spending to increase even as defense spending-to-GDP ratios have declined.[33] The defense budget for 2011–12 is estimated at 1.8 percent of GDP.[34] Overall, the Army accounts for the lion's share of total budgetary allocations. For example, in the fiscal year 2011–12, the Army accounted for 51 percent of the total military budget, followed by the Air Force with 28 percent, and the Navy trailing with 15 percent.[35] According to military analysts, Indian defense expenditures reveal three important trends: an increase in the share of capital outlays in the military budget; a rise in spending on research and development; and the largest share of capital outlays being spent on the Air Force.[36]

In spite of concerted efforts to enhance military performance, three primary challenges exist in the path of military readiness and of the ambitious goal of developing credible power projection capabilities. First, because of bureaucratic inefficiencies, the MoD has often underspent its capital budget, failing to allocate its procurement funds within the stipulated time period and, more tellingly, has not always spent the outlays in accordance with intended plans.[37] Second, and related to the first point, military readiness is far below levels stipulated as adequate for requirements of defense. These shortfalls call into question the goal of credible power projection capabilities in the near future.[38] Third, the armed forces are stretched thin as they battle domestic insurgencies in northeastern and central India and the Pakistan-supported proxy war in Kashmir that ebbs and flows. Pakistan and China pose potent external challenges. China's defense expenditures and modernization efforts dwarf those of India and even though relations with both countries have remained stable, there are important unresolved territorial issues that India has with China and Pakistan that could ignite violence if bilateral tensions were to mount.

Economic Strength

Since the turn of the twenty-first century, India has been in the process of gradually adding economic heft to its growing military power. India's strong economic performance led Goldman Sachs economist Jim O'Neill to predict in 2001 that the country would be poised to assume a major role in the global economy by 2050.[39]

The contrast with the past is stark because, from independence in 1947 through the 1980s, India had lumbered on at a very modest 3.5 percent average annual rate of growth, which an Indian economist had wryly dubbed "the Hindu rate of growth."[40] Thereafter, the gradual unshackling of the Indian economy from regimented government control resulted in steady gains reflected in higher rates of economic growth. With partial and incremental liberalizing reforms introduced in 1985, the growth rate was moved upward to 5.4 percent. But fiscal profligacy, in the form of government programs financed by deficit spending and borrowing, continued even as marginal tax rates and tariffs were lowered and private enterprise was unbound from the most stringent aspects of government regulation. This led to a major fiscal crisis in 1991 when the growth rate plummeted to an all-time low of 2.1 percent.

In late 1991, Indian foreign exchange reserves had dwindled to a point at which the country could not afford more than the cost of two weeks of oil imports. To obtain short-term loans from the West to cover immediate needs, India was forced to airlift all its gold reserves to London as collateral.[41] Compelled by economic exigencies to seek external assistance, India's newly elected Prime Minister Narasimha Rao, heading a minority government, informed his newly sworn cabinet in June 1991 of the country's dire financial crisis and of an IMF bailout package conditional on adoption of a program of structural adjustment. With the help of Finance Minister Manmohan Singh, Rao pushed forward the introduction of major fiscal and economic reforms. In an effort to boost exports, Manmohan Singh devalued India's currency (the rupee), lowered tariff and other barriers to trade, began dismantling the license *raj*, reduced tax rates, welcomed foreign investment, and lifted currency controls.

With these reforms, India turned its back on the Nehruvian Fabian socialist legacy and deregulated its economy. Even though the reforms slowed within a few years, the Indian economy grew at an average rate of 5.5 percent in the 1990s, reaching a high of 7.2 percent in 1999. Between 2000 and 2010, the economy grew at an average rate of 7 percent, recording a growth rate of 10 percent in 2010.[42] India's growth has been chiefly fueled by domestic consumption and growth in services. The services sector accounted for more than 50 percent of India's GDP in the mid-2000s.[43] India's vaunted strengths in the high technology sector and the English language skills of its educated population numbering in the tens of millions have made the country a prime destination for jobs outsourced by Western companies.

However, once the urgency of the fiscal crisis was blunted, the reforms introduced in 1991 lost momentum to forces of inertia and political machinations. Facing an election in 1996, Rao and his cabinet succumbed to populist pressures to slow down the disinvestment process and stymied Singh's efforts to proceed apace with the privatization of the public sector. Even so, Rao's party was defeated at the polls and the governments that followed did not pursue economic liberalization policies with the same zeal.[44] The Bharatiya Janata Party (BJP) government under Prime Minister Vajpayee, inaugurated in 1998, presided over a period of unprecedented growth, which, in the view of some analysts, occurred "despite the state" rather than because of it.[45]

With Singh's return, this time as Prime Minister, in 2004, reforms were once more on the agenda. However, the left-leaning parties in Singh's coalition government slowed or watered down the implementation of robust reforms. For instance, under pressure from parties of the left, the main opposition party (BJP), and small business, the Singh government in December 2011 suspended a decision to allow foreign retailers a 51 percent ownership stake in India's retail industry. Designed to attract sorely needed foreign direct investment (FDI), the indefinite suspension of this move has discouraged proponents of economic liberalism in India. The Chairman of the Indian Federation of Commerce and Industry lamented this reversal.[46] Citing UNCTAD's (United Nations Conference on Trade and Development) 2011 World Investment Report, an Indian news agency reported that China's 2010 FDI inflow at US$106 billion dwarfs that of India's at US$25 billion.[47] According to Indian analyst Gurcharan Das, India "cannot take its golden age of growth for granted. If it does not continue down its path of reform—and start to work on bringing governance up to par with its private economy—then a critical opportunity will have been lost."[48]

The country faces an uphill task in reducing its appalling poverty levels, upgrading the infrastructure, raising literacy rates, minimizing corruption, increasing the level of its public services, and making its bureaucrats and politicians accountable to the public. But until it can achieve this goal, its aggregate growth, however impressive, is likely to hold the country back from realizing its great power aspirations. As Indian observer Gautam Chickarmane remarked, "We would do well to remember that most of India's US$1.2 trillion GDP consumption is limited to about 300 million people. More than 800 million Indians . . . still live on less than US$2 a day."[49]

India's vaunted demographic dividend with large numbers of young people entering the labor force also presents a double-edged sword. Indian entrepreneur Nandan Nilekani noted that this dividend is "testing the resilience of India's policies and markets." Arguing that an aspiring young population numbering in the hundreds of millions could be a "massive engine of economic growth" and "determine how much of India's super-power potential the nation is able to realize," Nilekani cautions that there is one "hitch": "Government policies and programmes (sic) will have to get more efficient and more innovative very quickly if we are to arm these youngsters with the tools they will need to participate in, and boost the economy." [50]

The promise and challenge of India's economic story is aptly captured by Indian economist Piya Mahtaney who notes:

> India combines the achievements of a developed country with the challenges of a developing one and, in this sense, it is literally a nation of contrasts (indicating the country's track record of an impressive performance in certain sectors and persistent underachievement in some others).[51]

Soft Power Credentials

Soft power derives from the magnetic pull of a country's political ideology and institutions and a nation's cultural attractiveness. According to Joseph

Nye, influence that draws upon soft power allows its wielder to get other states to follow its preferences willingly, without added positive or negative inducements. A state possessing soft power attains desired outcomes because other states seek to emulate its values and its preferences.[52] Nye has argued that in the twenty-first century military power is less important than soft power. The latter can be understood in terms of the strength of a state's "narrative." Nye suggests that "[c]onventional wisdom has always held that the state with the largest army prevails, but in the information age it may be the state (or nonstates) with the best story that wins."[53] Nye's coinage of the term soft power was designed to demonstrate the continuing vitality of American power in the twenty-first century.

In the story of the twenty-first century rise of Asia, Indian politician Shashi Tharoor, borrowing from Nye, has argued that India's chief asset is the power of its example and the magnetism of its culture. As the world's largest democracy, India has held together a diverse national society with the strong thread of political pluralism. As Tharoor puts it:

> Our democracy, our thriving free media, our contentious civil society fora, our energetic human rights groups, and the repeated spectacle of our remarkable general elections, have all made of India a rare example of the successful management of diversity in the developing world.[54]

But he also notes that soft power alone cannot solve all of India's security problems, some of which can only be addressed through the application of hard power capabilities. Additionally, he argues that India needs to harness the power of its economic growth to lift the multitudes out of poverty because the claim to world leadership, especially on the basis of soft power, needs to be underpinned by a determined effort to solve the country's daunting internal problems.

In comparing India's emergent rise with China's established global rise, business journalist John Lee echoes Tharoor's assertion that India has significant soft power advantages over China. The currency of power, hard or soft, notes Lee, rests upon how "attractiveness and influence" within a region are "acquired and wielded." As a post-World War Two provider of public goods, the USA helped establish a regional order in Asia based upon the norms of open markets, multilateral cooperation, rule of law, and democratic governance. China is uncomfortable with several aspects of this order while India, by and large, is "fundamentally satisfied with the existing strategic order." This posture has been well-received by countries in the region, which have welcomed India as a "trusted strategic player." Lee, for instance, quotes Singapore's Foreign Minister George Yeo who stated, "We see India's presence as being a beneficial and benefecent one to all of us in Southeast Asia."[55]

But, like Tharoor, Lee points to India's significant weaknesses. Aggregate economic data obscure the extreme inequalities in income distribution, the weak physical infrastructure, and corruption in high places. Moreover, Lee notes, India is "weakly integrated into East and Southeast Asian economies."[56] Finally, as an open society, India is also unable to "shape" the message about the country in ways that authoritarian China often does. This has created, in Lee's view, a "perception gap" abroad over India's level of commitment to continued economic liberalization.[57]

In these discussions of India's soft power, however, there is a missing dimension: India's readiness to play the role of global leader and enhance its soft power credentials by fostering cooperative multilateralism at the global level. Here the record is mixed. India's assumption of a non-permanent seat on the UNSC allowed the country an opportunity to showcase its leadership. India's votes on UNSC resolutions in the wake of the 2011 Arab Spring movements are instructive. On 28 February 2011, India stepped away from its characteristic caution to back a UNSC resolution that imposed sanctions on Libyan leader Muammar Gaddafi that included a travel ban, a freezing of the assets of Gaddafi's inner circle, and referral to the ICC.[58] This vote was unanimous. Russia and China, which had strenuously opposed the resolution, supported it after the Arab League voiced strong concern over Gaddafi and when the permanent Libyan UN representative Abdurrahman Mohammed Shalgam urged support.

In a subsequent vote (UNSC Resolution 1973) on Libya in March that called for the institution a "no-fly zone" over Libya, India, joined Russia, China, Brazil, and Germany, and chose to abstain. While the resolution moved forward, India's abstention, in the face of US pressure and of mounting civilian deaths in Libya, was criticized for disregarding the "responsibility to protect" doctrine.[59] In light of such moves, together with Indian willingness to engage with the Burmese military leadership,[60] US Secretary of State Hillary Clinton, in a visit to India in July 2011, noted that as India takes its "rightful place in the meeting rooms and conference halls where the world's most consequential questions are debated," New Delhi also has to step up to the plate, assuming "increasing responsibilities, including the duty to speak out against violations of human rights."[61] In a similar vein, Meenakshi Ganguly, the South Asian Director of Human Rights Watch, urged India to "indicate an unwavering commitment to human rights and seek accountability for abuses" at home and abroad, wherever they may occur.[62]

In October 2011, India reprised its March 2011 abstention in the Libya vote to abstain again in the voting on a UNSC Resolution to impose sanctions against Syria for human rights violations. That China and Russia vetoed this resolution did not dilute the Indian failure to take a firm and principled stance against the use of violence by government forces against civilian protesters. India had coordinated its position on this resolution with two other emerging powers, Brazil and South Africa, which also abstained on the vote.[63] But in February 2012, perhaps stung by earlier criticisms, India supported a UNSC resolution calling for an end to violence and for an "inclusive Syrian-led political transition to a democratic, plural political system"[64]

India's reluctance to be a strong champion of democracy and human rights derives from multiple vulnerabilities. India is sensitive to the charge of human rights violations by Indian armed forces in Kashmir. More importantly, situated in a region with a democracy deficit and facing external security threats, strategic concerns have often trumped human rights issues in India's international outlook. India has viewed with rising concern China's "string of pearls" strategy of developing bases in countries around India's periphery that in New Delhi's perception has the objective of "containing" India. New Delhi, therefore, has sought to maintain links with countries like Burma and Iran, sanctioned by the West for political repression and human rights violations. Energy considerations feature highly in India's unwillingness to support stringent sanctions against Iran. India imports oil from Iran and is pushing ahead with the development of the North-South transportation corridor through that will link Indian ports by sea and land to the markets and resources of Central Asia, Russia, and Europe.[65]

However, as leaders in Asia assess the implications for their own countries of the Arab Spring movements for democracy, a changing political and economic dynamic may offer greater play for the "India model." As then Indian Foreign Secretary Nirupama Rao noted, "I think India has its strengths, has its capabilities and has its particularly Indian characteristics that appeal to a lot of our development partners, as you see in Africa where we are delivering on capacity building and where we provide scholarships for people to come and study in India. The whole democratic experience of India is something that appeals to a lot of our African partners, for instance, and in Southeast Asia."[66]

On environmental issues, Rao has argued that while the challenge of climate change requires an "urgent, coordinated, and collective global response," this response has to be based on principles of "equity" and "common but differentiated responsibility (CBDR) and respective capabilities." India has "one of the smallest carbon foot-prints in the world" and the country's "first and overriding priority" is to pursue economic development, to alleviate poverty and to address a severe energy deficit in order to overcome the enormous challenges in the path of bringing the benefits of India's economic growth to the poorer segments of the population.[67]

In respect to soft power, India's greatest strength comes from the example of its extraordinary success, against great odds, in sustaining a vibrant democracy since its emergence as an independent state in 1947.[68] But until India's growing development needs and external and domestic security vulnerabilities are addressed just as successfully, New Delhi's ability, on its own, to become a provider of global public goods is limited.[69] On the heels of its strong economic growth, India's emergence as a great power has come as a result of strong backing from the USA and other established powers, which see in New Delhi an important partner in the building of a liberal economic and security architecture in Asia and see in India a vivid example of viable democracy in the developing world.

Bilateral and Multilateral Engagement

India's conceptual map of the world draws upon ideas that can be traced to Kautilya's *Arthashastra*.[70] Viewing the geopolitical space around the country in terms of concentric circles of influence, India seeks to be the dominant power in South Asia, to be able to project power and influence in Greater Asia, to protect its interests in the larger Asian region from being undercut by other powers, and to be a player of consequence on the global stage. The *Annual Report 2010–11* of the Ministry of External Affairs prioritizes the safeguarding of national security and achievement of developmental goals in the context of a globalized and interdependent world and "given the stakes involved for India," seeks "dynamic engagement with a rapidly changing scenario in global affairs" and "emerging security and economic architectures."[71]

Having land or maritime boundaries with all South Asian countries (Bangladesh, Bhutan, Maldives, Nepal, Pakistan, and Sri Lanka) except Afghanistan, India geographically dominates the subcontinent, which New Delhi has long considered its sphere of influence. During the Cold War, the Indo-Pakistan conflict had been the single greatest obstacle to India's aspirations for a dominant role in this region. The wariness of smaller South Asian states of Indian power also served to check the play of India's influence. Over the course of the 1990s and 2000s, several circumstances—external and domestic—changed this dynamic. Externally, the end of the Cold War freed the India-Pakistan relationship from the bipolar straitjacket. As South Asian countries gradually began democratizing, ties with India improved. Domestically, in 1997, a more confident Indian Prime Minister Inder Kumar Gujral enunciated a new set of principles indicating India's willingness to shoulder asymmetrical responsibilities in trade with its smaller sub-continental neighbors, to respect the principle of non-interference, to uphold the territorial integrity of all states, to ensure that no state would allow its territory to be used to harm the interests of any other state, and to seek the peaceful bilateral settlement of disputes.[72]

Thus, while the India-Pakistan dispute continues, other countries in South Asia have sought to engage politically and economically with India. India has close ties with Bhutan and Nepal and has sought to strengthen connections with Bangladesh and Sri Lanka. With Afghanistan, India has established cordial ties underwritten by a committed development partnership. The India-Pakistan relationship, too, is improving gradually. The India-Pakistan composite dialogue begun in 2004 and suspended in 2008 after the terrorist attacks in Mumbai was restarted with a meeting between the respective prime ministers in Thimpu, Bhutan in April 2010. Bilateral meetings at the level of foreign ministers in Islamabad in July 2010 and foreign secretaries in Thimpu in February 2011 have sought to move forward the process of conflict resolution between the two countries.[73] There has since been a subsequent meeting of foreign secretaries of the two countries in July 2011 and a planned visit to Pakistan in June 2012 by India's External Affairs Minister S. M. Krishna.[74]

The creation of the South Asian Association for Regional Cooperation (SAARC) in 1985 provided India a framework within which both security concerns and issues of economic integration may be discussed. Interestingly, SAARC was founded on the initiative of Bangladesh, which along with smaller neighbors had sought to temper India's influence through enmeshment in a regional organization. As a result of Indian suspicions, SAARC did not demonstrate much vitality in its early years. A decade later, however, with India ready to shoulder "asymmetric responsibilities," the member countries took gradual steps toward integrating their economies. The introduction of the 1995 SAARC Preferential Trading Arrangement (SAPTA) and the 2005 South Asian Free Trade Area (SAFTA) are cases in point. Pakistan, which had implemented SAFTA provisions vis-à-vis all members except India, has indicated its willingness to move toward a full normalization of trade relations with India beginning in February 2012.[75]

In its quest for influence in the larger Asian region, India has reached out to countries in West, Central, and East Asia. Viewing countries in this area as part of India's "extended neighborhood," New Delhi has sought to build upon its customary friendly ties with the Gulf States and to deepen and diversify its relations with Central Asian countries. The "Look East" policy has pushed for a stronger interaction with East Asian countries with which India is becoming increasingly integrated. The trade turnover between India and the countries of ASEAN more than tripled between 2003–4 and 2009–10 from US$13.25 billion to US$44 billion. In August 2009, an India-ASEAN Trade-in-Goods (TiG) was signed in Bangkok as a precursor to an India-ASEAN Free Trade Agreement (FTA). The TiG came into force in January 2010.[76] Another initiative designed to link South and Southeast Asian countries in the Bay of Bengal region in multi-sectoral technical and economic cooperation is BIMST-EC (Bay of Bengal Initiative for Multi-Sectoral Technical and Economic Cooperation).[77]

India's relationship with China represents a complex mix of cooperation, competition, and conflict. The two countries signed a strategic partnership agreement in 2005, inaugurating a period of burgeoning ties. In 2010, China replaced the USA as India's largest trading partner. Unresolved territorial disputes, overlapping claims upon limited global energy resources, and competing global aspirations create friction in the Sino-Indian relationship even as the two countries cooperate in multilateral forums on global issues, such as climate change and the global financial situation in the wake of the 2008 economic crisis. India has strong strategic partnerships and cordial ties with all global centers of power—the USA, Russia, Japan, and the European Union.

New Delhi has made significant inroads in countries in Africa and Latin America, although China's presence and influence in both these regions dwarfs that of India. Through the Indian Technical and Economic Cooperation (ITEC) program, the Special Commonwealth Assistance for Africa Program (SCAAP), and the Technical Cooperation Scheme (TCS) under the Colombo Plan, India has reached out with development assistance to developing countries. Offering lines of credit (LoC) has been an important part of India's economic diplomacy in Africa, Asia, and Latin America, with a total of US$2.5 billion disbursed to countries in 2010–11.[78]

India is also an active participant in international organizations like the United Nations. In 2010, India was elected to serve a two-year term beginning in January 2011 as a non-permanent member of the UNSC, and has used its seat to push for reform of the body, among other issues. New Delhi has, for many years, sought permanent membership in the Security Council as a mark both of its growing global stature and economic strength. The Indian Army has taken part in 42 peacekeeping missions since its first commitment in Korea in 1950. India has 7,325 troops currently deployed to various UN missions, including several peacekeeping operations in Africa.[79] The Indian Navy is engaged in combating maritime piracy in the Indian Ocean region both on its own and in concert with the navies of other countries as a founding member of the Contact Group on Piracy off the coast of Somalia (CGPCS) established in 2009.[80]

In global financial multilateral organizations, such as the WTO, India has often joined with other emerging powers, primarily China, Brazil, and South Africa, to lobby for the economic interests of rising and developing countries. However, India has gradually shelved its strident tones in the WTO and has been more amenable to working within the multilateral framework of the trade regime. As Aseema Sinha has noted, participation in the WTO has led to a transformative change in trade policy and stimulated a "new bureaucratic politics, institutional innovation and activation of policy-expert linkages" that have helped in socializing India into liberal economic norms.[81]

The G20, formed in 1999, is another multilateral forum in which India is active.[82] At the 2011 Cannes meeting of the group, which was dominated by the crisis in the Eurozone, Prime Minister Manmohan Singh attested to India's interest in Europe's prosperity in light of an overall India-EU trade turnover of US$70 billion. Indian leaders, however, noted that any bailout funds from India to the Eurozone would be routed through the IMF after the coordination of a joint strategy with the BRICS countries. Indian analysts also remarked that New Delhi planned to use the IMF bailout terms for the Eurozone to leverage similar policies for developing countries. One senior Indian official was quoted as saying: "So far we have always maintained that the IMF tends to be softer to the developed economies when pulling them out of a crisis. That discrimination has to end and whatever position IMF takes now, should be the position for all developing economies."[83]

Institutionalized at the first meeting of foreign ministers on the margins of a United Nations General Assembly meeting in 2006, BRIC has functioned as an informal international forum for coordination of positions on global issues among emerging economic powers. South Africa joined this group in 2010, forming BRICS. At summits in Yekaterinburg, Russia, (June 2009), in Brasilia, Brazil (April 2010) and Sanya, China (April 2011), member countries sought to focus on common economic concerns while sidestepping their many political differences and have lobbied for an increased role for emerging and developing economies in decision making in international financial institutions.[84] India is also a member of a sub-set of BRICS—IBSA (India, Brazil, and South Africa)—a trilateral dialogue forum that brings together "three multicultural and multiethnic democracies, which are determined to contribute to the construction of a new international architecture, to bring their voice together on global issues, and to deepen their ties in various areas."[85] Predating BRICS by a few years, IBSA was founded in 2003.

Another grouping of Brazil, South Africa, India, and China (BASIC) was established in November 2009 as a negotiating group on climate change talks. At the December 2011 talks in Durban of the 17th Conference of the Parties (COP-17) of the United Nations Framework Convention on Climate Change, the emerging economies bargained hard and long. In tense negotiations, countries finally hammered a deal that built on important elements of the earlier Cancun Agreements, a second five-year commitment period (applicable mainly to EU countries) for the Kyoto protocol, and most importantly a consensus on formulating an agreement (albeit non-binding) by 2015 that would eliminate the distinction between Annex I (developed countries) and non-Annex I countries (emerging and developing economies) and bring all countries under a single legal regime by 2020.[86]

While India's strongest claim for influence is in the South Asian sub-region, India has made a robust play for influence in Greater Asia, has developed solid ties with all major centers of power, and has become an increasingly important player in regional and international multilateral organizations.

Conclusion

India's decision makers and its elite view India as a rising power but not all agree on the nature of the country's global role. Rahul Sagar has identified four competing visions extant among the Indian elite of India's place in the international system. *Moralists* would like to see India as an "exemplar of principled action"—a twenty-first century version of the "city on a hill." *Hindu nationalists* call for a muscular defense of Hindu civilization based upon the idea of *Hindutva*.[87] *Strategists* advocate an assertive championing of state interests through the development of strategic capabilities; and *liberals* favor an emphasis on the achievement of peace and prosperity through global economic engagement.[88] Since the 1990s, the liberal vision has guided the economic reform process in India even as strategists have made a case for arming India to weather the possibility of a two-front war in the future.

The proponents of all these competing visions continue to have an impact on decision making and their collective influence will exert a push-pull effect on future policy directions, which will be contingent both on domestic success in addressing the rising expectations of the population and upon the manner in which India's claims to great power status are received by the world's powerful states. Sagar suggests that were India's aspirations to be checked by the USA or China, such a move would unleash "radical fury" by serving to "confirm what Hindu nationalists and the strategists yearn for Indians to comprehend—that domination, rather than cooperation, must be the ultimate objective of a state seeking greatness."[89]

Such fears, however, may be overdrawn. India's current trajectory does not suggest much more than a moderately reformist approach both to international order and the architecture of global governance that calls for more inclusive rules allowing greater input into decision-making by rising states. As India has risen in stature in global councils, Indian leaders have been slowly shedding habits of the past when lecturing great powers on behalf of the non-aligned and the developing world constituted New Delhi's concept of leadership. As part of a globalized economy, India has generally demonstrated a strong commitment to a multilateral trade and security order and as a long-standing democracy has been a willing stakeholder in an international liberal order.

But Indian leaders have displayed a marked unwillingness to take strong positions on important global issues largely because New Delhi feels trapped between its strategic interests and its value claims. New Delhi's hesitance in taking strong and principled positions on international and global issues often undercuts its claim for leadership. As the uprisings in the Arab world unfolded in 2011–12, India chose a largely fence-sitting approach. In short, India has yet to demonstrate readiness to become a key player in the halls of global diplomacy. Additionally, India needs to develop the institutional resources that will anchor diplomacy and policy in sound strategic thinking. As one Indian observer noted acerbically, "India's foreign service of about 900 people is approximately the same size as Hungary's. Our think tanks and universities contribute next to nothing to the country's strategic debate. Welcome to a global aspirant without a strategic community."[90]

As regards dealings with states either labeled "rogue" or deemed to be gross violators of human rights by the West, India is often pulled in opposing directions due to the value divergence between the USA, which is the preeminent power in the international system and China, America's nearest peer competitor and India's long-time rival in Asia. As much as India's democratic credentials exert a value pull toward US positions, China's active courting of such countries, has led New Delhi to pursue engagement with these states to avoid military encirclement. For instance, Beijing's economic and military assistance to countries in India's extended neighborhood like Burma, Pakistan, Bangladesh, and Sri Lanka has secured important strategic benefits for China while constraining India's play for influence in Asia. Commitment to the value of strategic autonomy will keep India from a firm embrace of the USA even as competing, even conflicting, interests will limit India's dalliance with a Russia-China-India trilateral partnership. From a systemic perspective, only an overtly revisionist China would help forge elite consensus in India in favor of a firm and committed tilt toward the USA.

The long-term challenge for Indian leaders as they contemplate a larger global role also hinges upon how well they negotiate the clash between the demands of two Indias—the rising India as reflected in the country's growing aggregate economic and military power and the developing India characterized by widespread illiteracy, deep-seated poverty, and a rising demand for resources.

Endnotes

1 Nirupama Rao, Speech at the French Institute of International Relations (IFRI), (Paris, 5 May 2011), *Speeches/Statements* link, website of the Indian Ministry of External Affairs (MEA). http://www.mea.gov.in/

2 Omni-engagement in the post-Cold War world seems to be the preferred strategy of rising powers and contrasts with the strategy of "omni-balancing" identified by Steven David in his study of alliance patterns in the Third World during the Cold War. See *Choosing Sides: Alignment and Realignment in the Third World.* (Baltimore, M.D.: Johns Hopkins University Press, 1991).

3 On India's strategic partnerships, see Vidya Nadkarni, *Strategic Partnerships in Asia.* (London: Routledge, 2010).

4 In the Indian appellation, West Asia is used to refer to the Middle East.

5 System-level factors refer, for example, to the global distribution of power and international alliance systems. State-level factors constitute domestic variables such as political stability, level of economic development, and military strength.

6 As a reformist state in the international system, India sought to move away from power politics and alliances and toward a focus on peaceful resolution of conflicts through institutions like the United Nations.

7 For evidentiary documentation on the secondary containment of India by the US, see Baldev Raj Nayar, "A World Role: The Dialectics of Purpose and Power," in John W. Mellor, (ed). *India: A Rising Middle Power.* (Boulder, C.O.: Westview Press, 1979), 134–45.

8 Jawaharlal Nehru, "Inaugural Speech," Asian Relations Conference, (23 March 1947) in Shankar Saran, *Fifty Years after the Asian Relations Conference*, 27. http://tpprc.org/publication/fifty_years_after_asian_relations_conf-sharan–1997.pdf

9 The Aksai Chin region was also claimed by Chinese leaders who contested the legal standing of the 1914 Simla boundary agreement between Britain and Tibet that demarcated the border in north-western Kashmir between British India and autonomous Tibet.

10 Indira Gandhi was the daughter of Jawaharlal Nehru. She was assassinated in October 1984 by two of her Sikh bodyguards to avenge her June 1984 decision to storm the Golden Temple in Amritsar, Punjab—a site holy to Sikhs. Mrs. Gandhi's decision was taken in order to quell a separatist Sikh movement that had been gathering strength since the 1970s for the establishment of an independent state of Khalistan out of the Punjab region of India. Sikhism is an important monotheistic religion in India founded in the fifteenth century in Punjab.

11 The creation of Bangladesh out of the former East Pakistan came after domestic political battles in Pakistan over the 1970 election results led to a civil war between the Western and Eastern wings of Pakistan.

12 The Non-Proliferation Treaty was signed in 1968 and entered into effect in 1970. Five of its members joined as nuclear weapons states—the United States, the Soviet Union, the United Kingdom, France, and China. All other signatories abjured the option of developing nuclear weapons in return for a promise of assistance in developing nuclear energy subject to monitoring of such facilities by the International Atomic Energy Agency. The nuclear weapons states pledged to negotiate a graduated reduction of their nuclear weapons. India criticized this treaty as discriminatory because it allowed some signatories to hold on to their nuclear weapons.

13 The 1999 Kargil War started in May 1999 after Pakistani militants, according to accounts by Indian officials that have been corroborated by other governments, supported by regular Pakistani troops, infiltrated across the Line of Control in Kashmir that separates Indian-held Kashmir from Pakistan-held Kashmir. These incursions were repelled by the Indian armed forces. For

details, see "Kargil: What Does It Mean," in CSIS *South Asia Monitor*, No. 12. (19 July 1999), http://csis.org/files/media/csis/pubs/sam12.pdf

14 For details, see Robyn Meredith, *The Elephant and the Dragon*. (New York: W. W. Norton, 2007), 38ff.

15 K. J. Holsti, "National Role Conceptions in the Study of Foreign Policy," *International Studies Quarterly*, Vol. 14, No. 3. (September 1970), 3. For a detailed discussion of role theory, see the section on national role conceptions in the first chapter of this book.

16 See Dennis Kux, *India and the United States: Estranged Democracies*. (Washington, D.C.: National Defense University Press, 1992) and Richard L. Armitage, R. Nicholas Burns, and Richard Fontaine, *Natural Allies: A Blueprint for the Future of U.S.-India Relations*, Center for a New American Security, (October 2010), http://www.cnas.org/files/documents/publications/ CNAS_Natural%20Allies_ArmitageBurnsFontaine.pdf

17 Harsh Pant, *Contemporary Debates in Indian Foreign and Security Policy: India Negotiates Its Rise in the International System*. (New York: Palgrave Macmillan, 2008).

18 K. Alan Kronstadt, Paul K. Kerr, Michael F. Martin, and Bruce Vaughan, *India: Domestic Issues, Strategic Dynamics, and U.S. Relations*, Congressional Research Service (CRS) Report for Congress, (1 September 2011), 2–6, http:// www.fas.org/sgp/crs/row/RL33529.pdf

19 Ibid., 8.

20 Quoted in ibid. Emphasis added.

21 Ministry of External Affairs (MEA) *Annual Report 2010–11*: 90–2, Publications link, http://www.mea.gov.in/

22 Kronstadt et al, *India: Domestic Issues, Strategic Dynamics, and U.S. Relations*, 10.

23 Ibid., 10–11.

24 Ministry of Defence (MoD) *Annual Report 2010–11*: 2, http://mod.nic.in/

25 Ibid.

26 Ibid., 168.

27 Stephen P. Cohen, *India: Emerging Power*. (Washington, D.C.: Brookings Institution Press, 2001), 128.

28 Ibid.

29 K. Subramanyam, "Indian Defense Expenditures in Global Perspective," *Economic and Political Weekly*, Vol. 8, No. 26. (30 June 1973), 1155.

30 Laxman Kumar Behera, "India's Affordable Defence Spending," *Journal of Defence Studies*, Vol. 2, No. 1. (Summer 2008), 141. See also, Jasjit Singh, *India's Defence Spending: Assessing Future Needs*. (New Delhi: Knowledge World, 2001).

31 Averages computed from data on India between 1990 and 1999 in *The SIPRI Military Expenditure Database*, which include expenditure on paramilitary forces of the Border Security Force, the Assam Rifles, the Central Reserve

Police Force, and the Indo-Tibetan Border Force but does not include spending on military nuclear activities. http://milexdata.sipri.org/

32 Behera, "India's Affordable Defence Spending," 141. SIPRI data for the same decade shows a military expenditure of 2.74 percent. Defense data sourced from official Indian statistics on military expenditures do not include expenditure on paramilitary forces.

33 SIPRI 2010 Yearbook, 166, http://www.sipri.org/yearbook/2011/files/ SIPRIYB1104–04A–04B.pdf

34 "India's Defence Budget 2011–2012," *Defence Review Asia*, http://www. defencereviewasia.com/articles/98/INDIA-S-DEFENCE-BUDGET–2011–12 See also, Laxman Kumar Behera, "India's Defence Budget 2011–12: An Analysis," *India Strategic*. (March 2011), http://www.indiastrategic.in/ topstories960.htm

35 "India's Defence Budget 2011–2012."

36 Ibid. For instance, the share of capital outlays has increased from 23 percent of total military spending in fiscal year (FY) 2003–4 to 37 percent in 2004–5 and has stabilized at 34 percent since then. The capital budget, however, is projected to increase by 10 percent per year until FY 2015–16. The share of spending on research and development has quadrupled from 1.3 percent in FY 2001–2 to 5.6 percent in FY 2010–11 with the aim of spurring indigenous design and development efforts through public-private partnerships and by obtaining foreign technology through offset agreements. In terms of capital expenditures, the Air Force is the most capital-intensive, with the largest percentage share of capital outlays coming at the expense of the Army. See MoD *Annual Report 2010–11*, 166–7.

37 "India's Defence Budget 2011–2012."

38 For instance, the Air Force is operating with fewer than 30 squadrons from the authorized level of 39.5. Of envisaged force levels for naval vessels, the Indian Navy has 61 percent of frigates, 44 percent of destroyers, and only 20 percent of corvettes. See Ibid.

39 Jim O'Neill, *Building Better Global Economic BRICs*, Goldman Sachs, Global Economics Paper No. 66, (November 2001), http://www2.goldmansachs.com/ our-thinking/brics/brics-reports-pdfs/build-better-brics.pdf

40 Economist Raj Krishna quoted by Vijay Krishna in an essay titled "Raj Krishna" in Kaushik Basu, ed. *The Oxford Companion to Economics in India*. (New Delhi: Oxford University Press, 2007), 324.

41 Dietmar Rothermund, *India: The Rise of an Asian Giant*. (New Haven: Yale University Press, 2008), 81.

42 http://www.imf.org See downloadable data from IMF website. *World Economic Outlook Database* (country-level data on India of percent change in GDP at constant prices).

43 Gurcharan Das, "The India Model," in *Foreign Affairs*, Vol. 85, No. 4. (July/ August 2006), 7.

44 See Montek S. Ahluwalia, "Lessons from India's Economic Reforms." http://planningcommission.nic.in/aboutus/speech/spemsa/msa038.pdf

45 Das, "The India Model," 9.

46 See, "Market Reform in India: Off their trolleys," *The Economist*. (10–16 December 2011), 47.

47 "15 Nations with highest FDI inflows: India slips," (29 July 2011), http://www.rediff.com/business/slide-show/slide-show-1-nations-with-highest-fdi-inflows/20110729.htm

48 Das, "The India Model," 16.

49 Gautam Chickarmane, "Transforming Growth: The world will be wooing, watching," *Hindustan Times*, Mumbai. (1 January 2011).

50 Nandan Nilekani, "Transforming Demographics: A massive dividend, but can we cash in?" *Hindustan Times*, Mumbai. (1 January 2011).

51 Piya Mahtaney, India, China, and Globalization (New York: Palgrave Macmillan, 2007), 17.

52 Joseph Nye, *The Paradox of American Power: Why the World's Only Superpower Can't Go It Alone.* (Oxford: Oxford University Press, 2002), 8–12.

53 Joseph Nye, *The Future of Power.* (New York: Public Affairs, 2011), xiii.

54 Shashi Tharoor, "India's Strategic Power: 'Soft'" in *Global Brief: World Affairs in the Twenty-first Century.* (13 May 2009), http://globalbrief.ca/blog/features/soft-is-the-word/26

55 John Lee, "India's Edge over China: Soft Power," *Bloomberg Businessweek*. (17 June 2010), http://www.businessweek.com/globalbiz/content/jun2010/gb20100617_150774.htm

56 Ibid. This circumstance stems from India's refusal to join the Association of Southeast Asian Nations (ASEAN) at its inception in 1967 (Author's note).

57 Ibid.

58 Jyoti Malhotra, "Cautious India supports UNSC vote against Libya," *Business Standard*. (28 February 2011), http://www.business-standard.com/india/news/cautious-india-supports-unsc-vote-against-libya/426757/

59 Shirin R. Tahir-Kheli, "The Lopsided UN Security Council Vote on Libya," *The Daily Beast*. (19 March 2011), http://www.thedailybeast.com/articles/2011/03/19/un-security-council-vote-on-libya-why-bric-countries-abstained.html The "responsibility to protect" doctrine refers to the responsibility of governments to protect their populations from genocide, war crimes, crimes against humanity, and ethnic cleansing. Sovereignty in this view does not automatically confer upon states the right to non-interference in their internal affairs and indeed obligates states to protect their populations from violence. In the event of a breach of this responsibility, the international community is required to take any necessary action to prevent or stop harm to civilian populations. See Mike Abramowitz, "Libya and the Responsibility to Protect," (Event Summary, The Brookings Institution: Washington, D.C., 16 June 2011), http://www.brookings.edu/events/2011/0616_libya_responsibility.aspx

60 In February 2012, the US government announced the partial easing of sanctions against Burma (also called Myanmar) in response to democratic reforms initiated by the country's military-backed government. See, "USA Announces Limited Easing of Sanctions Against Burma," *VOA News*. (7 February 2012), Voice of America, http://www.voanews.com/english/news/asia/US-Announces-Limited-Easing-of-Sanctions-Against-Burma–138853474.html

61 US Secretary of State Hillary Clinton, "Remarks on India and the United States: A Vision for the Twenty-first Century," Chennai, India, (20 July 2011), http://www.state.gov/secretary/rm/2011/07/168840.htm

62 Meenakshi Ganguly, "Right Foot First: India at UNSC," *Deccan Chronicle*. (5 August 2011), http://www.deccanchronicle.com/editorial/op-ed//india-unsc-right-foot-first–350 See also, K. Alan Kronstadt et al., *India: Domestic Issues, Strategic Dynamics, and U.S. Relations*, 11.

63 In explaining the Indian position, Manjeev Singh Puri, India's deputy permanent representative to the United Nations said that New Delhi was unwilling to support far-reaching measures in the absence of credible information on the Libyan situation. Indian officials have not generally been supportive of military action in third countries. See Indrani Bagchi, "India abstains from UNSC vote on Libya no-fly zone," *The Times of India*. (11 March 2011), http://articles.timesofindia.indiatimes.com/2011–03–19/india/29145722_1_manjeev-singh-puri-resolution-libyan-foreign-minister

64 For text of the draft UNSC Resolution on Syria, see "Text of proposed UN Security Council resolution on Syria vetoed by Russia, China," *The Washington Post*. (4 February 2012), http://www.washingtonpost.com/world/middle-east/text-of-proposed-un-security-council-resolution-on-syria-vetoed-by-russia-china/2012/02/04/gIQAtKIipQ_story.html

65 Indrani Bagchi, "India-Iran oil corridor part of new great game," *The Times of India*. (13 March 2012), http://timesofindia.indiatimes.com/india/India-Iran-oil-corridor-part-of-new-great-game/articleshow/12239197.cms

66 Nirupama Rao, Indian Foreign Secretary, "Key Priorities for India's Foreign Policy," Address at the International Institute of Strategic Studies. (27 June 2011), Speeches/Statements link, http://www.mea.gov.in/

67 Ibid.

68 The only exception to this democratic norm was the period from 25 June 1975 to 21 March 1977 when Indian Prime Minister Indira Gandhi declaring a state of emergency, suspended civil liberties and imposed "President's Rule." Growing pressures from within and without impelled Mrs. Gandhi to call for elections in early 1977 when her party was voted out of office by a disillusioned electorate.

69 Public goods are indivisible and non-excludable entailing costs to the provider but minimal, if any, costs to the beneficiaries.

70 Kautilya, *The Arthashastra*, (ed.) by L. N. Rangarajan (New Delhi: Penguin Books, 1992). The Arthashastra (or science of the polity) was written by Kautilya (also known as Chanakya) in the fourth century B.C. Kautilya, who was a Brahmin minister in the court of Emperor Chandragupta Maurya, has

been called the Machiavelli of India for advocating a *realpolitik* approach in matters of foreign policy.

71 MEA *Annual Report 2010–11*, i.

72 See Bhabani Sen Gupta, "Gujral Doctrine: Security Dimensions of the Gujral Doctrine," Institute of Peace and Conflict Studies, New Delhi, (2 August 1997), http://www.ipcs.org/article/india-the-world/gujral-doctrine-security-dimensions-of-the-gujral-doctrine–2.html

73 MEA *Annual Report 2010–11*, i.

74 For text of the India-Pakistan Statement on the commencement of the Composite Dialogue, see *BBC News*. (6 January 2004), http://news.bbc.co.uk/2/hi/south_asia/3372157.stm On the resumption of high-level India-Pakistan contacts, see "Process of composite dialogue between Pak-India in interest of both countries: foreign secretaries," *South Asian News Agency*. (28 July 2011), http://www.sananews.net/english/2011/07/process-of-composite-dialogue-between-pak-india-in-interest-of-both-countries-foreign-secretaries/ and Sandeep Dikshit "India, Pakistan to continue dialogue process," *The Hindu*. (12 September 2011), http://www.thehindu.com/news/national/article2442284.ece

75 "Pakistan to normalise (sic) trade relations with India: Anand Sharma," *Daily News and Analysis* (*DNA*). (7 December 2011), http://www.dnaindia.com/india/report_pakistan-to-normalise-trade-relations-with-india-anand-sharma_1622639

76 MEA *Annual Report 2010–11*, p. vi.

77 For details, see BIMSTEC website, http://www.bimstec.org/

78 MEA *Annual Report 2010–11*, xiv.

79 MoD *Annual Report 2010–11*, 29.

80 MEA *Annual Report 2010–11*, 108.

81 Aseema Sinha, "Global Linkages and Domestic Politics: Trade Reform and Institution Building in India in Comparative Perspective," *Comparative Political Studies*, Vol. 40, No. 10. (October 2007), 1183.

82 The Group of Twenty Finance Ministers and Central Bank Governors were founded to bring together systemically important industrialized and developing economies to discuss key issues in the global economy.

83 Saikat Datta, "China the elephant in G20, India the confident dragon," *DNA*. (3 November 2011), http://www.dnaindia.com/india/report_china-the-elephant-in-g20-india-the-confident-dragon_1606768

84 "First BRIC summit concludes," *Deutsche Welle*. (16 June 2009), http://www.dw-world.de/dw/article/0,,4335954,00.html See also, Konstantin Rozhnov, "BRIC countries try to shift global balance of power," *BBC News*. (15 April 2010), http://news.bbc.co.uk/2/hi/8620178.stm The text of the Sanya summit is available on the website of the Center for Indian Political Research and Analysis (CIPRA), http://www.cipra.in/paper/BRICS_Summit_2011.html

85 For details, see the IBSA website, http://www.ibsa-trilateral.org/

86 For an unedited text version of the Durban Platform, see "UN climate change talks: full text of the Durban platform," *The Guardian*. (12 December 2011), http://www.guardian.co.uk/environment/interactive/2011/dec/12/durban-climate-change-conference-2011 global-climate-talks

87 Hindutva is based on the idea that all Indian citizens, whether Hindu or not, share a common cultural identity and heritage, which should be celebrated and should form the basis of a cultural nationalism.

88 Rahul Sagar, "State of Mind: What Kind of Power Will India Become?" *International Affairs*, Vol. 85, No. 4. (July 2009), 801.

89 Ibid., 816.

90 Pramit Pal Chaudhuri, "Transforming Strategy: India's strategic pieces of eight," *Hindustan Times*, Mumbai. (1 January 2011).

Bibliography

Abramovitz, Mike. "Libya and the Responsibility to Protect,": Event Summary, The Brookings Institution, Washington, D.C. 16 June 2011: http://www.brookings.edu/evemts/2011/0616_libya_responsibility.apsx

Ahluwalia, Montek. "Lessons from India's Economic Reforms," http://planningcommission.nic.in/aboutus/speech/spemsa/msa038.pdf

Armitage, Richard L., R. Nicholas Burns, and Richard Fontaine. *Natural Allies: A Blueprint for the Future of U.S.-India Relations*. Center for a New American Security, October 2010. http://www.cnas.org/files/documents/publications/CNAS_Natural%20Allies_ArmitageBurnsFontaine.pdf

Bagchi, Indrani. "India abstains from UNSC vote on Libya no-fly zone," *The Times of India*. (11 March 2011), http://articles.timesofindia.indiatimes.com/2011–03–19/india/29145722_1_manjeev-singh-puri-resolution-libyan-foreign-minister

—"India-Iran oil corridor part of new great game," *The Times of India*. (13 March 2012), http://thetimesofindia.indiatimes.com/india/India-Iran-oil-corridor-part-of-new-great-game/articleshow/12239197.cms

Basu, N. Kaushik (ed.) *The Oxford Companion to Economics in India*. (New Delhi: Oxford University Press, 2007).

Behera, Laxman Kumar. "India's Affordable Defence Spending," *Journal of Defence Studies*, Vol. 2, No. 148. (2008): 136–48, http://www.idsa.in/system/files/jds_2_1_lkbehera.pdf

BIMST-EC. http://www.bimstec.org/

Center for Strategic and International Studies (CSIS). "Kargil: What Does It Mean?" *South Asia Monitor*, No. 12. (19 July 1999), http://csis.org/files/media/csis/pubs/sam12.pdf

Chaudhuri, Pramit Pal. "Transforming Strategy: India's strategic pieces of eight," *Hindustan Times*, Mumbai. (1 January 2011).

Chickarmane, Gautam. "Transforming Growth: The world will be wooing, watching," *Hindustan Times*, Mumbai. (1 January 2011).

Clinton, Hillary. "Remarks on India and the United States: A Vision for the

Twenty-first Century," Chennai, India, (20 July 2011), http://www.state.gov/secretary/rm/2011/07/168840.htm

Cohen, Stephen Philip. *India: Emerging Power*. (Washington, D.C.: Brookings Institution Press, 2001).

Das, Gurcharan. "The India Model," Foreign Affairs, Vol. 85, No. 4. (2006): 2–16.

Datta, Saikat. "China the elephant in G–20, India the confident dragon," *Daily News and Analysis*. (November 3, 2011), http://www.dnaindia.com/india/report_china-the-elephant-in-g20-india-the-confident-dragon_1606768

David, Steven R. *Choosing Sides: Alignment and Realignment in the Third World*. (Baltimore, M.D.: Johns Hopkins University Press, 1991).

Deutshe Welle. "First BRIC summit concludes," (16 June 2009). http://www.dw-world.de/dw/article/0,,4335954,00.html

Durban Platform. "UN climate change talks: full text of the Durban Platform," *The Guardian*. (12 December 2011), http://www.guardian.co.uk/environment/interactive/2011/dec/12/durban-climate-change-conference–2011-global-climate-talks

The Economist. "Market Reform in India: Off their trolleys," (10–16 December 2011), 47.

Ganguly, Meenakshi. "Right foot first: India at UNSC," *Deccan Chronicle*. (2 August 2011), http://www.deccanchronicle.com/editorial/op-ed/india-unsc-right-foot-first–350

Gilpin, Robert. *War and Change in World Politics*. (Cambridge: Cambridge University Press, 1981).

Gupta, Bhabani Sen. "Gujral Doctrine: Security Dimensions of the Gujral Doctrine," Institute of Peace and Conflict Studies, New Delhi. (2 August 1997), http://www.ipcs.org/article/india-the-world/gujral-doctrine-security-dimensions-of-the-gujral-doctrine–2.html

Holsti, K. J. "National Role Conceptions in the Study of Foreign Policy," *International Studies Quarterly*, Vol. 14, No. 3. (1970): 233–309.

IBSA Website. http://www.ibsa-trilateral.org/

International Monetary Fund. *World Economic Outlook Database*. http://www.imf.org

Kautilya. *The Arthashastra*. Edited, rearranged, and translated with introduction by L. N. Rangarajan. (New Delhi: Penguin Books, 1992).

Krishna, Vijay. "Raj Krishna," in Kaushik Basu (ed.), *The Oxford Companion to Economics in India*. Revised Edition (New Delhi: Oxford University Press, 2007), 324–5.

Kronstadt, Alan K., Paul K. Kerr, Michael F. Martin, and Bruce Vaughan. *India: Domestic Issues, Strategic Dynamics, and U.S. Relations*. CRS (Congressional Research Service) Report for Congress. (1 September 2011), http://www.fas.org/sgp/crs/row/RL33529.pdf

Kux, Dennis. *India and the United States: Estranged Democracies* (Washington, D.C.: National Defense University Press, 1992).

Ladwig, Walter C. "India and Military Power Projection: Will the Land of Gandhi Become a Conventional Great Power? *Asian Survey*, Vol. 50, No. 6. (November/December 2010), 1162–83.

Lee, John. "India's Edge over China: Soft Power," *Bloomberg Businessweek*.

(17 June 2010), http://www.businessweek.com/globalbiz/content/jun2010/
gb20100617_150774.htm

Mahtaney, Piya. *India, China and Globalization: The Emerging Superpowers
and the Future of Economic Development* (New York: Palgrave Macmillan,
2007).

Malhotra, Jyoti. "Cautious India Supports UNSC vote against Libya," *Business
Standard*. (28 February 2011), http://www.business-standard.com/india/news/
cautious-india-supports-unsc-vote-against-libya/426757/

Meredith, Robyn. *The Elephant and the Dragon: The Rise of India and China
and What It Means for All of Us* (New York: W. W. Norton, 2007).

Ministry of Defence. *Annual Report 2010–11*. http://www.mod.nic.in/

Ministry of External Affairs. *Annual Report 2010–11*. Publications link, http://
www.mea.gov.in/

Nadkarni, Vidya. *Strategic Partnerships in Asia: Balancing without Alliances.*
(London: Routledge, 2010).

Nayar, Baldev Raj. "A World Role: The Dialectics of Purpose and Power," in John
W. Mellor (ed.), *India: A Rising Middle Power*. (Boulder, C.O.: Westview Press,
1979).

Nehru, Jawaharlal. "Inaugural Speech," Asian Relations Conference. (23 March
1947), in Shankar Saran, *Fifty Years after the Asian Relations Conference*,
22–30. http://tpprc.org/publication/fifty_years_after_asian_relations_
conf-sharan–1997.pdf

Nilekani, Nandan. "Transforming Demographics: A massive dividend, but can we
cash in?" *Hindustan Times*, Mumbai. (1 January 2011).

Nye, Joseph. *The Paradox of American Power: Why the World's Only
Superpower Can't Go It Alone*. (Oxford: Oxford University Press, 2002).

—*The Future of Power*. (New York: Public Affairs, 2011).

O'Neill, Jim. Building Better Global Economic BRICS. Goldman Sachs, Global
Economics Paper No. 66. (November 2001), http://www2.goldmansachs.com/
our-thinking/brics/brics-reports-pdfs/build-better-brics.pdf

Pant, Harsh. *Contemporary Debates in Indian Foreign and Security Policy:
India Negotiates Its Rise in the International System*. (New York: Palgrave
Macmillan, 2008).

Rao, Nirupama. Speech at the French Institute of International Relations. Paris, 5
May 2011. *Speeches/Statements* link, http://www.mea.gov.in/

—"Key Priorities for India's Foreign Policy," Address at the International Institute
for Strategic Studies, (27 June 2011). Speeches/Statements link. http://www.
mea.gov.in/

Rediff.com. "15 Nations with highest FDI inflows: India slips," (29 July 2011),
http://www.rediff.com/business/slide-show/slide-show–1-nations-with-highest-
fdi-inflows/20110729.htm

Rothermund, Dietmar. *India: The Rise of an Asian Giant*. (New Haven: Yale
University Press, 2008).

Rozhnov, Konstantin. "BRIC countries try to shift global balance of power," *BBC
News*. (15 April 2010), http://news.bbc.co.uk/2/hi/8620178.stm

Sagar, Rahul. "State of Mind: What Kind of Power Will India Become?"
International Affairs, Vol. 85, No. 4. (July 2009), 801–16.

Sharma, Anand. "Pakistan to normalise (sic) trade relations with

India," (7 December 2011). http://www.dnaindia.com/india/
report_pakistan-to-normalise-trade-relations-with-india-anand-sharma_1622639
Sinha, Aseema. "Global Linkages and Domestic Politics: Trade Reform and
Institution Building in India in Comparative Perspective," *Comparative
Political Studies*, Vol. 40, No. 10. (October 2007), 1183–210.
Singh, Jasjit. *India's Defence Spending: Assessing Future Needs*. (New Delhi:
Knowledge World, 2001).
SIPRI. *Military Expenditure Database*. http://milexdata.sipri.org
SIPRI. *2010 Yearbook*. http://www.sipri.org/yearbook/2011/ files/SIPRIYB1104-
04A-04B.pdf
South Asian News Agency. "Process of composite dialogue between Pak-India in
interest of both countries: Foreign Secretaries," (28 July 2011), http://www.
sananews.net/english/2011/07/process-of-composite-dialogue-between-pak-
india-in-interest-of-both-countries-foreign-secretaries/
Subramanyam, K. "Indian Defense Expenditures in Global Perspective,"
Economic and Political Weekly, Vol. 8, No. 26. (30 June 1973), 1155–8.
Tahir-Kheli, Shirin. "The Lopsided UN Security Council Vote on Libya," *The
Daily Beast*. (19 March 2011), http://thedailybeast.com/articles/2011/03/19/
un-security-council-vote-on-libya-why-bric-countries-abstained.html
Tammen, Ronald L. et al. *Power Transitions: Strategies for the Twenty-First
Century*. (New York: Chatham House Publishers, 2000).
Tharoor, Shashi. "India's Strategic Power: 'Soft'" in Global Brief: World Affairs in
the Twenty-First Century. (13 May 2009), http://globalbrief.ca/blog/features/
soft-is-the-word/26
VOA News. "US Announces Limited Easing of Sanctions Against Burma," (7
February 2012), http://www.voanews.com/english/news/asia/US-Announces-
Limited-Easing-of-Sanctions-Against-Burma–138853474.html

CHAPTER SEVEN

Russia in the New Distribution of Power

Tatiana Shakleina

Russia is often defined as a world power rising after a period of decline. This definition is not quite correct. The notion of a "rising power" has a different meaning for Russia as compared, for instance, to China, India, Brazil, Argentina, South Africa, Indonesia, and other big countries (Turkey and Iran are also often considered to be very close to the status of rising powers). In the nineteenth and twentieth centuries the territory of the contemporary Russian Federation was the core of the Russian Empire and of the Soviet Union correspondingly. Thus it carries the legacy of a historic great power heritage, and the problem for contemporary Russia is to preserve and consolidate its great power potential. For other rising powers, it is more a question of acquiring a new higher status in world politics as they either never played the role of a global actor (Brazil, India), or played such a role in the distant past (China).

This raises two important questions. The first question is whether this enlarged community of great power actors (and rising ones) manages either to modify the old order to make it more suitable for them, or establishes a new one where they will play a bigger governing role.[1] The second question is how new powers of the twenty-first century reconcile their interests and differing views on global, regional and national development and manage to consent on methods and forms of global regulation.

In this chapter we shall analyze what options Russia has as a great power player and assess Russia's perspectives on the ability of the country to maintain its role as a major global and regional actor.

Russia's International Strategy: Views and Actions

After 1991 there were many debates in Russia on the choice of its interna
tional strategy. The issue centered on whether to continue a great power
policy similar to that of the USSR, or to change the historic paradigm
and join the so-called "community of civilized nations" (of the West).
In describing Russian foreign policy discourse, one needs to note that
the operational code of American scholars and politicians is different
from the one used by most Russian scholars. Notions and criteria used
by non-Russian scholars to describe and analyze Russian foreign policy
thinking and to interpret Russian views on international relations do
not take into account the intellectual autonomy determined by history,
tradition, and the complex contemporary stage of its development.

Visible difference in organizational resources[2] between the USA and
other great powers and the unilateralism and domination of the USA in
world politics gave rise to expectations among American scholars of intellectual subordination (partial or complete) of other countries and their elites
to Western (especially American) theories of international relations.[3] These
expectations were not realized in Russia and other countries (for instance,
in China and Brazil). Only a small segment of the Russian intellectual elite
embraced the American view of world development and accepted a sub-
ordinated, reactive position. The majority accepted only some ideas while
maintaining adherence to their own national political culture and traditions
and fashioned their own worldviews.

This was certainly the case with Russian scholars of international
relations, even though Russian political science and international relations
developed under very strong Western (British and American) influence.
These disciplines are in their formative period in Russia and therefore accept
many ideas from Western theoretical traditions, but Russian international
relations scholars seek to develop a uniquely Russian school of thought
that does not necessarily reflect or fully coincide with imported (American)
theories.[4] Russian liberalism and conservatism contain a number of characteristics in common with American theory and practice, but also embody
distinctive characteristics. Russian liberals and especially conservatives
differ in many ways from American liberals and conservatives.[5]

Liberals and Conservatives in Contemporary Russia

Some Russian Studies specialists in the USA continue to divide Russian
analysts and politicians using the categories of "Slavophiles" and
"Westernizers." This division is obsolete and leads to confusion when
we so characterize the contemporary Russian intellectual and political

community. The dominant majority fall within "liberal-conservative, and/
or "idealist-realist" categories.[6] In the real world of politics and political
discourse we can hardly find "pure" types. Among Russian *liberals* we
can distinguish between "liberal-internationalists" and "liberal-realists."
Among Russian *conservatives* who think in realist terms, we can identify
"liberal conservatives" or "conservative internationalists" and "traditional
conservatives."

The difference between liberal-internationalists and liberal-realists is
very small. Liberal-internationalists acknowledge the unipolarity of the
world and America's global leadership. They accept the universal character
of Western values and institutions. They assert that domestic policy and
domestic problems are of primary importance, and object to contemporary Russia's pursuit of a great power policy. They believe that Russia
has a historic opportunity to solve problems (in the areas of healthcare,
education, social security, economy, etc.) that had to be "postponed"
because the USSR pursued a global strategy that demanded a giant's share
of the country's resources.

Liberal-realists agree with liberal-internationalists on the subject of
values and orientation to the West because they believe that Russia should
not oppose the dominant international trends of globalization and democratization. However, they emphasize the importance of foreign rather than
domestic policy in Russia's successful reformation and revival. Liberal-
realists as well as liberal-internationalists associate Russia with the West in
general, and with Europe in particular. For these scholars, relations with the
USA are vitally important, and seeking any alternative partner in the East
(China) is counterproductive or dangerous.[7]

Liberal conservatives are experts and politicians who are intellectual
liberals, but strongly adhere to realism in politics and to strong statehood
(*gosudarstvenniki*). In the foreign policy sphere, liberal conservatives
emphasize the need to preserve everything positive from Russian history
and great power political culture, restore Russia's influence in world
politics, and consolidate its organizational resources. In domestic policy,
they consider the country's primary task as strengthening the federation and
the power structures both in the center and in the subjects of the federation,
and moving Russia in the direction of a highly developed country economically and technologically with a high living standard for its citizens.

Liberal conservatives support the concept of a polycentric world order
where the USA docs not play a dominant (or hegemonic) role. They do not
deny that the USA is the strongest center of power in the contemporary
world, but do not agree that America is an acknowledged and indisputable
global leader.[8] Liberal conservatives declare that the nation-state and
national sovereignty are very important and cannot be forcefully destroyed
and violated. They draw attention to the fact that through policies of
forceful democratization foisted on other states with the use of military

force, often justified in the name of humanitarian intervention, some people improve their lives by making lives of other people worse and instead of a community of prosperous states we can get an explosive mix.[9]

Liberal conservatives state that Russia's great power status is a reality and the country should continue with an international strategy in accordance with its historic traditions, political culture and attributes of a great power. They stress that Russia has a complex civilizational position, and therefore cannot but have a pragmatic policy of strong ties with countries in the West and in the East. The civilizational character of the Russian state, they argue, should not be conflated with the issue of "Russia's special way" or "unique role." They point out that globalization and democratization cannot make the world absolutely homogeneous. Countries are different, and the "common cultural value set" of Western countries cannot be made the model for the rest of the world, which is made up of countries with different cultures, social and political systems, ideologies, and socio-anthropological characteristics of people ("*chelovecheskiye kachestva*" or "national character"). This is an important theoretical question that should not be overlooked and its neglect will not necessarily make Russia and the USA complementary partners in world politics. The same is true of other countries, China in particular, which is very distinct from other nation-states.[10]

Liberal conservatives acknowledge that the world is a field of competition for natural resources and influence, and see the task of Russian policy makers as working to ensure a favorable environment and conditions for Russia's economic development and security and the growth of its influence in regional and world politics.

Russian Foreign Policy: Stages and Perspectives

At different periods one or the other intellectual and political group has prevailed in decision-making, exerting specific influence on Russia's policy abroad and at home. One can distinguish between three such stages: 1992–5, 1996–2008, and 2009–12.

In 1992–5 Russia pursued a one-dimensional course aimed at achieving closer and broader cooperation with the West—the USA and European countries. Russia became a member of the International Monetary Fund (1992), of the so-called "political G8" or Group of 8 (1994) where it did not have full membership until 1998, and of the Council of Europe (February 1996). After the dissolution of the USSR, academic research went into a stage of decay and dismantlement, so the impact of expertise on foreign policy was minimal, if any. The Minister of Foreign Affairs Andrei Kozyrev failed to heed the advice and analysis of academic institutions ("think-tanks" and university centers). Liberal-internationalists who prevailed in decision making were simultaneously certain and hopeful that a non-Communist Russia striving for the creation of a democracy and a market economy would be viewed with favor in the USA and Europe and would receive substantial financial support, akin to the Marshall Plan for Europe after World War Two, to fulfill liberal political and economic reforms. They were willing to accept any terms and conditions of the so-called "victors" in the Cold War while the majority of the Russian elite and the population did not accept Western interpretations of the end of the Cold War.

Liberal-internationalists and liberal-realists did not form a united political group. Liberal-internationalists who were strongly represented in financial and economic structures did not view Russia's role in world politics through the lens of geopolitics and realism. Liberal-realists, on the other hand, did. Among their adherents were Gennady Burbulis, Sergey Shakhrai, and Boris Yeltsin who were the "architects" of the Commonwealth of Independent States (CIS) that replaced the Soviet Union in December 1991. They continued to view the Russian Federation—the successor of the Soviet Union—as a great power. They saw themselves as leaders of a great power and thus saw no need to change the historic paradigm of Russia's world and regional strategy. As a liberal-internationalist, Kozyrev did not support a great power policy for Russia but he had to conform to the vision of the liberal-realists in the Yeltsin government and tailor his official language to declared official strategy. He abandoned his willingness to be treated as a "junior partner" of the USA and insisted on an "equal or strategic partnership," stating that Russia would not stand any paternalism.[11]

The first *Foreign Policy Conception of the Russian Federation* was presented in 1992 and approved by President Yeltsin in 1993.[12] It was a long formal document; however, its contents did not provide an accurate portrayal of the international situation that Russia faced after 1991 and did not clearly formulate Russia's plans and ambitions in a geopolitically changed situation. Even though the CIS was defined as the number one priority in the Russian foreign policy, Russian liberal-internationalist experts and politicians, in practice, did not consider the post-Soviet countries to be the main focus of Russia's policy. They seemed sure that these states would inevitably return to Russian patronage, would remain dependent on its natural resources and its security umbrella. Liberal-internationalists denied the importance of Central Asian republics for Russia[13] and thought it necessary to maintain close relations only with former European republics, such as Ukraine, Belarus, and to a lesser degree with Georgia, Armenia and Azerbaijan.[14] Their major aim was to bring Russia into European organizations and establish good relations with the USA. As a result, by 1995–6 the CIS was in deep political and economic crisis, leading the President of Kazakhstan Nursultan Nazarbayev to address Russian leaders and leaders of other post-Soviet countries with a warning of the possible dissolution of the Commonwealth.[15]

Liberal-realists, on the contrary, considered it very important, even vital, to keep the post-Soviet space under Russia's economic and political influence and sustain Russia's military presence in that region. They hoped that the USA would acknowledge Russia's legitimate interests and would not challenge Russia's presence and influence in post-Soviet countries. This did not happen and Russia was severely criticized for its actions during internal political conflicts in Moldova (Trans-Dniester conflict in 1993) and in Georgia (Georgia-Abkhazia conflict in 1993–4).[16] Further disappointment to liberal-realists came in 1994 when President Clinton announced the enlargement of NATO to include former communist countries in Europe.

By 1995–6 it was clear that hopes for Russia's easy admission into the "Western civilized world" were rootless. Credits and investments from the USA and Europe did not come to Russia. Russian military operations that began in December 1995 in the course of a war in Chechnya (a constituent republic within the Russian Federation seeking independence) complicated the domestic political situation and dramatically damaged Russia's image in the world. Criticism of Russia's domestic and foreign policy abroad started to grow, the population in Russia was increasingly dissatisfied with the way the country was going, and the CIS needed reforms. President Yeltsin was re-elected in 1996, but many liberals who worked with him over the course of 1989–90 were forced to leave because their political reputations were ruined. In the parliamentary (Duma) elections of 1999 and 2003 all liberal parties lost favor with the electorate and did not win seats in the Duma. However, many political leaders who were liberal-internationalist in orientation and who worked for the government during Yeltsin's first term either kept their positions or got new ones (for instance, Minister of Finance Alexei Kudrin, Minister of Economics German Kokh, Head of RAO UESR (Unified Energy System of Russia) Anatoly Chubais, Vice-Prime Minister Viktor Khristenko, and Head of ROSATOM (State Nuclear Energy Corporation) Sergey Kiriyenko, along with many others).

Many liberal-realists who expressed foreign policy views very similar to the ones articulated by the liberal conservatives supported the foreign policy approach of Evgeny Primakov who was appointed Minister of Foreign Affairs in 1996 to replace Kozyrev. Primakov outlined a multi-vector Russian policy of equidistance between the West and the East, was more realistic regarding the prospects for Russia's partnership with the West and sought to reestablish relations with Asian and Latin American countries, primarily with China, India, Brazil.[17] Being a realist, he played a decisive role in domestic debates on NATO in 1995–7 and strongly supported signing the "Founding Act on Mutual Relations, Cooperation and Security between the Russian Federation and the North Atlantic Treaty Organization" in 1997, defeating strong and vocal opposition from many in Russia's political and academic community.

In 1998 Primakov was appointed Prime Minister and Igor Ivanov was appointed Russian Foreign Minister. Ivanov continued the multi-vector policy initiated by his predecessor. Criticism of Russia and of Primakov in the USA (and also in Russia by liberals) grew, especially after March 1999 when he canceled his visit to the USA in March 1999 after NATO's decision to start a military operation in Serbia (bombardment of Belgrade). This demonstration by Primakov of Russia's disagreement with American actions was not only viewed with disfavor abroad, but also divided Russian experts and politicians. However most interpretations of Primakov's motives failed to recognize that his opposition to NATO's Balkan operation was not only about supporting the Serbs, but was also a demonstration of Russian disagreement with the concept of "humanitarian intervention" in a foreign country with the use of military force. Primakov's reaction reflected the attitude of a majority of Russians on the issue of national sovereignty. By the end of 1990s, liberal conservatives constituted a majority of politically active elite. President Yeltsin's resignation in December 1999 and appointment of Vladimir Putin as the Acting President suggested that Russia was ready to pursue a stronger and more independent policy.

In 2000, Putin was elected President and in the same year a revised version of the *Foreign Policy Conception of the Russian Federation* was adopted.[18] The document stated that Russia's great power status was a reality and the country should therefore continue to pursue an international strategy in accordance with its historic tradition, political culture, and attributes of a great power. The document also asserted that the world was multipolar (or polycentric).[19]

The *Conception of 2000* incorporated many ideas expressed by liberal conservatives and by Putin himself.[20] One of them was that Russia's geostrategic position at the center of Eurasia[21] defined its "new globalism," suggesting that the challenges for Eurasian countries and for Russia were not only of continental, but also of a global character because many Eurasian states were caught up in energy and criminal networks and were the sites where the interests of many countries clashed. Russia could not ignore the areas to the South and to the East, as most of them were politically unstable and likely to become so in the future, requiring constant Russian attention and involvement regionally in order to maintain stability along Russian borders. The growing threats of terrorism, drug and arms trafficking, WMD (weapons of mass destruction) proliferation was making the Asian vector of Russian foreign policy both important and challenging.

During 2001–8, liberal conservatives who determined Russia's policy tried to stop the destructive and disintegrationist tendencies inside the CIS. Organizations established after 1991 under the framework of the CIS were either restructured or replaced with new ones with broader tasks aimed at closer cooperation to meet growing challenges in the economic and security spheres. In October 2000, the Eurasian Economic Community was established (with Belarus, Kazakhstan, Kyrgyzstan, Russia, and Tajikistan as members. Uzbekistan was a member only between 2006–8). In October 2003, the Collective Security Treaty Organization (CSTO) became a broader collective security organization replacing the 1992 Collective Security Treaty that was a defensive grouping (with Armenia, Belarus, Kazakhstan, Kyrgyzstan, Russia, Tajikistan, and Uzbekistan since 2006 as members). In September 2003, Russia, Kazakhstan, Belarus and Ukraine signed the "Agreement on the Establishment of Common Economic Space" (ratified in May 2004). Russia was accepted into the Central Asian Cooperation Organization (May 2004). In 2010, the Customs Union of Belarus, Kazakhstan and Russia started functioning. Russia enlarged its military presence in Central Asia by establishing an air base in Kyrgyzstan in 2003 and a military base in Tajikistan after the countries signed the agreement on the changing status of the Russian 201st division stationed there since 1990s.

China was accorded a higher status in Russian policy and several new bilateral agreements were signed. Russia has to coordinate its policy in Eastern Asia and in Central Asia with China because no regional security and economic problems can be resolved without considering Chinese interests and concerns. Russia and China signed the "Treaty of Good Neighborly Relations, Friendship and Cooperation" in July 2001. In June 2001 Shanghai Cooperation Organization (SCO) replaced the "Shanghai Forum" established in 1996 (with Russia, China, Kazakhstan, Kyrgyzstan, and Tajikistan as founding members and Uzbekistan as a new member). The SCO has two equally powerful states as members—Russia and China. The interests of these two countries often do not coincide, preventing the SCO from becoming an influential regional organization. Russia and China adhere to the idea of a polycentric world structure, but China is not very active in new institution-building, does not support Russia in its criticism of NATO's out-of-area reach, and did not use its considerable influence in the WTO to speed up Russian membership in that body.[22]

China is interested in enlarging its economic influence in Central Asia, which encroaches upon Russian interests in that region. China does not support widescale security initiatives and collective action to fight terrorism, drug-trafficking, and criminal networks. China also objects to enlargement of the SCO, for instance, by inviting the USA as an observer, as Russia has suggested, and is not very enthusiastic about inducting India as a full member of the SCO. However the SCO has been successful in Central-Eastern Asia through the organization of regular summits among political leaders. India, Iran, and Pakistan were given observer status in the SCO in 2005, and Mongolia had been invited as an observer in 2004. Russia is also an active participant in the BRICS multilateral forum of emerging powers. One can state that if the member states of the SCO and BRICS were to coordinate their activities, these bodies have the potential of becoming meaningful regional organizations with considerable global impact.

In the context of Russia's multi-vector policy, the USA remained a very important vector. Russian and American presidents sought to establish friendly and constructive relations and regularly held summit meetings. Bill Clinton and Putin met in June 2000 in Moscow during Clinton's visit to Russia and in September 2000 in New York during Millennium Summit. In 2001, there were two meetings between Presidents Putin and George W. Bush. The two met in Ljubljana, Slovenia in June, and in Genoa, Italy in July. After the terrorist attacks in September 2001 in New York and Washington, D.C., President Putin was one of the first leaders to express sympathy and offered Russian cooperation in the struggle against terrorism (in the form of logistical support and intelligence information). In November 2001, President Putin visited the USA. In May 2002 President Bush came on an official visit to Moscow where the two leaders signed the "Treaty between the Russian Federation and the USA on Strategic Offensive Reductions." Also in May 2002, Russia and NATO signed "Declaration by Heads of State and Government of the Russian Federation and NATO Member States" that established the NATO-Russia Council, which formalized the basis for a Russian voice in NATO. In June 2002, Russia became a full member of the G8 economically developed countries.

However disagreements remained. The December 2001 US announcement about the unilateral American withdrawal from the ABM (Anti-Ballistic Missile) Treaty of 1972 caused serious strains in the bilateral relationship, which were exacerbated by the US invasion of Iraq in 2003 and by the second round of NATO enlargement in March 2004. By 2006–7 relations between the countries were in crisis when both sides publicly expressed their dissatisfaction with the policies of the other. The USA expressed serious concerns over the nature of the emerging political system in Russia, particularly the lack of democracy; Russia's policy towards post-Soviet countries, which the USA defined as a "new imperialism"); and over its assertiveness in energy sphere.[23] American concerns were summarized in the report of the Council on Foreign Relations titled "Russia's Wrong Direction: What the USA Can and Should Do," which was made public in May 2006.[24] In a speech in Munich in 2007, President Putin offered Russia's view of the state of bilateral relations and of American foreign policy. In this speech he offered counterpoints to the arguments made in the Council's report.

Characterizing the nature of Russian-American relations over time, liberal conservatives pointed out that in 1986–91 relations between the USSR and the USA were of a "non-confrontational equal partnership" type and between 1992–9, Russia was cast in the position of "junior partner." In the 2000s, although the Bush administration declared Russia to be a partner in the anti-terrorist campaign, this cooperative potential was not realized. Russia's return to global assertiveness was not met with enthusiasm in the USA and Europe. American scholars stated that it was necessary to admit that a strategic or equal partnership with Russia was not possible because neither the USA nor Russia were willing or able to change their historic paradigms. But some scholars argued that the two countries could and should sustain constructive and cooperative relations wherever and whenever possible.[25]

Despite problems in foreign policy and the not quite successful implementation of economic and social programs, Russia could boast of certain positive achievements in the economic and political consolidation of the country and in the development of positive relations with many countries. In its words and actions, Russia firmly declared and tried to prove that it remained a serious, independent and strong player.[26] Changes in Russia's foreign policy approach were reflected in a number of foreign policy documents. On June 27, 2006 President Putin addressed the Ambassadors and Permanent Representatives at a meeting in the Foreign Ministry. He declared that "Russia must take responsibility for global and social-economic development according to its status and potential." This idea was repeated in the *Review of Russian Foreign Policy* published by the Ministry of Foreign Affairs on 28 March 2007.[27]

As Russian analysts concluded, Putin's speech could be considered as a new formulation of the first global doctrine of the Russian Federation (a new document was adopted in 2008). Five points of the new doctrine deserve recognition:

First, that Russia was against any kind of confrontation and would not participate in any "Holy alliances." Russia favored civilizational dialogues without any emphasis on ideology.

Second, that Russia would conduct a policy of diversification using the most favorable methods, mechanisms, trends, actors, campaigns, markets, etc. to achieve success and economic profit for the country.

Third, that globalization processes would accelerate the formation of a multipolar world order with positive and negative consequences, which would have to be taken into account when great powers planned their policies.

Fourth, that Russia recognized that the nature and sources of threats to Russia's security had changed since the 1990s, when the main threat had been of an internal character relating to the stability of the federation and economics. In the 2000s, on the other hand, the threats were more of an external character: the growth of instability at the global and regional levels due to a rise in regional conflicts; the threat of proliferation of nuclear weapons and the possibility of a new stage in the arms race; and the growing tendency to violate the UN Charter and intervene militarily in sovereign countries or interfere in their internal affairs (change of political regimes).

Finally, that Russia would support global collective governance by leading world powers through multilateral diplomacy.

Putin's successor as president was Dmitri Medvedev who came to power in 2008. Medvedev followed in the track of the liberal conservatives.

Russia looked both to the West and the East. Medvedev sought to avoid any confrontation with the West but made it clear that he would not stand systematic attempts of the USA and NATO to establish absolute dominance over Russia, to deprive Russia of having an independent policy, and that he would not make one-sided concessions.[28] Russia strongly opposed further NATO enlargement and welcomed NATO's decision temporarily to stop further enlargement. In 2008, President Medvedev put forward an initiative to establish a new system of collective security in Europe with Russia's participation. In 2009, Russia presented the "Project of the European Security Treaty,"[29] which did not get support in the USA and Europe.[30] Russia, for its part, disapproved of the NATO policy of regime change and expressed serious concerns with its new strategy of 2010, which extended the scale of NATO's political and security activities.[31] The problem of an ABM system deployed in Europe remained unsolved. The USA ignored Russia's concerns and suggestions to establish a common ABM system (Russia and Azerbaijan suggested as a possible site for such a system in Gaballa, Azerbaijan). The USA continued negotiations with several European countries, including Latvia, Lithuania, Estonia, and Georgia, which were willing and ready to have elements of an ABM system on their territories.

However, US-Russian bilateral relations did not become confrontational. Summits and negotiations continued. The Russia-NATO Council continued work after a short interval caused by the disagreements on the conflict between Russia and Georgia in August 2008.[32] WTO negotiations continued. The Presidential American-Russian Committee (The Obama-Medvedev Committee) was established in 2009 and START–3 (Strategic Arms Reduction Treaty) was ratified in 2010.

In 2009 economic and social issues became the focus of presidential policy. Russia started to put into effect a state program of economic modernization and innovation. The *Strategy of the Development of Russia till 2020* stated: "Russia proved many times that it is able to achieve what seemed to many impossible. ... It has recovered after the chaos of the 1990s, after the economic devastation and disintegration of the former system. ... Today we put forth a very ambitious goal to achieve a qualitative change of living standards, a qualitative change of the country, its economy and social conditions." [33]

This shift to domestic economic problems was favorable for liberals. The influence of liberal-realists and liberal-internationalists who continued working in government structures and had strong positions in big business started to grow. They began to exert larger influence on foreign policy decision-making. And since most of them were Western-oriented, the American and European directions of Russia's policy started to get more attention. In 2009 Russian liberal-realists put forward the idea of an "enlarged West" with Russia as the third center of the Western system of states. They declared that the establishment of a stable world order would be possible only on the basis of an "enlarged West" which included Northern America, Australia, New Zealand, the European Union, Russia, the former Soviet republics that were not members of the EU and Latin American countries. This new enlarged community of states, they argued, would require new security and economic institutions: a new security organization as a substitute for NATO, and a new economic organization similar to the EU but much broader with the membership of Russia, Brazil, Argentina, Mexico, Ukraine etc.[34]

At the same time, the economic and social situation in Russia was worsening. The fulfillment of requirements needed to join the WTO aggravated the negative conditions existing in the country reflected in a severe rise in prices for everything; a critical situation in Russian agriculture and in the steel and automobile and mining industries; a decline in the healthcare and social security areas; a low standard of living because of low salaries and constant rise of prices, etc. Skepticism was growing and many expressed doubts about the rationality of joining the WTO, as well doubts about the effectiveness of Bretton-Woods institutions, such as the IMF in preventing and dealing with economic and financial crises. In 2010, the countries of the BRIC group agreed to do payments in their national currencies to broaden cooperation and to protect their countries from dependence on the American dollar.

By 2011, with the liberals on the ascendance, the influence of the liberal-realists and liberal conservatives was close to equal. They had similar views on domestic issues but differed on foreign policy. Further consolidation of liberal political influence and survival of the liberal-conservative consensus was possible only in the event that the Russian government and the ruling elite were to adhere to further strengthening Russia's great power status.

Russia Among the Great Powers of the Twenty-first Century

Great powers of the twenty-first century exhibit different characteristics and are not equal in their cumulative power. The concept of a "great power" represents a special category that includes many factors. A contemporary great power is a country that possesses traditional characteristics of a great power, such as territory, natural resources, population, intellectual resources, economic, military, technological potential, and high cultural and educational potential. A great power today is a country that is independent in conducting its domestic and foreign policy aimed at safeguarding national interests, is able to exert visible influence on macro regional and world politics, and on the policies of other countries, and has the will and potential for realization of its great power strategy. Moreover, a great power must have a historic tradition of thinking and acting globally, a tradition and culture of exerting influence on world politics, and acting as a dominant or very active and influential player.[35] Does Russia possess the characteristics that can testify to its status of as a great power?

Russia and the Traditional Characteristics of Great Powers

Russia remains the largest country in the world, in terms of its geographical size, and one of the richest in *natural resources*. This fact cannot be overlooked because in the contemporary world possession of resources is of vital importance. Richness in natural resources has a two-fold effect: trade brings a lot of money to the country but "easy money" strengthens corruption and does not necessarily facilitate advanced technological development, which was the case for Russia in the 1990s. The other concern is that shrinkage of resources in the world in general facilitates and aggravates competition for resources, and in Russia, in particular, where it is the source of influence and money.

It is true that natural resources are diminishing, and Russia is pressed by time to fulfill its economic and political reforms. However, Russia still possesses large explored (known) resources. Moreover, there are huge resources on its territory that are still not known. Geological exploration of new fields and further extraction of resources will be much cheaper on Russian territory, than for instance in the Arctic Ocean or the area near the North Pole (where Russia also has vast territory). So, shrinkage of resources is not a major problem for Russia. But it is a problem for countries without sufficient resources, for instance, China, India, and some European countries. The challenge for Russia is to enlarge exploration, modernize the resource industry, and use this "resource factor" for the benefit of the country, for economic modernization; and to use natural resources smartly for achieving success and consolidating its position as a great power.

Territory is also very important. Those who deny the importance of traditional characteristics in general, and territory in particular, state that the population of the Russian Federation is too small and shrinking every year, that huge territories are very sparsely populated and can be lost in the near future to migrants from more populous neighboring states, like China. This maybe a challenge in the future, and the threat for Russia might be a failure to solve its demographic problem and maintain control of its vast territories. However, at present, Russian exerts complete control of its entire territorial expanse.

Richness in territory and natural resources prevented Russia from severe aggravation of its economic and social situation in the years following the dissolution of the Soviet Union, with all its dramatic consequences. At the macro level, richness in natural resources saved the Russian economy from complete collapse, and at the micro level, territory with resources (free land, forests, rivers, lakes, etc.) helped people to survive, overcome unemployment and shortage of money, and start small businesses. Shortage of territory and resources for countries with large populations can become a source of instability, crisis, and decline, often leading to aggression. The challenge for Russia now is to move away from dependence on resource exports, to make the economy modern and effective, and to improve the social conditions of the populace.

Russia remains the second mightiest *military power* in the world, though it lags far behind the USA in its military budget and in the development of advanced military technologies. Russia is not among the leaders in military expenditures, its arsenal is getting old, and it does indeed have serious problems with modernization of its military forces and arms. Military reform is proceeding with great difficulties and there is not enough money for the development of new advanced types of weapons. Nevertheless, the period of deep crisis has passed and federal expenditures for social programs for military personnel have been increased (salaries, pensions, living conditions, social benefits, fighting corruption, growth of spending for Research and Development, etc.).

Russia and the USA have comparable military capabilities: they are comparable quantitatively in nuclear arsenals, in their first-strike ability, ABM systems, and in the ability to destroy the other.[36] American experts have noted that Russia is the only country in the world capable of destroying the USA.[37] Other nuclear states are still far behind in their nuclear and general military capability. Russia demonstrates steady support for the NPT; however, some nuclear states did not join the NPT, for instance, India and Pakistan. Russia, together with the USA, continues positive initiatives started during the Cold War in the sphere of arms control and reductions of nuclear weapons (START). Rising nuclear powers—China and India—are in the process of enlarging their military arsenals, and the problem for Russia and the USA is to decide how to continue their bilateral reduction initiative and where to stop, while they cannot influence these two rising powers.

The economy is the weakest point for Russia. The country managed to survive after the end of the Soviet economic system. The Soviet economic heritage was very controversial: what was left to Russia was enough to sustain a modest level of economic development and survival for the population, but it was not enough to remain in the ranks of the most developed countries and be able to participate in global and macro-regional decision making on financial and economic issues. In the growth rate of industrial production, Russia lags behind China, India and Brazil, which occupy the 5th, 7th, and 15th positions in GDP growth rate respectively, while Russia is 88th; they occupy the 12th, 17th and 10th positions in industrial production growth rate, while Russia is 25th; China is now the second largest economy in the world; Russia lags behind all leading world powers in the development of advanced technologies.[38]

One can continue with the list of figures that look very unfavorable for the Russian Federation today. However, one should be careful with figures. High rates of industrial growth cannot always be viewed as a characteristic of great power status. One needs to answer the following questions: (1) Does one need to compare Russian economic figures with those of China, for instance, where the population is near 1.5 billion, and production must grow tremendously to satisfy the increasing needs of its population? (2) What might be the overall consequences of such a tempo and scale of economic development? (3) Does one necessarily need to compare all the countries, especially highly developed states, and even Russia, with China?

Not only quantitative, but also qualitative, results are of primary importance. Russia does not need the same quantities, but does need to catch up with the most developed countries in the development of advanced technologies. Russia still possesses impressive scientific potential as a legacy from the USSR and what she managed to keep in 1990s and to develop in 2000s. But science and research face a critical situation. Russia lags behind the USA, China, India, Germany and many other countries in expenditures on science and research. If Russia does not fulfill the declared program of modernization and reinforcement of its scientific and technological development, its decline might become an irreversible process.

The strong point for Russia is its *culture and education*. The Russian population is 100 percent literate (secondary education) despite all the setbacks resulting from the dismantlement of the common system of education that existed in the USSR. The generally poor financial and economic situation in the country in the 1990s did not allow the country to maintain the previous high level and scope of the educational system and many secondary schools, colleges and universities found themselves in severe financial crisis and did not have enough money to pay teachers' salaries and provide necessary support for the teaching process. The change in the country's political system and political ideology brought radical changes in content (teaching programs and textbooks) and methods of education. While the emergence of new private colleges and universities that appeared after 1991 was a positive development, these institutions did not always adhere to high academic standards.

The introduction of paid college and university education also had an impact on the number of students (at the state universities half of the students get free education, and the rest are paying students). In the 2000s, the situation started to change as universities got more financial support in the form of federal funds, grants from federal and local governments, and from big business structures, which were interested in getting highly qualified specialists. The number of those who travel to study abroad is not large. The real challenge is making Russian university education compatible with standards at European and American universities (the so-called "Bologna process"—complete reorganization of Russia's university system and university standards, which will fully correspond with European standards—is close to its finishing and Russian students already get 4+2 university education in the majority of state and private universities and diplomas with Bachelor's and Master's degrees similar to European standards); stopping the decline of secondary education in the provinces; and making Russian universities attractive to foreign students (the current number is not large, with students coming from the CIS and Asian countries).

In summary, one may say that despite the fact that Russia ranks on the lower end of the scale on some characteristics of great power status, such as advanced technology, demography, or ranks average in such areas as economy, science and research, the country still possesses many assets in the form of territory, natural resources, military potential, culture, and education.

In addition to the traditional elements of great power status there are two very important and distinctive features that mark a contemporary great power: (1) the historic experience and the tradition and culture of exerting a decisive or visible influence on world politics and to determine or very actively participate in the formation of world order; and (2) the ability to pursue an independent domestic and foreign policy aimed at safeguarding national interests. A great power actor must have a culture of thinking globally and have the will and capability to act globally. These two characteristics cannot be ignored, as great power policy cannot grow only on a foundation of economic or military might and it takes a historically long period of time (in the past it took centuries) to form and develop a great power culture. The Russian state was established and lived with this culture throughout different stages of its historic development—as Kievan Rus (until the Mongol-Tartar invasion in the thirteenth century), the Russian State (*Rossiiskoye Gosudarstvo*) in the fifteenth–seventeenth centuries, the Russian Empire from the eighteenth to the beginning of the twentieth centuries (1917), the Soviet Union (till 1991), and as the Russian Federation since that time. The Russian historic paradigm has always been that of a great power, though its role in world affairs changed with the change in the scope of world politics. Among contemporary great powers Russia is not the mightiest, but remains influential at global and regional levels.

A general picture of great power characteristics among the five acknowledged great powers is presented in Table 1.

Note: +/- *or* -/+ means that this characteristic of a great power is controversial and may cut both ways—positively and negatively. It contains either achievements or potential while at the same time exhibiting quite visible deficiencies. For instance, Russia has significant technological and science and

Table 1 Power characteristics among the five acknowledged great powers.

Parameters of a great power	USA	China	India	Brazil	Russia
Territory	+	+/-	+/-	+	+
Natural resources	+/-	-	-	+	+
Population	+	+/-	+/-	+	-
Military potential	+	+/-	+/-	-	+
Economy	+	+/-	+/-	+/-	-/+
Advanced technologies	+	+/-	+/-	-/+	+/-
Science & Research	+	+/-	+/-	-	-/+
Education	+	-	-	-	+
Culture	+	+/-	+/-	-/+	+
Tradition to act globally	+	-/+	-	-	+

research potential as a legacy left after the Soviet Union. However, it does not sufficiently and effectively develop modern advanced technologies, lags behind other developed countries in R&D, and is not a member of the OECD. Still, in a number of fields Russia remains highly developed, for instance, in space technologies and research and military technologies. While China and India have fairly large territories, their geographical size is not commensurate with their large and growing population, which can create migration pressures for Russia from China, for instance. In these countries, the economies are rather strong but due to a large and poor population, economic effectiveness and prosperity can be difficult to achieve. The same can be said about education, which remains a big problem for India, Brazil, and China; whereas in Russia the population remains very well educated, despite the fact that Russia is spending less for education than other great powers.

The table shows that only the USA possesses all characteristics of a great power. The other four great powers have pluses and minuses, making them comparable both in achievements and losses. Only time will show which of them will manage to become full-fledged powers on par with the USA, and whether there will be more than one superpower. At present such a prospect seems unlikely. Much depends not only on the desire and efforts of a great power to achieve a higher position, but also on the general situation in the world, which does not seem stable and fully predictable. It is not clear what the relations will be between Russia and China, or whether the bipolar order will return with the USA and China as the two poles, or whether Chinese adherence to multipolarity and cordial interaction with the largest Eurasian country—Russia—will continue.

Russia's relations with countries of the BRIC group remain rather controversial. The four leading powers are united by the desire to play a more visible role in the world, are eager to grow economically and militarily (though Brazil is still not quite certain about that), and want to be present in the main regulating international structures. However, they are not certain whether BRIC (or BRICS) should acquire the status of a legal structure with accepted rules and obligations of interaction to advance and defend interests of states that do not belong to NATO and EU. The absence of collective will is explained by existing constraints, which every country has: Russia (social-economic), India (social-economic), China (social-economic and political), and Brazil (social-economic and civilizational).

The establishment of a new collective center of economic and political power uniting non-Western great powers depends on India's and Brazil's choice to be more independent from the USA, on China's will to exert its influence in full and not only in economics, on Russia's success in overcoming social and economic unevenness in its development, on the honest acceptance of multi-polarity by the USA accompanied by an acknowledgement of the importance of great power cooperation for the resolution of global problems, and of regional organizations willing and capable of sustaining security and stability.

Endnotes

1 In this chapter we refer to the definition of "world order" given by Alexei Bogaturov, a well known Russian specialist in the theory of international relations: "The world order is the system of interstate relations regulated by: a number of *principles* of international behavior accepted by the majority of states or by the great powers; generally accepted *norms* developed according to these principles and *sanctions*, also by the *potential of this majority of states or great powers,* together with the *institutions* established by them, which are empowered to implement accepted norms and sanctions; and by the *political will* of the main actors to use this potential in full to sustain the established order. See: Alexei Bogaturov, *Great Powers in the Asia Pacific: History of International Relations in East Asia after World War Two 1945–95 (Velikiye Derzhavi na Tikhom Okeane).* (Moscow: Institute of the USA and Canada Studies, 1997), 40.

2 In Russian discourse, the category of "organizational resource" is used as one of characteristics of a contemporary great power. It means that this or that country has the potential, ability and will to influence world and regional politics and the policies of different countries and organizations, and that it can change them dramatically. The USA ranks highest in its organizational resource capacity in the twenty-first century and quite visibly influences global and regional politics and the policies of different countries, albeit to a different degree in the case of the latter. For instance, the policies of many European countries—both big and not so big—demonstrate great dependence on US policy as in the US-European consensus on military or so-called humanitarian interventions aimed at democratization of non-democratic countries (such as in the former Yugoslavia in the 1990s, Iraq in 2003, Libya in 2011, etc.). In the case of great powers—China, Russia, India—US influence is much less strong than on such countries as Canada, Mexico, Great Britain, Poland, Romania, the Baltic states, Ukraine, Georgia, Pakistan. The USA also has the greatest influence in many international and regional organizations, including the UN, NATO, WTO, G20, NAFTA. America's biggest organizational resource—the resource of a superpower—however, is not absolute. The USA, in turn, is also influenced by the policies of various countries and organizations, though at present this influence has not changed its policy dramatically (there has been no major paradigm change). But it often makes fulfillment of certain US plans and operations either impossible, or poses serious obstacles.

3 The main disagreement between Russian (not all, as we see in the analysis) and US scholars is not on basic IR (International Relations) theories but on one important issue—the structure of the world order and the way it is constructed. It is the debate between adherents of a unipolar or monocentric order where the USA is the pole that defines (or dictates) the formation of new world order institutions and norms and the behavior of other actors. The polycentric character of world structure was acknowledged by many US scholars only in 2008. See, for instance: Richard Haass, "The Age of Nonpolarity: What Will Follow U.S. Dominance," *Foreign Affairs,* Vol. 87, No. 3. (May/June 2008), 44–56. The majority of Russian (and Chinese) scholars had already in the 1990s persistently stressed the polycentric character of the world order, and did not accept the right of the USA to define the place and role of other countries in the new order and dictate the rules of political, economic, ideological, or military interaction and behavior at all levels of world politics. Some Russian scholars also stressed the difference between the category of a power pole and center of power. See, for instance: Eduard Batalov "Novaya Epokha–Noviy Mir" (New Epoch–New World), *Svobodnaya Mysl*, Vol.1, no. 1. (January 2001), 4–13.

4 The Russian IR school of thought developed, to a very great extent, under the influence of Western theories and is very young as compared to British and US schools. However, Russian IR scholars have attempted to develop indigenous ideas in analyzing and describing the contemporary world and world history. Some of them, for instance, Alexei Bogaturov, Mikhail Khrustalev, Nikolai Kosolapov, and Alexei Voskressenski have developed their own analytical

frameworks and have offered their own conceptions and views of international relations and of the foreign policies of various countries, particularly Russia, the USA, China, and other states. They acknowledge that there may be different approaches to the structure of world order and of the ways of its construction but argue that the result should be the product of collective interaction. A detailed analysis of the Russian school of thought is presented in the following books: Andrei Melville and Tatiana Shakleina (eds), *Russian Foreign Policy in Transition: Anthology* (New York and Budapest: Central European University Press, 2005); A. Umland (ed.), *New Directions in Russian International Studies.* (Stuttgart: Ibidem-Verlag, 2005); Tatiana Shakleina, Rossia i SSHA v Novom mirovom poriadke (*Russia and the USA in the New World Order. Debates in Russian and American Academic and Political Communities. 1991–2002.*), (Moscow: Institute of the USA and Canada Studies, 2002).

5 See: Edward Batalov, *O Philosofii Mezhdunarodnikh Otnosheniy (Philosophy of International Relations).* (Moscow: NOFMO, 2005); Edward Batalov, *Russkaya Idea i Amerikanskaya Mechta (The Russian Idea and The American Dream)* (Moscow: Progress-Traditsia, 2009).

6 In this chapter we do not analyze political conservatism in its extreme manifestations. These ideas do exist in Russia but are not numerous and not popular. Those who "dream" of a monarchist empire or a "new USSR" are very few, have not taken any practical steps and have no support in society (religious conservatism is a special and separate subject).

7 For instance, see Viktor Kremenyuk, "Rossia Vne Mirivogo Obschestva" (Russia Outside World Society), *International Trends*, Vol. 4, no. 3. (September-December 2006), 52–61 http://www.intertrends.ru Vladimir Kulagin, "Mir i Zapad v Rossiiskoy Politologii" (The World and the West in Russian Political Science), *International Trends*, Vol. 4, no. 3. (September-December 2006), 97–105, http://www.intertrends.ru

8 Russian liberal conservatives draw attention to the fact that US policy toward targeted countries can change their political and economic development dramatically, either by slowing it down or pushing it forward. They define this kind of policy as "manipulating leadership." According to such an interpretation of the US leadership, US and Western strategy are viewed in terms of actions aimed at reducing opportunities for Russia's recovery and reassertion of its regional and global influence. See: Alexei Bogaturov, "Liderstvo i Decentralizatsia v Mezhdunarodnoy Sisteme" (Leadership and Decentralization in International System), *International Trend*, 4, no. 3. (September-December 2006), 5–15, http://www.intertrends.ru

9 Edward Batalov, "Anthropology of International Relations," *International Trends*, Vol. 3, no.2 (May-August 2005), 12, http://www.intertrends.ru Andrei Kokoshin, *Realniy Suverenitet* (Real Sovereignty). (Moscow: Europe, 2006).

10 Nikolai Kosolapov, "Svoboda I Nesvoboda v Globalnom Miroporiadke" (Freedom and Lack of Freedom in Global World Order), *International Trends*, Vol. 2, no. 3. (September-December 2004), 16, http://www.intertrends.ru

11 Andrey Kozyrev, "Strategy for Partnership" in: *Russian Foreign Policy in Transition. Concepts and Realities*, Andrei Melville and Tatiana Shakleina (eds). (New York and Budapest: Central European University Press, 2005), 193–206.

12 The *Foreign Policy Conception of the Russian Federation*, 23 April 1993, in *Russian Foreign Policy in Transition. Concepts and Realities*, Andrei Melville and Tatiana Shakleina (eds). (New York and Budapest: Central European University Press, 2005), 27–64.

13 The subregion of Central Asia in the Russian discourse includes: Kazakhstan, Uzbekistan, Tajikistan, Kyrgyzstan, Turkmenistan. In US literature, Central Asia is sometimes defined differently as a larger subsystem including Afghanistan, Pakistan and some other countries.

14 "Russia's Interests in the CIS" (Interesi Rossii v SNG), *International Affairs* (*Mezhdunarodnaya Zhizn*), no. 9, 1994, 14–35; Vadim Tsymburski, "Russia's National Interests" (Natsiolalniye Interesi Rossii), *Vestnik of the Moscow State University, Social and Political Studies Series*, Vol. 12, no. 3. (1994), 7–9.

15 "Russia's Interests in the CIS" (Interesy Rossii v SNG), *International Affairs*, No. 9, (1994), 14–35. Nursultan Nazarbayev. "Russia Could Have Become the Core of the Commonwealth, But Didn't" (Rossia Mogla Bi Stat Sterzhnem Sodruzhestva, No Ne Stala), *Nezavisimaya Gazeta*. (16 January 1997).

16 See: Tatiana Shakleina, "Russian Policy toward Military Conflicts in the Former Soviet Union," in Bruce Parrott (ed.) *State Building and Military Power in Russia and the New States of Eurasia*. (New York: M. E. Sharpe, 1995), 83–107.

17 Evgeny Primakov, "On the Horizon—A Multipolar World: International Relations on the Eve of the twenty-first Century," *Nezavisimaya Gazeta*. (22 October 1996).

18 The *Foreign Policy Conception of the Russian Federation*, 28 June 2000, in Andrei Melville and Tatiana Shakleina, (eds) *Russian Foreign Policy in Transition. Concepts and Realities*. (New York and Budapest: Central European University Press, 2005), 89–104; The *Foreign Policy Conception of the Russian Federation*. (2008), http://www.mid.ru

19 The formulation of a new foreign policy strategy was preceded by debates in Russian political and expert communities on the issues of Russia's national identity, national interests, and the nature of the world system after the Cold War. These debates were not seriously analyzed by US scholars, and the fact of *historic continuity* in international strategy was not always taken into account. Russia was viewed as "a loser," a declining power that would need a lot of time to restore its high international status (if ever). In Russia, there was no consensus on the national identity issue and its role in the post-Cold War world. This lack of a coherent political position among the ruling elites in 1990s did not contribute to a better understanding of post-Soviet Russia by other world and regional players and prevented Russia from fashioning an effective and understandable policy. See: Tatiana Shakleina, "Russia Between East and West" in Dmitri Katsy (ed.) *International Relations: from Local Changes to Global Shifts*. (St. Petersburg: St. Petersburg State University Press, 2007), 125–36.

20 For an elaboration of the "Putin Doctrine," see Vladimir Putin, "Russia at the Turn of the Millennium," *Nezavisimaya Gazeta*. (30 December 1999).

21 The term "Eurasia" is used differently in Russian and US political discourse. In Russia "Eurasia" refers to the Continent, representing a geographic category. Russia and other post-Soviet states are part of Eurasia, and for convenience this subsystem is defined as "Malaya Evrazia" (Small Eurasia).

22 Russia was finally admitted to the WTO in December 2011.

23 In 2006 Russia turned off gas supplies to Ukraine because it did not pay for those supplies on time and regularly stole gas from the main pipeline and sold it to European countries for higher prices when Russia sold gas to Ukraine for lower than established world prices. The same problem of non-payment was repeated in 2008 with Ukraine. In 2009–11 Belarus could not pay in time for gas and electricity and Russia temporarily turned supplies off.

24 *Russia's Wrong Direction: What the USA Can and Should Do*, Report of an Independent Task Force (Council on Foreign Relations, 2006), www.cfr.org

25 Eugene Rumer and Angela Stent, *Repairing US–Russian Relations: A Long Road Ahead*. (INSS–CERES, April 2009).

26 Anatoly Torkunov, "Rossiiskaya Model Demokratii i Sovremennoye Globalnoye Upravlenie" (Russian Model of Democracy and Contemporary Global Governance), *International Trends*, Vol. 4, No. 1. (January/April 2006), 28–9, http://www.intertrends.ru

27 President Putin, *Speech at the Meeting with Ambassadors and Permanent Representatives of the Russian Federation*, Ministry of Foreign Affairs of the Russian Federation. (27 June 2006), www.kremlin.ru/text/ appears/2006/06/107802/html; Ministry of Foreign Affairs of the Russian Federation, *Review of Foreign Policy*. (28 March 2007), www.mid.ru/ brp_4nsf/sps/3647dA97748A106BC32572AB002AC4DD

28 Alexei Bogaturov, "Khochesh Otkritoy Systemi–Stroy Zakritiy Blok?" (In Case One Wants an Open System–Build up a Closed Bloc?), *Nezavisimaya Gazeta– Dipcourier*, 15 June 2009 http://www.ng.ru Sergei Rogov, "'Perezagruzka' v Otnosheniykh Mezhdu Rossiey i SSHA Prodolzhaetsa" ("Reset" in Relations Between Russia and the USA Continues) *Nezavisimaya Gazeta—NVO*, 25 September 2009, http://www.ng.ru Anatoly Torkunov, "Slovo i Delo v Otnosheniyakh SSHA s Rossiey" (Word and Deed in Relations Between the USA and Russia), *Izvestia*. (31 March 2009), http://www.izvestia.ru/comment/ article3126869/index.html

29 *Proekt Dogovora o Evropeiskoy Bezopasnosty* (European Security Treaty Project). (29 November, 2009), http://www.mid.ru/ns-dvbr.nsf/dveurope/968BF E5F5D506083C325767E003CEEAE

30 *Remarks on the Future of European Security*, Hillary Rodham Clinton, Secretary of State, L'Ecole Militaire, Paris, France. 29 January 2010, http:// www.state.gov/secretary/rm/2010/01/136273.htm *DOD News Briefing with Secretary Gates, Navy Adm. Mullen, Secretary Clinton, and Secretary Chu from the Pentagon*. (6 April 2010), http://www.defense.gov/Transcripts/ Transcript.aspx?TranscriptID=4599

31 *Active Engagement, Modern Defense.* Strategic Concept for the Defense and Security of the Members of the North Atlantic Treaty Organization adopted by Heads of State and Government in Lisbon, Portugal. (19–20 November 2010), http://ww.nato.int/cps/en/natolive/official_texts_68580.htm

32 Russian military forces entered into conflict with the Georgian army after Georgians attacked Russian peacekeepers and the population of South Ossetia. South Ossetia and Abkhazia were autonomous units in the Georgian Soviet Republic in the Soviet Union. After the dissolution of the USSR they declared independence from Georgia—South Ossetia in May 1992 after the military conflict with Georgia, and Abkhazia in 1994 also after the military conflict with Georgia. After the defeat of the Georgian army in August 2008, Russia recognized the two republics as independent states.

33 Vladimir Putin, *"O Strategii razvitia Rossii do 2020 goda" (On the Strategy of the Development of Russia till 2020)*, Speech at the Meeting of the State Council, Kremlin: Moscow (8 February 2008), http://archive.kremlin.ru/text/appears/2008/02/159528.shtml Dmitri Medvedev, *"Poslaniye Federalnomu Sobraniyu Rossiiskoy Federatsii" (Address of the President to the Federal Assembly of the Russian Federation).* (12 November 2009), http://президент.рф/transcripts/5979

34 Vyacheslav Inozemtsev, "Konturi Postkrizisnogo Mira" (Contours of the World after the Crisis), *Russia in Global Politics*, No. 3. (May-June 2009), http://www.globalaffairs.ru/numbers/38/11949.html

35 No country is completely free in the realization of its policy, even the USA. But within existing objective restrictions, countries possess different degrees of freedom in the conduct of their domestic and foreign policies. As a review of contemporary international relations shows, not many countries possess this freedom. Great powers must be able to safeguard this political freedom.

36 Andrei Kokoshin and Alexei Bogaturov (eds) *Rossia v Formirovanii Mezhdunarodnoy Systemi Profilaktiki Rasprostranenia Oruzhiya Massovogo Porazhenia (Russia in the Formation of the International System to Control Proliferation of Weapons of Mass Destruction).* (Moscow: URSS, 2008), 14–35; 72–138.

37 One of the main arguments of US experts about Russia is that it is the only country in the world that is capable of destroying the USA. See: *An Agenda for Renewal. US–Russian Relations*, A Report by the Russian and Eurasian Program of Carnegie Endowment for International Peace. (Washington, D.C.: CEIP, 2000).

38 The figures are taken from the CIA website: https://www.cia.gov/library/publications/the world factbook/rankorder/2003rank.html

Bibliography

Aldred, Ken and Martin A. Smith. *Superpowers in the Post-Cold War Era.* (New York: St. Martin's Press, 1999).

Aslund, Anders and Andrew Kuchins. *Pressing the "Reset Button" on U.S.-Russia Relations.* (Washington, D.C.: Center for Strategic and International Studies – Peterson Institute for International Economics, March 2009), http://www. petersoninstitute.org

Barnett, Thomas. *The Pentagon's New Map: War and Peace in the Twenty-First Century.* (New York: G. P. Putnam's Sons, 2004).

Bogaturov, Alexei. *International Relations in Central-Eastern Asia: Geopolitical Prospects for Political Cooperation.* Working Paper (Washington, D.C.: The Brookings Institution, Center for Northeast Asian Policy Studies, June 2004), http://www.brookings.edu

—"Russia's Priorities in Northeast Asia: Putin's First Four Years." *Northeast Asia Survey.* (Washington, D.C.: The Brookings Institution, 2004), 84–103, http://www.brookings.edu

—"The Syndrome of 'Absorption' in International Politics." in Andrei Melville and Tatiana Shakleina (eds) *Russian Foreign Policy in Transition: Anthology.* (New York and Budapest: Central European University Press, 2005), 291–310.

Carnegie Endowment for International Peace. *An Agenda for Renewal. U.S. – Russian Relations.* A Report by the Russian – Eurasian Program of the Carnegie Endowment for International Peace. (Washington, D.C.: CEIP, 2000), http://www.ceip.org/pubs

Council on Foreign Relations. *Russia's Wrong Direction: What the United States Can and Should Do,* Report of an Independent Task Force, 2006, http://www.cfr.org

Donaldson, Robert H. and Nogee, Joseph L. *The Foreign Policy of Russia: Changing Systems, Enduring Interests.* (Armonk, N.Y.: M.E. Sharpe, 2009).

The Foreign Policy Conception of the Russian Federation, 2000 in Andrei Melville and Tatiana Shakleina (eds), *Russian Foreign Policy in Transition, Anthology.* (New York – Budapest: Central European University Press, 2005), 27–64.

The Foreign Policy Conception of the Russian Federation, 2008, http://www.mid.ru

Gaddis, John L. "History, Grand Strategy and NATO Enlargement." *Survival,* Vol. 40, No. 1. (Spring 1998), 145–51, http://www.survival.org

Gupta, A. and S. Cherian. *The Second Bush Presidency: Global Perspectives.* (Delhi: Dorlong Kindersley, 2006).

Haass, Richard. "The Age of Nonpolarity. What Will Follow U.S. Dominance?" *Foreign Affairs,* Vol. 87, No. 3. (May/June 2008), 44–56.

Kuchins, Andrew (ed.). *Russia after the Fall.* (Washington, D.C.: Carnegie Endowment for International Peace, 2002).

Layne, Christopher. *The Peace of Illusions. American Grand Strategy from 1940 to the Present.* (Ithaca: Cornell University Press, 2006).

Legvold, Robert (ed.). *Russian Foreign Policy in the 21st Century & the Shadow of the Past.* (New York: Columbia University Press, 2007).

Lieven, Anatol. *America Right or Wrong: An Anatomy of American Nationalism.* (New York and London: Harper Perennial, 2005).

Melville, Andrei and Tatiana Shakleina (ed.). *Russian Foreign Policy in Transition: Anthology.* (New York – Budapest: Central European University Press, 2005).

NATO. *Active Engagement, Modern Defense.* Strategic Concept for the Defense and Security of the Members of the North Atlantic Treaty Organization adopted by Heads of State and Government in Lisbon: Portugal. (19–20 November 2010), http://ww.nato.int/cps/en/natolive/official_texts_68580.htm

Parrott, Bruce (ed.). *State Building and Military Power in Russia and the States of Eurasia.* (New York: M. E. Sharpe, 1995).

Putin, Vladimir. "Russia at the Turn of the Millennium" *Nezavisimaya Gazeta*, December 30, 1999, in Andrei Melville and Tatiana Shakleina (eds), *Russian Foreign Policy in Transition: Anthology.* (New York and Budapest: Central European University Press, 2005), 221–34.

Rumer, Eugene and Angela Stent. *Repairing U.S. – Russian Relations: A Long Road Ahead.* (Washington, D.C.: INSS – CERES, April 2009).

Shearman, Peter (ed). *Russian Foreign Policy Since 1990.* (Boulder, C.O.: Westview Press, 1995).

Shakleina, Tatiana. "Foreign Policy Studies: Role and Impact on Decision-Making in the U.S. and Russia" in Dmitri Katsy (ed.), *International Relations: The Field of Vision and Persistence of Politics.* (St. Petersburg: St. Petersburg University Press, 2008), 191–200.

—"Russia Between East and West" in Dmitri Katsy (ed.), *International Relations: from Local Changes to Global Shifts.* (St. Petersburg: St. Petersburg State University Press, 2007), 125–36.

Tsygankov Andrei P. and Pavel A. Tsygankov (eds), *New Directions in Russian International Studies.* (Stuttgart: Ibidem-Verlag, 2005).

US Department of Defense. *DOD News Briefing with Secretary Gates, Navy Adm. Mullen, Secretary Clinton, and Secretary Chu from the Pentagon.* (6 April 2010), http://www.defense.gov/Transcripts/Transcript. aspx?TranscriptID=4599

CHAPTER EIGHT

Brazil as an Emerging Power in the Twenty-First Century

João Augusto de Castro Neves

Introduction

Mainly because of its size and abundance of natural resources, Brazil has always believed in the inevitability of its great power role in the world, from the heyday of its monarchic imperium in the nineteenth century to the more candid power project (known as *Brasil Potência*) rhetoric of the military regime (1964–85). Since the end of the Cold War, however, the country has hesitatingly grappled with that idea. Initially faced with the challenges of democratization and mainly focused on achieving domestic economic stability, Brazilian foreign policy was somewhat constrained by domestic priorities and thus left with little leeway to operate actively in global affairs throughout most of the 1990s.

Despite persistent economic inequalities, in the past decade or so the overall domestic situation (political, economic, and social) has improved considerably and Brazil, like other emerging powers, has become more assertive regionally and globally. As the country redefines its own national interests in ever-expanding terms, its foreign policy goals are increasingly placed under scrutiny, inside and outside Brazil. Is the country's fate closely linked to that of other Western powers and its Western hemisphere neighbor, the USA, or does Brazil hold particular aspirations in a changing global order? What are the main drivers behind Brazil's rise? What role does the region (South America) play in Brazilian foreign policy? What are the main challenges and priorities the country faces in the twenty-first century?

In light of those questions, this chapter will seek to address Brazil's process of adaptation to the post-Cold War international order and examine Brazil's role as an emerging power in the twenty-first century.

Adaptation to the Post-Cold War World

The post-Cold War period ushered in a period of change for Brazil. After a gradual and negotiated return to democracy in the 1980s, the country entered into a process of adaptation to the "New World Order" in the early 1990s. Brazil, like many emerging countries, embraced a series of international norms, ranging from economic liberalization to the control of nuclear weapons, and from the respect for human rights to a more progressive approach towards environmental matters.

Nevertheless, for a large country like Brazil, this process was no small feat. Brazilian policymakers surely felt the winds of change that came with the end of the Cold War, but certainly they could not foresee if those winds would set the country on a clear course and bring about a new paradigm of foreign policy. The uncertainty towards the sudden shift in the international balance of power and the resilience of traditional national values and beliefs of its governing elite resulted in what seemed as an intricate combination of incorporation and resistance to the international system of the turn of the century.[1]

Moreover, Brazil is a country deeply concerned with concepts and values such as autonomy and national development. To instill a bundle of liberal ideas into the framework of the Brazilian national project, those concerns had to be somehow challenged and loosened. This process began with the administration of President Fernando Collor de Mello (1990–2), who accepted the modernization rhetoric and bluntly promised to take Brazil into the First World. What followed was a broad agenda of economic reform and liberalization and a cluster of foreign policy initiatives aimed at regaining the country's international credibility. Between 1990 and 1992, Brazil became more receptive to the General Agreement on Trade and Tariffs (GATT) negotiations, ratified the International Covenant on Civil and Political Rights, hosted the United Nations Conference on Environment and Development in Rio de Janeiro, in 1992, and agreed, with Argentina, on a set of measures to control nuclear proliferation.

Although his tenure as president was brief and some of his policies short-lived, Collor de Mello, rather awkwardly, introduced into the Brazilian policymakers' mindset the tension between old values and new ideas.[2] The nationalistic approach that had framed Brazilian economic policies and foreign policy throughout much of the second half of the twentieth century seemed long out-of-date in an era of growing economic interdependence and globalization.[3]

For the most part, the idea of a foreign policy that would lead Brazil into the mainstream of international society remained active during the rest of the 1990s. From its inauguration, President Fernando Henrique Cardoso's administration (1995–2003) pushed forward an agenda of economic reform that included macroeconomic stabilization (the *Real* plan)[4], privatization of state-owned enterprises, deregulation, and trade liberalization. Outside the economic realm, Brazil joined the Missile Technology Control Regime (MTCR) in 1995, ratified the NPT in 1998, and began, in that same year, to recognize the Inter-American Human Rights Court and the ICC.

But it is noteworthy that Brazil's responsiveness to the dominant norms of the post-Cold War world did not fully set aside the traditional concerns that guided its foreign policy. In order to justify its international choices at home, the Cardoso government revamped a very distinct notion of autonomy. What many considered a shift from a national development paradigm to a neoliberal paradigm was construed by Cardoso and the Brazilian foreign policy establishment as a necessary adaptation to a new and ever-changing global order, an order of "undefined polarities."[5] The idea of "autonomy through distance," that prevailed during much of the Cold War bipolarity, was replaced with the notion of "autonomy through participation." While the former was the cornerstone of inward-looking economic policies and a rather skeptical and mildly revisionist foreign policy, the latter provided the basis for national development through economic liberalization and for international credibility through receptiveness to international norms.[6]

There was something of substance behind this wordplay. Brazil's acceptance of the dominant norms of the post-Cold War world contrasted quite clearly with Argentina's wholehearted conversion towards liberal claims in the 1990s.[7] On the economic front, while Argentina reinforced its liberal credentials by adhering relatively quickly to the Washington Consensus[8], in Brazil liberalization was regulated by the resilience of traditional concerns with national development and autonomy. The free trade rhetoric that molded the creation, in 1991, of Mercosur, the regional economic bloc that includes Argentina, Paraguay and Uruguay, gradually yielded to an idea of a regional bloc as an instrument to realize traditional *national* goals. That seemed to be the prevailing logic behind Brazil's growing resistance to the initiative led by the USA to create the hemispheric Free Trade Area of the Americas (FTAA), during the Bill Clinton and George W. Bush presidencies in the mid-to-late 1990s and early 2000s.

On the political front, there were also signs of ambiguity. Brazil's move towards the core of the liberal order did not seem to be driven by its leaders' conviction that the international order was legitimate. In fact, as US hegemony and unilateralist US foreign policy became more evident, especially after President George W. Bush's emphasis on the "War on Terror," so did Brazil's disapproval of the international status quo. The focus was not so much on the goals of the international order, but on the means by which these objectives were realized. The ratification of the NPT, after decades of fierce opposition, combined with the subsequent resistance to adhere to the Additional Protocol to the treaty,[9] underlined the notion that Brazil was finally trying to change the system from within. The country's embrace of numerous international norms in other areas was followed by renewed calls for the democratization of the structures that framed international relations.

What were the reasons behind this subtle yet multifaceted process of adaptation? First, there were the material constraints. In a context of domestic economic vulnerability—debt, hyperinflation—and a series of international financial crises in the 1990s—in Mexico, Southeast Asia, Russia, Argentina—Brazil's leaders saw the embrace of liberal market-based norms as a necessary means to regain international credibility and support of the international community for economic reform at home.[10] The economic model of autonomous development and import substitution had lost its effectiveness and appeal in the late 1980s. Through this lens, one may argue that it was mainly necessity, and not so much conviction, that pushed Brazil towards the core of the liberal post-Cold War order.

But there were also domestic political factors in operation. The democratization process that started in the 1980s pointed to a more pluralistic foreign policy. On the one hand, the inclusion of more actors in the decision-making process created the incentive to broaden the scope of Brazilian foreign policy with more interest and concern with "new" issues like human rights, environment and the like. Moreover, liberal theories tell us that democratic regimes are more prone to cooperate with one another. The stress on the political economy of democratic transition sheds some light on the regionalization process launched by Brazil and Argentina and that later became Mercosur. It is widely believed that the political and strategic rapprochement between those two countries in the late 1970s and early 1980s—and the trade liberalization that it entailed—gained momentum and support from political and economic elites when both countries entered into a quasi-simultaneous process of democratic transition in the mid–1980s. In this case, democracy helped put an end to the strategic rivalry and paved the way for greater economic integration.[11]

On the other hand, the existence of a somewhat autonomous and insulated state bureaucracy, the Brazilian Ministry of External Relations (known as *Itamaraty*), indicated an inclination towards continuity of its foreign policy. Despite the emergence of new and more vocal societal actors, such as NGOs and businesses, and even of competing state bureaucracies, like Congress or other ministries with foreign policy agendas, the *Itamaraty* kept playing a predominant role in the formation of Brazil's international agenda. By setting an informal network with those new actors in its own terms, the *Itamaraty* was able to sift through new ideas and locate them in terms of the traditional values that guided the country's foreign policy. To some extent, this dominant domestic structure helps explain the tension between old values and new ideas, and the intermittently mild strain of international activism during the 1990s.

Another way to approach this somewhat ambiguous behavior is to observe the official domestic discourse to justify Brazil's foreign policy options in the past two decades. The thought of Brazil as a "not-so-Western" country or rather as a country situated in the "Far West" had crossed the mind of several leaders, like former minister Azeredo da Silveira,[12] long before the end of the Cold War. Even when Brazil seemed to tread the path towards the core of the liberal post-Cold War order, there was a need to point out the piecemeal tempo at which those options were implemented. More frequent, however, were the government's efforts to show that it was somehow possible and interesting to seek room for autonomy on the fringes of the liberal order.[13]

To a large extent, what happened in the first decade of the twenty-first century reinforced some aspects of Brazil's ambivalent adaptation and its strain of international activism. On the internal side, the Brazilian economy benefitted from sound economic policies and from a much more stable global economy throughout most of the decade. As a result, the Lula administration (2003–11) was able to free Brazilian foreign policy from the usual material constraints and revamp the idea of a national grand strategy based on principles of social justice, inside and outside Brazil, as will be discussed below.

On the external side, the affirmation of US unilateralism introduced by the Bush Doctrine created more tension between Brasilia and Washington on matters like the invasion of Iraq in 2003 and the role of the United Nations Security Council, sidelined in the conflict. That led not only to a restored and yet more explicit campaign for a permanent seat in that body, which is perceived by Brazil as a tantalizing symbol of international power oligarchy, but also towards a more active role in UN peacekeeping operations (United Nations Stabilization Mission in Haiti, MINUSTAH) and what became the basis of a South-South diplomacy, which basically meant a deeper engagement with countries in South America,[14] Africa, and Asia. It also fostered an unambiguous effort to try to increase Brazil's leverage on global issues, such as the Middle East peace process and the Iranian nuclear program.[15] In line with that strategy was also the effort to seek an emerging powers coalition and initiatives such as the BRICS, BASIC, pertaining to climate change negotiations), and IBSA, which emphasizes development and democracy. The main goal of these initiatives is to try to coordinate the interests of the developing world on multilateral issues.

Main Drivers Behind Brazil's Rise

When one talks about rising powers in the twenty-first century it is legitimate to wonder whether it is a scholarly fad or even 1970s redux, when international turbulence caused by the Vietnam War and the oil crisis helped bring about concepts such as devolution and key countries[16] (from a US perspective) and the strategic importance of a less friendly or even defying emerging world (the oil producing states in that particular case). In the case of Brazil, the same skepticism seems even more suitable. In the early 1970s, the military regime that ruled the country (1964–85), backed by a impressive surge of economic growth (a period referred to as the economic miracle), had launched an unambiguous national project of power (known in Portuguese as *Brasil Potência*), which also included plans to enhance Brazil's nuclear capabilities. Fast forward to the first decade of this century and add to the suspicion an elevated and more ambitious foreign policy rhetoric fueled by several years of consistent economic growth and underpinned by a highly popular and charismatic leader, President Luiz Inácio Lula da Silva (2003–11).

Although it is a prudent measure to consider Brazil's rise—or any country's, for that matter—reversible, it is also important to recognize that there are more sound drivers at play behind Brazil's recent rise than the provisional factors aforementioned. The first consistent pillar that sustains Brazil's status as a regional and emerging power in the twenty-first century is domestic political stability. After the return to democracy in the 1980s, the country underwent a series of major political events that constituted a steppingstone towards institutional stability. It began with a negotiated and peaceful transition to democracy and the proclamation of the 1988 constitution, which gave voice to a multitude of political and societal interests. Soon after, an important test for Brazil's incipient democratic institutions was the legal ousting of the first popularly elected president in decades, Fernando Collor de Mello (1990–2).[17] The following years showed a remarkable progress in terms of power transition. Besides being the first president to be granted the possibility of serving a second four-year term, Fernando Henrique Cardoso (1995–2003) was succeeded by Luiz Inácio Lula da Silva (2003–11), a leftist opponent and former labor union leader. Democracy was reinforced in the span of two decades, as every major political force in Brazil had their turn at the governmental helm.

A second driver behind Brazil's global rise is economic stability. Since the early 1990s, a series of economic reforms began to take shape. The established protectionist stance, so common throughout most of the twentieth century, yielded to trade liberalization policies, which were gradually implemented at the multilateral level (GATT and later the WTO) and the regional level (Mercosur). As a consequence of increased competition on the domestic market, Brazilian companies were forced to seek more efficiency. Many important, yet inefficient, state-owned enterprises were privatized, some of which, in the following years, became known as "national champions" (such as Vale mining company and Embraer aircraft manufacturer, to name a few) with an increasing international role. Macroeconomic stabilization policies, such as the Real Plan (1994), reined back hyperinflation and paved the way for comprehensive public sector reform and more fiscal responsibility and transparency. As the years went by and administrations changed, most of these stabilization measures not only survived the domestic political dispute, but crystallized into a third rail of Brazilian politics.

Two consequences stemmed from this economic stability. First, the economic reform policies of the 1990s and early 2000s placed the country in an advantageous position to benefit from a favorable international economic environment. From 2000 to 2009, Brazil's GDP expanded at the fastest rate since the end of the Cold War—3.3 percent a year against a rate of 1.7 percent during the 1990s.[18] The combination of global economic expansion with an increased demand for commodities (mainly from China) pushed Brazilian exports to record-high levels and turned the country into a global agricultural powerhouse. Even with the international financial meltdown of 2008–9, the country's economy remained relatively resilient to the crisis. Second, the sustainable economic growth of the past decade, combined with a cluster of social policies implemented by the government (such as the cash transfer program known as *Bolsa Família*), led to a successful process of poverty alleviation and the emergence of a new Brazilian middle class. In fact, according to a recent study, in 2008 Brazil's middle class corresponded to nearly 50 percent (almost 95 million people) of the total population in the country, the highest rate in history.[19]

What do these changes mean in terms of Brazilian foreign policy? On the political front, the strengthening of Brazilian democratic institutions since the mid–1980s has led to increasing public debate on policy planning, and thus to greater government accountability in general. On the economic side, liberalization and sustainable economic expansion has increased trade and investment flows, thus exposing Brazilian companies and society as a whole to the ebb and flow of the global market. As a consequence, foreign policy issues, which were traditionally restricted to power elite circles, have unequivocally acquired a more popular and salient role in Brazilian political life—such as in electoral disputes and congressional debates. In fact, some numbers are able to pick up on Brazilian society's newfound interest in international relations.[20] All in all, the perception of society as a whole of political stability combined with sustainable economic growth has seemed to unleash Brazil's desire—and potential—to become a more influential player on the international stage. Illustrative of this is a 2008 survey of the views of Brazilian elite on foreign policy issues. When compared to the previous study made in 2001, the data show an increase in support for Brazil's more prominent role in international affairs (from 74 percent in 2001 to 85 percent in 2008) and also a slight increase in what was an already high confidence that Brazil will become more powerful in the future (91 percent from 88 percent in 2001).[21]

Despite these remarkable accomplishments, several aspects of Brazil's emergence are raising concerns among part of the Brazilian political and economic elite and even in the international community. As Brazil asserts itself internationally, it is not yet clear how this growing economic power will translate itself into political clout in the twenty-first century. In reality, since the early 1990s, more often than not Brazil has shown that its process of adaptation to the post-Cold War environment is the outcome of an intricate combination of systemic and domestic factors. As a result, an elevated degree of ambivalence has obfuscated a precise appraisal of long-term foreign policy goals. In the past two decades, for example, relations between Brazil and the USA have been marked by relative distance and considerable friction, as is usually the case when there is US military presence or political influence in the region—in Colombia and Honduras, among others. In South America, despite the ambitious rhetoric, Brazil has shown a limited interest in strengthening regional institutions. With regard to most international regimes (trade, human rights, climate change, and nuclear proliferation), besides being somewhat limited by the domestic concerns for the national interest, Brazil's embrace of transnational norms is accompanied by a mildly revisionist stance towards the stratification of international power. In most cases, Brazil has incorporated the transnational norms that constitute theses regimes, but not without some resistance, pointing to the asymmetries between the established powers and the less powerful. With regard to climate change and trade, the concern is with the economic development of poorer nations. With regard to human rights and disarmament, the concern is with the violation of sovereignty of less powerful countries.

Foreign Policy Priorities and Challenges

Regional Engagement

Since the early 1980s Brazilian foreign policy has revamped its interest in South America. The rapprochement with Argentina that began in the late 1970s ended decades of strategic rivalry between the region's largest countries, a process initiated by Brazil's and Argentina's military regimes and which gained momentum as the two countries quasi-simultaneously treaded the path of democratization. By the end of that decade, not only had both states renounced their nuclear race and secured a bilateral nonproliferation regime, but they also had in place an ambitious framework of political and economic cooperation. In 1991, this framework became the core of the Asunción Treaty, which, along with Paraguay and Uruguay, established a time frame for the creation of Mercosur.

For Brazil, there were initially two fundamental ideas behind the creation of Mercosur. First, the regional bloc was seen as of strategic importance to "lock in" Argentina and put a definitive end to the nuclear rivalry[22] as well as to provide a degree of institutional stability to smaller neighbors, namely Paraguay.[23] Second, there was the notion that Mercosur could work as a protective shield against negative externalities of global capitalism, such as volatile trade and financial flows. In a way, for an economy that relied for decades on the model of industrialization via import substitution, there was a strong belief that gradual regional integration could provide an environment for policies designed to somehow manage globalization and protect the Brazilian economy from external shocks and from an unbridled competition. As intraregional trade flows rose approximately fivefold in the 1990s, these ideas gained ground among the inner and outer circles of Brazilian foreign policy establishment.[24]

There were other incentives at play behind Brazil's regional activism, two of which stemmed directly or indirectly from the USA. First, as a cluster of US initiatives (such as the Initiative for the Americas, launched by President George W. Bush in 1990, the FTAA, proposed by President Clinton in 1994, and free trade negotiations with Mexico, Colombia, Chile, Peru, and Central American countries) aimed at Latin America in the 1990s began to gain acceptance in the region, Brazil increased its efforts to form a defensive coalition with its Mercosur partners and Venezuela. In the end, these efforts led to a shift in Washington's trade strategy towards the region in the 2000s, from a multilateral single undertaking approach (the logic behind the FTAA negotiations) to a hub-and-spoke approach of bilateral FTAs.

Second, according to Brazil's assessment, US foreign policy under George W. Bush created unexpected openings for Brazil in the regional arena. As the War on Terror pulled the attention of the USA elsewhere, it also created a favorable environment for more political engagement among Latin American countries, especially during the Lula administration (2003–11). New regional institutions, such as the Union of South American Nations (Unasur) and the South American Defense Council (CDS) were created not only to facilitate interaction among neighboring countries, but also to exclude the USA from these mechanisms. There were other novel initiatives, some aimed at seeking a new regional consensus on many issues (Latin American and Caribbean Summit), some intended to emphasize the South-South aspect of Brazil's diplomacy (Africa-South America Summit, held in Nigeria, in 2006; South American and Arab Countries Summit, held in Brasilia, also in 2006). These summits, along with a cluster of emerging powers initiatives, were aimed at trying to coordinate the interests of the developing world (the global South) on multilateral arenas.

Although Brazil strives to be perceived as the leader of South American integration, significant political and economic obstacles lie in the way. On the political side, as deep ideological differences among government leaders in the region persist and even intensify, the political cost to maintain and strengthen regional institutions rises. Most of these differences rest on how each leader relates to the USA. Moreover, disputes between Colombia and two of its neighbors, Venezuela and Ecuador, regarding narco-terrorist and paramilitary activities, for example, underline how perceptions toward regional security risks differ. To avoid an impasse that would obstruct its creation, the South American Defense Council was thus forced to minimize the importance of the issue. In a sense, these quarrels put pressure on Brazil to assume the role of ad hoc mediator between contestants, rather than that of a country that is willing to pay the costs to provide public goods necessary to lead a common regional project, such as economic and political stability.

On the economic side, the obstacles to more regional integration are also clear. Although Mercosur was designed, from its inception, to become the main axis of integration in South and even Latin America, the bloc's expansion has been limited. Even though full membership is permitted to any Latin American country that requests admission, no country has ever requested it, aside from Venezuela.[25] The main reason behind this is Mercosur's unconvincing credentials as an open regionalism mechanism. In order to gain full membership, countries would have to forgo their own trade policies and agreements to abide by the bloc's more protectionist rules (this would be the case for all countries that have signed FTAs with countries outside the region). Therefore, in order for Mercosur expansion to occur, candidates would have to adjust their trade policies to a more protectionist environment or Mercosur would have to lower its own trade tariffs. Furthermore, even if new members were to join, rather than increase the bloc's bargaining power, they would most likely enhance internal contradictions that stand in the way of current negotiations, such as the Mercosur-EU trade talks. Since Mercosur's decision-making process is by consensus, the inclusion of new members would increase the number of veto players. To avoid this risk, the bloc would have to adopt a EU-style of decision-making (i.e. majority voting) and/or directly deal with the economic asymmetries and trade disputes that exist today between member countries. Therefore, as Mercosur seeks a horizontal expansion, it will be pushed to address to shortcomings of its vertical institutionalization. So far, despite the more ambitious rhetoric, Brazil has shown a lack of enthusiasm to delegate sovereignty to regional bodies. Moreover, for a country that claims that its regional leadership role is benevolent, the fact that Brazil has for the most part of the past decade sustained trade surpluses with every

South American nation except Bolivia may be seen by neighboring leaders as a sign of political insensitivity, if not thoughtless hypocrisy.

Dealing with US Hegemony

Since the end of the Cold War Brazil has shown less enthusiasm to engage with the USA than have other Latin American countries like Mexico, Chile, Colombia and Argentina (this last one especially in the 1990s). On the other hand, Brazilian leaders have manifested a considerably milder anti-American rhetoric than some leftist or so-called Bolivarian regimes in the region, such as Venezuela, Bolivia, and Ecuador. In a sense, the bilateral relations of the past two decades have been marked by considerable friction and relative distance or, as some may call it, an attitude of benign indifference.[26]

In the early 1990s there were important overtures to bilateral agreements on issues such as the negotiation of the Brazilian foreign debt and the recognition of US intellectual property rights. Furthermore, as was discussed above, during the implementation of the plan (*Real* Plan, 1994) to stabilize the Brazilian economy, it is reasonable to affirm that the country's foreign policy was constrained by an overarching economic imperative. In the crisis prone international financial environment of the 1990s, Brazil could not afford to sustain an unfriendly relationship with the US administration and with multilateral organizations, such as the International Monetary Fund (IMF).[27]

Nevertheless, the furthering of economic cooperation was limited by domestic concerns in both countries. After failed attempts to establish a FTAA in the 1990s, Brazil and the USA still have made little progress toward cooperation on more promising issues, such as biofuels. Outside the economic realm, there were few developments throughout most of the period. In 2010 the two countries signed a defense agreement, the first since 1977,[28] which was aimed at promoting cooperation in the fields of research an development, logistics support, technology security, acquisition of defense products and services, and engagement in combined military training and joint military exercises. While the treaty does not entail major practical shifts in the military relationship, it is important because it may pave the way for other relevant agreements and a significant increase in negotiations between both countries' arms industries.

The defense agreement was also important because it sheds some light on other aspects of the bilateral relationship. The timing of the agreement, for example, had some political significance, because it showed that, despite recent misunderstandings, cooperation between the two largest democracies in the Western hemisphere was possible. While the deal was signed, Presidents Obama and Lula were drifting apart on a number of issues, like

Brazil's lack of condemnation of the situation of political prisoners in Cuba, the solution to the political crisis in Honduras, and the talks on a new round of sanctions on Iran at the UN Security Council.

Although the defense agreement is not likely to alter the stances both countries hold on those issues, at least it sent three important political signals. First, as it re-established a much-needed framework of cooperation between Brazil and the USA, the agreement helped dampen the anti-American rhetoric present in sectors of Brazil's left-of-center administration (first with President Lula, now with President Dilma Rousseff) and in its foreign policy bureaucracy (the *Itamaraty*). Second, the deal may be read as part of an effort by Brazil to show neighboring countries that it is possible to engage in a cordial and strategic relation with the USA while maintaining regional agreements such as the UNASUR and the South American Defense Council intact. The Brazilian government, when announcing the defense agreement with the USA, explicitly mentioned the regional bloc's charter as the cornerstone of any understanding between the region and other countries. Third, by reaching an important agreement with the USA, Brazil is trying to move away from the general belief that its role as an emerging power and as a frequent challenger of the post-Cold War global order is nothing more than a revamped anti-American rhetoric. To say that there is anti-Americanism in the Brazilian political landscape—there certainly is—is not the same as to affirm that any move by Brazil that may go against US general interests.

That said, what are the prospects for an engagement between Brazil and the USA in the near future? One concern that is likely to increase is the growing asymmetry between Brazil and its neighbors and how the USA will perceive this. As Brazil's rise becomes more sustainable (in political, economic and social terms, as discussed above), the country will, intentionally or not, exert more influence in the region. As of 2009, for example, Brazil's GDP accounted for more than 50 percent of South America's GDP. From a US perspective, that process may lead to a redefinition of the framework of its relations with Brazil. Today, the USA still tries to forge a broad yet tentative Latin American agenda. This framework, however, does not seem suitable to encompass every aspect of a more strategic engagement with an emerging regional power with global aspirations. Recent US overtures towards India may point to a possible direction for future Brazil-US relations. This idea, in fact, seems to be the logic behind a recent comment by an important US official, who stated that "as Brazil becomes more assertive globally and begins to assert its influence, we are going to bump into Brazil on new issues and in new places…it is challenging for both of us because it means we have to rethink how we understand our relationship."[29]

This process, however, may take time. President Obama's trip to Brazil in 2011, for example, although generally positive, fell short of Brazil's expectations for a revamped strategic relationship. Receptive gestures aside, it seems that what is perceived by Brazilian leaders as a relative US disregard of Brazil's new global status works against any significant change in the relationship. In fact, the recent past suggests that for Brazil the shortest path to the center of the US strategic field of vision has been through friction and controversy, as was the case with Brazil's posture on the Iranian nuclear program and on the aforementioned regional issues (Honduras, Colombia etc.).

Rising China: Partner and Competitor

In 2004, an exchange of state visits between President Lula and President Hu Jintao underlined the growing importance of China for Brazilian foreign policy in the twenty-first century. As the Brazilian foreign minister stated at the time: "We are talking about a relationship between the largest developing country in the Western hemisphere with the largest developing country in the Eastern hemisphere."[30] But it is in the trade exchange that bilateral relations have shown a remarkable boost in the past decade. Fueled by the impressive growth of its economy, Chinese demand for natural resources pushed the price of commodities to record-high levels, a process that greatly benefited Brazil's economy. Brazilian exports to China went from US$1.1 billion in 2000 to US$21 billion in 2009. By 2010, China became Brazil's main trading partner, surpassing the USA.[31]

However, in the past few years the bilateral trade relationship has shown some difficulties, especially for Brazil. Although China became Brazil's main trading partner, Brazil does not figure among China's top ten trading partners. Moreover, the relations between the two countries constitute in fact not a South-South exchange (or a balanced exchange between developing countries), as the official Brazilian rhetoric may lead one to believe, but actually an increasingly North-South relationship—Brazil as basically a commodity exporter and as an importer of manufactured goods from China. While approximately 79 percent of Brazilian exports to China in the first quarter of 2010 were basic goods (mostly soy, iron ore, and oil), Brazil's imports from China are mostly electronic goods and capital goods. In 2000, 49 percent of Brazilian exports to China were basic goods. This, however, was not an obstacle for Brazil to become one of the first major world economies to grant China market economy status in 2005, a measure that limits safeguard mechanism at Brazil's disposal.

According to a recent study by the National Development Bank of Brazil (BNDES), these figures strongly suggest two unfavorable economic trends for Brazil. First, it confirms the changing nature of the bilateral exchange, a shift from labor-intensive imports to knowledge- and technology-intensive imports from China. Second, the study points to the correlation between the import coefficient from China and the competitiveness of Brazilian products abroad. The Brazilian sectors (knowledge- and technology-intensive) that have shown a significant increase of Chinese imports have also shown a lack of competitiveness in global markets. One may draw two different readings from this. First, Brazil's growing comparative advantage to produce and export basic goods may be seen as a result of a growing Chinese economy. In a less favorable light, however, this specialization of the Brazilian economy is due to increased difficulties to compete with Chinese products elsewhere.[32] As a matter of fact, Brazil's has been losing ground to China in traditional markets for Brazilian manufactured goods, such as the USA and Latin America.

In light of this, a diverse coalition of Brazilian stakeholders, of government officials and the private sector, are becoming more vocal and critical of China and its impact on the Brazilian economy. Also, as they observe China's actions in other regions, like Africa and other Latin American countries, it becomes clearer that China regards Brazil much more as a source of natural resources than a partner in the political and strategic sense. Although both countries have benefited from trade exchanges in the recent past, (some) Brazilian authorities are realizing that there are serious risks in the relationship with China that should be dealt with, such as currency wars, trade deficits, competition in third markets, investments laws etc.

Information that was disclosed recently by *WikiLeaks* furthers the argument. According to official reports by the US government on the perception of Chinese scholars and Latin American diplomats posted in China, the economic crisis of 2008/9 and the changing global economic balance for power forced China to diversify its export market and target more developing countries. The document, however, stresses two caveats to this strategy. First, the increasing perception by Chinese scholars and Brazilian diplomats that China's interests in Latin America remain primarily economic and with the main goal of securing natural resources. Because of this, China is facing an image problem in the region, which it would have to address by taking Latin American interests more into account. The growing anti-China lobby in Brazil's industrial sector is but an example of the difficulties ahead. Second, according to the report, many interests between China and Latin America's most developed economies do not overlap, "because many Chinese exports compete directly with exports from Latin America."[33]

Although China and Brazil have shown considerable degrees of coordination on multilateral negotiations such as climate change and the Doha Round of the WTO, trade relations between the two countries point to a more multifaceted arrangement. Clearly there are those who underscore the win-win situation of the bilateral exchange, with both countries capitalizing on their areas of comparative advantage. But as the exchange becomes more asymmetrical (in China's favor), it is reasonable to ponder whether Brazilian officials will alter their stance towards China in order to attend to rising domestic distributive conflicts between winners and losers in that relationship. Furthermore, another reasonable line of questioning is whether the bilateral imbalance, if it persists, will affect Brazil and China's multilateral trade coordination at the WTO and other international groupings, such as the financial G20 and the BRICS.

In light of the differences displayed above, China will pose a constant challenge to Brazilian policymakers. Although the two countries may be defined generally as emerging or regional powers with global ambitions, this definition itself does not provide a framework capable of capturing all the nuances of the relationship. Actually, by some standards (i.e. nuclear weapons status) China is already deemed a great power.[34] When it comes to the political and strategic realms, for example, if the difference of interests is not so clear all the time, the contrast of power resources between both countries in most international arenas is stark—as is the case in topics such as nuclear proliferation, United Nations Security Council reform, regional security, climate change etc. In fact, a closer look at the regional context provides some clues as to the differences between the two countries regarding international security. Whereas strategic rivalry is an outdated concept in South America ever since the Brazilian-Argentinian nuclear rapprochement of the 1980s, China still faces a classic security dilemma in its own region, with potential rivalries emerging from Japan, India and even Russia, but also with the constant military presence of the USA. This fact alone makes the Brazil-China bilateral relationship a kaleidoscope of different colors.

China's growing presence in Latin America and in other regions where Brazil has interests at stake (such as Africa) is already becoming a major issue for Brazilian foreign policy. The main challenge for Brail in the years to come will be how to forge a strategy with China that combines the cooperation of the coalition of emerging powers (BRICS, G20 etc.) in multilateral arenas while simultaneously maintaining a degree of autonomy to deal with the more competitive aspects of the bilateral relationship.

Conclusions

Rising powers have become more than secondary players in the international arena of the twenty-first century. As obvious as their importance to regional stability is, these countries seem to be extending their reach well beyond regional boundaries. Their increasing influence on global issues, such as the recent talks on a new international financial architecture, and on the future of international regimes, like trade, climate change, human rights, and disarmament, are but examples of this new role. How these countries will relate to the established powers, how will they interact with each other, how will they influence the regions around them and how will international institutions and regimes assimilate these powers are some of the main questions that will guide international relations scholarship in the following years. As for Brazil, although the answers to these questions are not yet clear, it is possible to infer several trends of Brazilian foreign policy in the beginning of the twenty-first century.

As the country strengthens its domestic material capabilities, it will seek to expand its influence abroad through overlapping and often bumpy tracks. First, there is the regional track of pursuing a stable political and economic environment in South America in order to build a regional consensus on many global affairs. Second, there is the challenge to update the framework of engagement between Brazil and the USA, in order not only to coordinate joint solutions to regional problems, but also to avoid clashes between the two largest democracies in the Western hemisphere. Third, there is the multilateral international institutions track, where Brazil will maintain its strategy to increase its global leverage and balance between furthering its own interests while representing the interests of other developing and/or emerging nations.

How each of these tracks develops will depend mostly on how Brazil's leaders understand the concept of autonomy in the contemporary world. Brazilian International Relations scholarship frequently alludes to the concept to label different moments of Brazilian foreign policy. The concept, however, is often accompanied by qualifiers such as distance ("autonomy through distance," or equidistance between the two superpowers in the Cold War), participation ("autonomy through participation" in international regimes after the Cold War), and, more recently, diversification ("autonomy through the diversification" of partners, mainly in the developing world).[35] While some may say that the main difference between the last two is rhetorical, others see a shift from a generally more satisfied international behavior to a more explicitly revisionist foreign policy. As former president Cardoso put it: "in terms of foreign policy, President Lula and I stand on the same place, on the fringe of the liberal order. The difference being that I am on the fringe looking in and he is on the fringe looking out."[36]

Endnotes

1 Flávia C. Mello, *Regionalismo e Inserção Internacional: Continuidade e Transformação da Política Externa Brasileira nos anos 90.* (Unpublished doctoral dissertation, University of São Paulo), 2000: 1–23.

2 The Brazilian Congress impeached President Collor de Mello in 1992, due to corruption allegations.

3 For an extensive assessment on Brazilian foreign policy throughout much of the twentieth century, see José Augusto Guilhon de Albuquerque (ed.), *Crescimento, Modernização e Política Externa* (vol. 1) and *Diplomacia para o Desenvolvimento* (vol. 2): *Sessenta Anos de Política Externa Brasileira (1930–90)*. (Cultura: São Paulo, 1996). See also Riordan Roett, *The New Brazil* (Washington, D.C.: Brookings Institution Press: 2010).

4 In 1994, as finance minister, Cardoso oversaw the implementation of a new currency (the *Real*).

5 Celso Lafer and G. Fonseca, Jr., "Questões para a Diplomacia no Contexto Internacional das Polaridades Indefinidas," in Gelson Fonseca, Jr. and Sergio Nabuco de Castro, *Temas de Política Externa Brasileira II*, 2nd edn. (São Paulo: Ed. Paz e Terra, 1997): 49–78.

6 Autonomy is a key concept used to understand and analyze Brazilian foreign policy in the twentieth century. During most of the Cold War, the idea of "autonomy through distance" roughly meant an effort to balance relations with both superpowers. The concept remained active, despite its fuzziness, in the 1990s and 2000s, as "autonomy through participation" (in international regimes) and "autonomy through diversification" (of partners). See Tullo Vigevani and Gabriel Cepaluni, *Brazilian Foreign Policy in Changing Times: The Quest for Autonomy from Sarney to Lula*. (Plymouth: Lexington Books, 2009).

7 José Arbilla, "Arranjos Institucionais e Mudança Conceitual nas Políticas Externas Argentina e Brasileira (1989–94)." Contexto Internacional 22, n. 2 (July/December, 2000), 337–85.

8 The Washington Consensus was a set of market-friendly policies that were generally advised by multilateral financial institutions, such as the International Monetary Fund and the World Bank, to developing economies in the 1990s.

9 In 2008, the Brazilian government published its National Defense Strategy, in which it explicitly states that the country will not sign any additional instruments to the Non-Proliferation Treaty.

10 Fernando H. Cardoso, *The Accidental President: A Memoir*. (New York: Public Affairs, 2006).

11 For more on the dynamics of democratization, liberalization and regionalization, see Edward Mansfield and Helen Milner, (eds), *The Political Economy of Regionalism*. (New York: Columbia University Press, 1997).

12 Azeredo da Silveira was Brazil's minister of External Relations from 1974 to 1979. After that, he was Brazil's Ambassador to the USA (1979–83).

13 For a comprehensive study on Brazilian foreign policy during the 1990s, see João Augusto de Castro Neves, "No limiar da ordem global: O Brasil depois da Guerra Fria (1989–2001)" (On the fringe of global order: Brazil after the Cold War (1989–2001)), unpublished PhD thesis, University of São Paulo, 2012.

14 See Rafael Villa and Manuela Viana, "Security Issues during Lula's Administration," *Revista Brasileria de Politca Internacional 53*, Special Edition, 2010: 91–114.

15 See João Augusto de Castro Neves and Matias Spektor, "Obama and Brazil" in Abraham Lowenthal, et al, (eds), *Shifting the Balance: Obama and the Americas*. (Washington, D.C.: Brookings, 2011).

16 For a more recent assessment on the importance of key developing countries for US foreign policy, see Robert Chase, Emily Hill, and Paul Kennedy, eds., *The Pivotal States: A New Framework for U.S. Policy in the Developing World*. (New York: W. W. Norton, 1999).

17 The Brazilian Congress impeached President Collor de Mello in 1992, due to corruption allegations. Vice-President Itamar Franco (1992–95) succeeded President Collor.

18 Source: Brazilian Bureau of Geography and Statistics (IBGE), www.ibge.gov.br

19 According to the Getúlio Vargas Foundation's Center for Social Policies (CPS-FGV), there are five classes in Brazil: A, B, C, D and E; middle class (C) income ranges from R$1126 to R$4854 a month (US$662 to US$2855; dollar at R$1.70), see http://cps.fgv.br/pt-br/banco-de-dados?area=11&tipo=P&pesquisa=All

20 According to a Pew Research poll (September 2010), 77 percent of Brazilians believe that the country already is (24 percent) or will eventually become (53 percent) a superpower. Only 20 percent do not believe that Brazil will play an important part in world affairs. Another opinion poll conducted by the IBOPE group (March 2010) showed that five of the six most remembered news stories by Brazilians in that period were somehow related to foreign policy: President Lula's trip to Haiti (mentioned by 12 percent), Lula's trips abroad (12 percent), Lula's trip to Cuba (7 percent), secretary Hillary Clinton's visit to Brasilia (6 percent), and Lula's comments on the Iranian nuclear program (5 percent).

21 In Amaury de Souza, *A Agenda Internacional do Brasil*. (Rio de Janeiro, Editora Campus, 2009).

22 In 1991, Brazil and Argentina created a safeguard Agency for Accounting and Control of Nuclear Materials (ABACC).

23 It is important to observe that Brazil's largest hydroelectric dam, Itaipu, is a bi-national undertaking with Paraguay. Mercosur countries signed a protocol on democratic commitment in 1998 (Ushuaia Protocol).

24 Another indisputable success was Mercosur's democratic clause, which proved essential to help prevent a coup d'état in Paraguay in 1998.

25 As of January 2011, the Paraguayan Senate has yet to cast its vote on Venezuela's admission as a full member of Mercosur.

26 Castro Neves and Spektor, 2011, 43.

27 In fact, in 1998, Brazil received a US$41.5 billion IMF-led international support program, IMF's largest-ever loan at the time.

28 Because of disagreements on human rights issues and US pressure on the Brazilian nuclear program, the Brazilian military regime unilaterally denounced the defense treaty with the US in 1977.

29 Tom Shannon, US Ambassador to Brazil, "Brazil Asserts its Role on Iran," *Financial Times*. (14 May 2010).

30 *"Parceria com chineses não é ameaça aos Estados Unidos, afirma Amorim"* (Partnership with China is not a threat to the United States, says Amorim), *Folha de Sao Paulo*. (24 May 2004). The same piece cites Amorim, former Brazilian foreign minister, as saying that the strategic partnership between the two countries will reinforce coordination in other international negotiations.

31 Source: Brazil's Ministry of Development, Industry and Trade (MDIC).

32 A recent study by the Brazilian National Development Bank (BNDES): *Visão do Desenvolvimento: o efeito China sobre as importações brasileiras* (the China effect on Brazilian imports), n. 89. (2010). Moreover, according to IBGE (the official Brazilian Institute of Geography and Statistics), the industrial sector share of Brazil's GDP fell to 15.5 percent in 2009, the lowest figure since 1947.

33 See cable 09SHANGHAI170, China's Growing Trade and Investment ties with Latin America, (15 April 2009), http://wikileaks.ch/cable/2009/04/ 09SHANGHAI170.html

34 Although I acknowledge that part of the International Relations literature may classify Brazil as a regional power and China as a great power (Buzan, 2004), I focus on more general attributes that translate into a non-hegemonic—yet emerging—position in the post-Cold War international system (Hurrell, 2006).

35 Autonomy through diversification of partners is how Vigevani and Cepaluni (2009) label President Lula's foreign policy.

36 Interview with Matias Spektor, 2010.

Bibliography

Albuquerque, José A. Guilhon. *Crescimento, Modernização e Política Externa* (vol. 1) and *Diplomacia para o Desenvolvimento* (vol. 2): *Sessenta Anos de Política Externa Brasileira (1930–1990)*. (São Paulo: Cultura, 1996).

Arbilla, José M. "Arranjos Institucionais e Mudança Conceitual nas Políticas Externas Argentina e Brasileira (1989–94)." Contexto Internacional 22, n. 2 (July/December, 2000), 337–85.

Buzan, B. *The United States and the Great Powers: World Politics in the Twenty-First Century*. (Cambridge: Cambridge University Press, 2004).

Cardoso, Fernando H. *The Accidental President: A Memoir*. (New York: Public Affairs, 2006).

Castro Neves, João Augusto de and Carlos Pereira. "Brazil and China: South-South Partnership or North-South Competition?" (Brookings Foreign Policy Paper, April 2011).

Castro Neves, João Augusto de and Matias Spektor. "Obama and Brazil" in Abraham F. Lowenthal, Theodore J. Piccone, and Laurence Whitehead (eds), *Shifting the Balance: Obama and the Americas*, 1st edn. (Washington, D.C.: Brookings Institution Press, 2011): 43–54.

Chase, Robert, Emily Hill, and Paul Kennedy. *The Pivotal States: A New Framework for U.S. Policy in the Developing World*. (New York: W. W. Norton, 1999).

Hurrell, Andrew. "Hegemony, liberalism and global order: what space for would-be great powers?" *International Affairs*, 82 (1), (2006), 1–19.

Lafer, Celso and Fonseca Jr., G. "Questões para a Diplomacia no Contexto Internacional das Polaridades Indefinidas (Notas Analíticas e Algumas Sugestões)," in Gelson Fonseca Jr. and Sergio H. Nabuco de Castro, *Temas de Política Externa Brasileira II*, 2nd edn, org. (São Paulo: Ed. Paz e Terra, 1997): 49–78.

Mello, Flávia C. Regionalismo e Inserção Internacional: Continuidade e Transformação da Política Externa Brasileira nos anos 90. (Unpublished doctoral dissertation, University of São Paulo, 2000).

Roett, Riordan. *The New Brazil*. (Washington, D.C.: Brookings Institution Press, 2010).

Vigevani, Tullo and Gabriel Cepaluni. *Brazilian Foreign Policy in Changing Times: The Quest for Autonomy from Sarney to Lula*. (Plymouth: Lexington Books, 2009).

Villa, Rafael D. and Manuela Viana. "Security issues during Lula's administration: from the reactive to the assertive approach." *Revista Brasileira de Política Internacional* 53, special edition. (2010), 91–114.

CHAPTER NINE

Conclusion: Global Leadership in the Twenty-First Century

Vidya Nadkarni and Norma C. Noonan

The Evolving International Landscape

The essays in this volume testify to a rapidly changing international arena. The case studies have profiled rising as well as established powers. This volume has focused on the BRIC states because the shift in economic power toward these rising states has gradually begun to reshape the global economic playing field.[1] This shift in economic power presages geopolitical changes and transnational challenges as the energy-hungry economies of China and India begin to compete for ever-larger shares of depleting global energy and water resources. While other fast growing economies, such as Turkey, Mexico, Indonesia, and South Africa have the potential to emerge as strong regional players, they have yet to make a strong impact globally.[2]

The essays confirm that the world is in flux. The established powers—the USA, Europe, and Japan—remain formidable players on the world stage. Brazil, China, and India have continued to show impressive growth and have weathered the 2008 global economic crisis better than Western economies. Critics of Russia contrast the economic dynamism of Brazil with Russia's conservatism and its dependence on revenues from gas and oil. But economist Jim O'Neill continues to see great potential in Russia's future and argues that if the Russian economy is diversified, it could not only move ahead of the others in the BRIC pack but also European countries.[3]

What is clear is that the twenty-first century will be a time of accelerated transformation in the power relationships among the world's major states.

In a little over two decades the international system has moved from a bipolar to a unipolar and now to a multipolar structure. In 1990, few would have predicted that Brazil would be counted among major global players, that the USA would be widely perceived as in decline, and that Russia would be struggling to maintain a place among the top powers. One could well have predicted that China and India, by virtue of their large size and huge populations, would be among the great powers if they could solve their major problems, but few would have predicted the degree to which Japan has treaded water in the past two decades.

In many ways, the world of 1990 with two superpowers was a simpler world and easier to understand. But the simplicity, in part, came from looking only at the surface of the international political situation. The overlay of the bipolar ideological struggle masked other developments, such as the quietly rising powers in the background, the rise of non-state security threats, and transnational challenges like climate change. Who, in 1990, would have guessed that the Soviet Union would implode within two years, that Japan would suffer severe economic setbacks in the early 1990s, adversely affecting the country's progress for the next two decades, and that the rise of non-governmental terrorist networks would become a significant factor in international politics? From the present vantage point, the future seems both bright and slightly cloudy for each of the countries reviewed in this volume. No country has totally unblemished prospects, but none seem to have insurmountable obstacles to prevent their continued success.

What is Global Leadership?

One of the most important underlying questions that the authors in this volume have addressed has been the nature of global leadership. What does it mean to be a global leader in the interstate system? Hard capabilities in the form of economic and military power have to be joined with the *will* to exercise power. More importantly, power has to be translated into influence. The exercise of power and the costs of leadership are minimized if subordinate states accept the legitimacy of that power. As Italian political philosopher Antonio Gramsci noted, a hegemonic social order that rests on a foundation of moral and intellectual authority and voluntary acceptance is more enduring because it is seen as legitimate.[4] The contrast during the Cold War between a coercive Soviet hegemony in Eastern Europe and a cooperative American hegemony in Western Europe is instructive. The provision of public goods in the form of security and an open US market for exports made American dominance acceptable in Western Europe, Japan, South Korea, and countries in Southeast Asia. The USA used its position of power to entrench its economic value preferences by establishing multilateral institutions to anchor the principles of open trade and international monetary stability.

In the twenty-first century, the demands on global leadership are greater. Transnational problems that cannot be resolved through single country initiatives demand structures of global governance that promote multilateral cooperation. Such structures entail costs and demand leadership. While the USA remains the world's unmatched power in terms of hard capabilities, the burden of fighting two wars in Afghanistan and Iraq, of financing a worldwide system of military bases, of managing surging trade deficits with China among other countries, and of dealing with a burgeoning national debt have severely restricted its ability to continue providing public goods to allies and other states in terms of providing security and an open market. In the areas of the international economy, security, climate change, and human rights, American leadership is faltering. China and other emerging powers have been caught in a vise as they simultaneously claim the prerogatives of a great power on some matters while demanding exemptions as developing states on issues ranging from trade to climate change.

All the contributors to this volume agree that we are living in a world where the hierarchic ordering of states is in a phase of prolonged transition and that there are multiple and overlapping value contestations regarding norms relating to sovereignty, human rights, and democracy. No single power is thus able to provide authoritative global leadership on the functional issues of trade, security, and the environment. This chapter sums up the major conclusions that may be drawn from the book.

International Economy

The contrast between the respective roles of the USA and China as the sovereign debt crisis in Europe first unfolded is telling. Whereas US President Barack Obama had played a key role at the April 2009 London summit meeting of the Group of 20 (G20) when leaders devised a common plan of coordinated action[5] to address the fallout from the 2008 economic crisis, two years later, the USA remained on the sidelines while China became the focus of attention. The 3 November 2011 G20 summit[6] that began in Cannes, France in the long shadow of the 2008 global financial crisis and the gathering economic maelstrom in the Europe, provided a stark tableau of an economically buffeted Europe attempting to save the Eurozone and stave off the possibility of sovereign defaults by Portugal, Ireland, Greece, Spain, and Italy contrasted with a China flush with cash but wary of stepping in to rescue Europe.[7] Sitting on a three-trillion-plus dollar pool of foreign exchange reserves, China politely rebuffed requests from Germany and France to purchase Eurobonds and add its economic heft to the bailout package for Greece.[8]

In a globalized world where China has become the factory that manufactures consumer goods that are exported around the world, demand abroad for such products provide important fuel for the engine of the Chinese economy. The Chinese leadership could have used Europe's time of need to demonstrate global leadership by stepping in as a provider of public goods in much the same way as the USA did with the Marshall Plan for Europe in 1947. Faced then with a war-torn Western Europe struggling to get back on its feet in the face of an ideologically divided continent, the USA, which had emerged economically unscathed after World War Two, crafted a two-pronged strategy of a realist-oriented military containment of the Soviet Union and of a liberal-oriented economic plan to rebuild and strengthen Western European economies. Funds from the Marshall Plan that were funneled into Europe were channeled back to the USA to buy American-manufactured products that were in great demand in economically devastated Europe. The USA earned both good will and dollars and was simultaneously able to shore up Western defenses against the Soviet Union.

One may ask whether this represented a missed opportunity for China to demonstrate global leadership. But what is clear is that the situations then and now are vastly different because China remains a relatively poor country. The Chinese economy "accounts for less than 10 percent of the global GDP at present, while the USA and Europe make up well over 50 percent."[9] While Beijing theoretically did have a unique opportunity to showcase its rhetoric of "peaceful rise" by extending a benign helping hand to a Europe that is a prime destination point for Chinese exports, China, as Suisheng Zhao notes in this volume, is wary of exercising global economic leadership prematurely, as it juggles the competing demands of a great power with the concerns of a developing state.

Ensnared in the mesh of a lingering economic crisis, the USA, Europe, and Japan have been unable to perform the role of benefactors but are too wealthy to be supplicants. Under these conditions, the wealthy developed countries dealing with bruised economies are no longer able to play the role of economic savior. The ship of the international economy is now captained not by the G8 but by the G20, which includes both developed and emerging economies.

International Security and Human Rights

On the intersecting issues of international security and human rights, the greatest transnational post-Cold War security challenge has come from terrorism. The close connections between terrorism, organized crime, and drug trafficking have focused renewed efforts at multilateral cooperation to manage these problems. But progress on interstate cooperation has been slow because of concerns over sovereignty. Plural definitions of the national interest have rendered difficult the ability of any one state to provide leadership on this issue. The United Nations therefore has become the central site for international collaboration on terrorism. As Thakur and Weiss state: "The United Nations has become the forum of choice for regime negotiation and norm promotion in countering international terrorism, one of the most contested policy issues."[10]

The threat of terrorism and the resultant rollback of civil liberties in democratic societies have raised concerns among scholars and civic activists in the USA about the rise of a surveillance state and ignited a debate over the proper balance between liberty and security.[11] In authoritarian polities, terrorism has often provided the rationale for greater policing by the state over its citizens. For instance, the 2001 Shanghai Convention on Combating Terrorism, Separatism, and Extremism noted that these three problems were linked.[12] In this view, the protection of territorial integrity and security of states from these triple threats permitted, indeed called for, vigilant and forceful efforts against its perpetrators.

The liberty-security conundrum at the national level finds its international counterpart in the sovereignty-human rights debate that impinges on issues of international security. China and Russia, in particular, have vociferously objected to a view of international security based on the presumption that state sovereignty may be violated under certain conditions. During debates in the United Nations Security Council over Libya and Syria, both countries, sometimes joined by India, have opposed in principle any resolutions that would involve the infringement of state sovereignty. In their own country, Chinese authorities have clamped down harshly on anti-government protests in Tibet, Mongolia, and other restive provinces. Such value contestations raise interesting questions about the nature of an international order that may reflect the interests and value preferences of countries like China and Russia.

Contested values also lie at the heart of differences between established and emerging powers on how best to deal with the security challenge represented by Iran's nuclear program.[13] Russia and China have urged diplomatic negotiations as the best approach to dealing with Iran's suspect uranium enrichment program and would oppose any violation of sovereignty that the option of using force would imply. Additionally, China and India, which need energy to fuel their growing economies, have balked at supporting a stringent sanctions regime against an oil-exporting Iran. Concern over maintaining high levels of economic growth are also at the heart of the differences in approach on climate change between the USA and European countries on the one hand and emerging powers on the other over their joint or several responsibilities.

International Environment

In the competing demands between environmental protection and economic development, emerging economic powers have tended to come down on the side of development. The challenge of climate change and the reductions in carbon emissions required to mitigate global warming has raised questions over the just allocation of economic burdens. Adversely affected by a protracted and stubborn economic crisis, the established powers have insisted on shared sacrifice and have been unswayed by the protestations of China and India that the economic priorities of late developers and the per capita rate of carbon emissions merit special exemptions. The USA, troubled by ballooning debt, a structural budget deficit problem, persisting trade deficits, and a public unwilling to shoulder additional international burdens, has not been in a position to take the lead in creating an effective international environmental regime.

The pace of multilateral cooperation has therefore been glacial. The 2011 United Nations Climate Change Conference in Durban, South Africa concluded with a decision to adopt a universal legal agreement by 2015 that would be binding on developed and developing countries and would come into force after 2020. Upon the conclusion of the Durban conference, David Symons, director of an environmental consultancy firm provided this assessment:

> Many political agreements put off the difficult actions for the next regime and that appears to be the reality for the Durban platform. No one should underestimate the difficulty of arriving at a legal agreement between the developed and developing countries, let alone one that for the first time includes China, India, Europe and America.[14]

In a move designed to show some leadership on this issue, US Secretary of State Hillary Clinton in February 2012 announced the launching of a Climate and Clean Air Coalition as part of a "new global effort to fight climate change, protect health, improve agricultural productivity, and strengthen energy security."[15] Joined by representatives from Bangladesh, Canada, Mexico, Sweden, Ghana, and the United Nations Environment Program, Secretary Clinton noted that the Coalition representing the "first international effort of the kind" would "conduct a targeted, practical, and highly energetic global campaign to spread solutions to the short-lived pollutants worldwide."[16]

The Price of Power

As the USA has learned in recent decades, the price of power is high. Global leadership demands great costs and great sacrifices. The Soviet Union paid the ultimate price for the relentless global pursuit of power and influence. The combination of subsidizing its East European, Asian, African, and Cuban protégés combined with the high cost of maintaining its military machine strained the Soviet economy. In the process of addressing the financial toll that the quest for power demanded, the Soviet Union unraveled. The USA also paid a heavy economic cost for its victory in the Cold War competition with the Soviet Union and in the last two decades has perhaps paid an even heavier price in undertaking two expensive wars in Afghanistan and Iraq as part of the "war against terrorism."

Global power and influence cannot be attained without great cost. The aspiring global powers thus far have not had to spend vast sums of money to provide security as a public good. The USA, for instance, provided a defense umbrella that shielded its allies in Europe and Asia from security threats. This security guarantee freed Europe and Japan to pursue economic development and welfare goals because they did not bear the burden of global military responsibility. In the last two decades, China has become the world's factory and has focused on economic development goals. Beijing has directed rising military expenditures to targeted national security goals. With military modernization, the Chinese military has become powerful. But, unlike the USA, China has not been involved in extraordinarily expensive wars and foreign interventions that tend to deplete national coffers; this has allowed its leaders to accumulate considerable foreign exchange reserves. The USA, by contrast, is dealing with a burgeoning national debt and chronic budget deficits.

One may argue that until the present time, the rising powers and established powers like the European countries and Japan have had the privilege of selective involvement in global issues. China demonstrated that in its 2011 refusal to bail out Europe. The option of selective involvement—about when and how to be engaged in solving global issues—is a luxury that all great powers would naturally prefer. But for a great power to have a global impact, the willingness to exercise global leadership is must. The USA practiced selective involvement prior to 1945 and its global influence was circumscribed because of that choice. Europe has practiced it since 1945, as has Japan. The BRIC countries have all practiced selective engagement since the 1990s. The irony of selective involvement is that when a country participates only in situations that it deems essential to its national interests, it may be less influential when it does choose to act. A state cannot be on the sidelines most of the time and expect to be the recognized global leader when it chooses to act or be involved.

The price of becoming a dominant power calls for a state to be involved and willing to be involved in a wide array of situations not necessarily of its choosing. The issues may range from economic and military to humanitarian. Selective involvement is not an option for a would-be great power. China appears to be the most likely candidate for superpower status but thus far does not seem inclined to assume the mantle of global leadership. The twenty-first century, which appears to be characterized by multiple great powers facing a wider range of transnational challenges than before, may be the post-superpower era. If the last half of the twentieth century featured two superpowers in a bipolar world, the twenty-first century may be characterized by regional superpowers or great powers, none of which has predominant power. Several decades hence, we may be headed toward a world with seven to ten peer powers with no clearly defined dominant or leading state. Each is likely to command respect, but none will have preponderant power or influence and each may opt for selective involvement as a modus operandi.

The Primary Challenges Ahead

The primary challenge ahead for the USA, as Norma Noonan has pointed out, is how to adapt to a world of rising powers. In the near future, the BRIC countries will be joined by other "growth economies," primarily Mexico, Indonesia, South Korea and Turkey as claimants to influence in the world. As Stewart Patrick has observed,

> The world is entering a chaotic era. Global visions will compete, norms will shift, and yesterday's rule takers will become tomorrow's rule makers.[17]

And if the challenge for the USA is to learn to accommodate the rising powers, the challenge for the latter is to understand that with great power comes great responsibility.

Endnotes

1 Jim O'Neill, "BRICs rapid growth tips the global balance," *The Telegraph*. (20 November 2011), http://www.telegraph.co.uk/finance/financialcrisis/8902824/Jim-ONeill-BRICs-rapid-growth-tips-the-global-balance.html

2 See Karen Brooks, "Is Indonesia Bound for the BRICs? How Stalling Reform Could Hold Jakarta Back," *Foreign Affairs*, Vol. 90, No. 6. (November/December 2011), 109–18; Hugh Pope, "Pax Ottomana?" *Foreign Affairs*, Vol.

89, No. 6. (November/December 2010), 161–71; Jim O'Neill, *The Growth Map: Economic Opportunity in the BRICs and Beyond* (London: Penguin, 2011).

3 Stefan Wagstyl, "Jim O'Neill: Russia could surprise us all," *Financial Times*. (28 November 2011), http://blogs.ft.com/beyond-brics/2011/11/28/jim-oneill-russia-could-still-surprise-the-world/#axzz1poFI9u7U

4 Joseph Femia, "Gramsci, Machiavelli, and International Relations," *Political Quarterly*, Vol. 76, No. 3. (July-September 2005), 342–43.

5 Steve Schifferes, "G20 leaders seal $1tn global deal," *BBC News*. (2 April 2009), http://news.bbc.co.uk/2/hi/business/7980394.stm

6 The Cannes summit of the G20 was the sixth summit since President George W. Bush convened the first such summit in November 2008 in the wake of the 2008 global economic crisis. The London summit in April 2009 was followed by summits in Pittsburgh, Toronto, and Seoul. See Stewart M. Patrick, "Six Criteria for G20 Success in Cannes," Expert Brief, Council on Foreign Relations, (2 November 2011), http://www.cfr.org/economics/six-criteria-g20-success-cannes/p26399

7 Catherine Bremer, "China to hold sway at G20 Cannes summit," *Reuters*. (31 October 2011), http://www.reuters.com/article/2011/10/31/us-g-idUSTRE79U61Z20111031

8 China's reluctance may have stemmed from excessive economic caution or from fears of domestic opposition to such a move, especially in the wake of the expected leadership transition in 2012 when the fourth generation leadership team of President Hu Jintao and Premier Wen Jiabao is expected to cede their respective positions to the fifth generation leaders Vice president Xi Jinping and Vice Premier Li Keqiang. See also, Damian Grammaticas, "Why China won't save the world," *BBC News*. (2 November 2011), http://www.bbc.co.uk/news/15550691

9 Ibid.

10 Ramesh Thakur and Thomas G. Weiss, "United Nations 'Policy': An Argument with Three Illustrations," *International Studies Perspectives*, Vol. 10, No. 1. (2009), 26.

11 Russell Hardin, "Civil Liberties in the Era of Mass Terrorism," *The Journal of Ethics*, Vol. 8, No. 1. (2004), 77–95.

12 The Shanghai Cooperation Organization (SCO) is a regional grouping made up of Russia, China, Kazakhstan, Kyrgyzstan, Tajikistan, and Uzbekistan. The text of the Shanghai Convention on Combating Terrorism, Extremism and Separatism is available on the SCO website, http://www.sectsco.org/EN/show.asp?id=68

13 The Iranian government claims that their nuclear program is designed for peaceful purposes while the USA and European countries believe that Iran is embarked on a quest to acquire nuclear weapons. See, "Iran's Nuclear Program," *The New York Times*. (6 March 2012), http://topics.nytimes.com/top/news/international/countriesandterritories/iran/nuclear_program/index.html

14 Quoted in Fiona Harvey and Damian Carrington, "Durban climate conference agrees deal to do a deal—now comes the hard part," *The Guardian*, US Edition. (12 December 2011), http://www.guardian.co.uk/environment/2011/dec/12/durban-climate-change-conference-2011-southafrica

15 Hillary Rodham Clinton, "Remarks at the Climate and Clean Air Coalition to Reduce Short-lived Climate Pollutants Initiative," Washington D.C. (16 February 2012), http://www.state.gov/secretary/rm/2012/02/184061.htm

16 Ibid.

17 Stewart Patrick, "Irresponsible Stakeholders? The Difficulty of Integrating Rising Powers," *Foreign Affairs*, Vol. 89, No. 6. (November-December 2010), 44.

Bibliography

Bremer, Catherine. "China to hold sway at G20 Cannes summit," *Reuters*. (31 October 2011), http://www.reuters.com/article/2011/10/31/us-g-idUSTRE79U61Z20111031

Brooks, Karen. "Is Indonesia Bound for the BRICs? How Stalling Reform Could Hold Jakarta Back," *Foreign Affairs*, Vol. 90, No. 6. (November-December 2011), 109–18.

Clinton, Hillary Rodham. "Remarks at the Climate and Clean Air Coalition to Reduce Short-lived Climate Pollutants Initiative," Washington D.C. (16 February 2012), http://www.state.gov/secretary/rm/2012/02/184061.htm

Femia, Joseph. "Gramsci, Machiavelli, and International Relations," *Political Quarterly*, Vol. 76, No. 3. (July-September 2005), 341–9.

Grammaticas, Damian. "Why China won't save the world," *BBC News*. (2 November 2011), http://www.bbc.co.uk/news/15550691

Hardin, Russell. "Civil Liberties in the Era of Mass Terrorism," *The Journal of Ethics*, Vol. 8, No. 1. (2004), 77–95.

Harvey, Fiona and Damian Carrington. "Durban climate conference agrees deal to do a deal—now comes the hard part," *The Guardian*, US Edition. (12 December 2011), http://www.guardian.co.uk/environment/2011/dec/12/durban-climate-change-conference-2011-southafrica

New York Times. "Iran's Nuclear Program," *The New York Times*. (6 March 2012), http://topics.nytimes.com/top/news/international/countriesandterritories/iran/nuclear_program/index.html

O'Neill, Jim. "BRICs rapid growth tips the global balance," *The Telegraph*. (20 November 2011), http://www.telegraph.co.uk/finance/financialcrisis/8902824/Jim-ONeill-BRICs-rapid-growth-tips-the-global-balance.html

—*The Growth Map: Economic Opportunity in the BRICs and Beyond*. (London: Penguin, 2011).

Patrick, Stewart M. "Irresponsible Stakeholders? The Difficulty of Integrating Rising Powers," *Foreign Affairs* Vol. 89, No. 6. (November-December 2010), 44–53.

—"Six Criteria for G20 Success in Cannes," Expert Brief, Council on Foreign Relations, (2 November 2011), http://www.cfr.org/economics/six-criteria-g20-success-cannes/p26399

Pope, Hugh. "Pax Ottomana?" *Foreign Affairs*, Vol. 89, No. 6. (November-December 2010), 161–71.

Schifferes, Steve. "G20 leaders seal $1tn global deal," *BBC News*. (2 April 2009), http://news.bbc.co.uk/2/hi/business/7980394.stm

SCO website. http://www.sectsco.org/EN/show.asp?id=68

Thakur, Ramesh and Thomas G. Weiss. "United Nations 'Policy': An Argument with Three Illustrations." *International Studies Perspectives* Vol. 10, No. 1 (2009), 18–35.

Wagstyl, Stefan. "Jim O'Neill: Russia could surprise us all," *Financial Times*. (28 November 2011), http://blogs.ft.com/beyond-brics/2011/11/28/ jim-oneill-russia-could-still-surprise-the-world/#axzz1poFI9u7U

GLOSSARY

American Exceptionalism: A term used to express several interrelated concepts about the United States in world affairs. It has been used to refer to the United States' inclination to see *its* norms, rather than international norms, as its operational foundation in US foreign policy. It has also been used to refer to a belief that the United States, unlike other great powers in history, is immune to the decline and fall syndrome.

Arc of Freedom and Prosperity: In a major policy address in November 2006, then Japanese Foreign Minister Taro Aso indicated that Japan had decided to follow the path of "value-oriented diplomacy" and help establish an "arc of freedom and prosperity" along the outer rim of Eurasia. Japan's foreign policy shift placed greater emphasis on what it identified as the universal values of democracy, freedom, human rights, rule of law, and market economies. The foreign minister's statement specified that Japan would support countries such as Cambodia, Laos, and Vietnam in Southeast Asia, along with the countries of Central Asia and those in the Caucasus region such as Georgia and Azerbaijan, to move down the road to peace and happiness through economic prosperity and democracy.

Arthashastra: An ancient Indian treatise on various aspects of statecraft written by Kautilya around the fourth century B.C. He is considered to be the earliest exponent of realpolitik or politics based on pragmatic rather than ethical considerations.

Beijing Consensus: A model of economic policy based on the China model of state-led capitalism, suggesting a greater role for the state in the economy, in contradistinction to the market-friendly approach of the Washington Consensus traditionally supported by the United States.

Bolshevik Revolution: Inspired by communist ideology, this Russian revolution in October 1917 followed the February 1917 revolution that had overthrown the tsarist monarchy. Led by Vladimir Lenin, the Bolsheviks (a faction of the Russian Social Democratic Labor Party) toppled the Provisional Government that had been established after the abdication of Tsar Nicholas II. The goal of the Bolsheviks was to assist in bringing about the world communist revolution.

Brasil Potência: A project put forth by Brazil's military regime in the late 1960s and early 1970s to promote rapid economic expansion while increasing the country's international clout. The project aimed at fostering jingoism among the population in order to garner support for its political goals, which included a military nuclear program.

Brazil, Russia, India, China, South Africa coalition (BRICS): An acronym created in 2001 by an investment bank to denote this group of dynamic emerging markets. A few years later, the leaders of these countries decided to confer a political yet not-institutionalized dimension on the group. The BRICS countries have held several high-level meetings to exchange information while aiming at coordinating interests on several global issues, such as finance and trade, among others.

Brazil, South Africa, India, China (BASIC): A coalition of developing economies (Brazil, South Africa, India, and China) that was created in 2009 to cooperate in international climate talks. The main aspiration of the group is to try to represent the interests of the developing world in the negotiations with the developed economies.

Bretton Woods System: Established in 1944 with 44 member states after a conference held in Bretton Woods, New Hampshire, the Bretton Woods system created an international basis for currency exchange by linking the dollar to gold (US$35 for an ounce of bullion). Other member states agreed to a fixed exchange rate by tying their currencies to the dollar. This fixed exchange rate system collapsed when President Richard Nixon in 1971 effectively stopped the convertibility of the US dollar to gold. The institutional mechanisms created under the auspices of the Bretton Woods system—the International Monetary Fund, the World Bank, and the General Agreement on Tariffs and Trade (since 1995, the World Trade Organization)—continue to operate.

Bumai Xifang de Zhang: An "important change witnessed in Chinese foreign policy in 2009 in comparison with past years," according to one Chinese scholar, which suggests that "China no longer bends in response to Western pressure and heeds what the West thinks about its behavior undertaken in pursuit of its interests."

Central Asian republics: In Russian literature and in this chapter, the term Central Asia refers to a group of five countries: Kazakhstan, Uzbekistan, Kyrgyzstan, Turkmenistan, and Tajikistan. Very often this term is used as a broader group of countries including Afghanistan and Pakistan.

Checkbook diplomacy: A term used to describe international policy that openly uses economic aid and investment between countries to carry diplomatic favor. The term has been used to describe Japanese and German international involvement during and after Gulf War I. Both countries were unable to commit troops to the coalition because of restrictions placed into their constitutions when they were drawn up under allied occupation following World War Two.

Chinese Communist Party: The incumbent, founding and ruling political party of the People's Republic of China. At present, it claims to follow a doctrine of "socialism with Chinese characteristics." Its leading status is mentioned in the preamble of the PRC Constitution. The standing committee of its *politburo* is PRC's actual policymaker.

Common but Differentiated Responsibility: This principle, upheld by India, China, and Brazil at the world climate talks, is based on two ideas: the common heritage of humankind and the notion of equity in international law. The first idea comes from the belief in the common or shared responsibility of all states for the protection of the environment and the second idea recognizes the historical differences in the contributions of developed and developing countries to global environmental problems and the differences in their economic and technical capacity to contribute toward the solution.

Common Market of the South (MERCOSUR): Established in 1991 between Argentina, Brazil, Uruguay, and Paraguay (Venezuela is negotiating its full membership). Although its aim is to become a common market, Mercosur is still an imperfect customs union. The bloc, however, has created an overarching institutional framework for cooperation in areas that go beyond the economic realm.

Commonwealth of Independent States (CIS): The CIS was established on 8 December 1991 after three Soviet republics—the Russian Federation, Belarus, and Ukraine—signed the "Belovezhskiye Agreements" on the dissolution of the Soviet Union. These agreements were signed in a place close to Minsk, the capital of Belarus, called Belovezhskaya Puscha. On 21 December 1991, in Alma-Ata, capital of Kazakhstan, other Soviet republics joined the CIS and signed a special Protocol on their membership. In 1991 the CIS included: Azerbaijan, Armenia, Belarus, Kazakhstan, Kyrgyzstan, Moldova, Russian Federation, Tajikistan, Turkmenistan, Uzbekistan, and Ukraine. Georgia did not join the CIS in 1991, but became its member in 1993 after the Georgian-Abkhazian war, and in 2008 left the organization.

Conference of the Parties (COP): These are the Parties to the United Nations Framework Convention on Climate Change (UNFCCC), which advances implementation of the Convention through decisions taken at periodic meetings. The seventeenth session (COP 17) took place in Durban, South Africa in November 2011. COP 18 will be held in Doha, Qatar in November-December 2012.

Core Interest(s): A concept developed in response to what Beijing perceives as the daunting internal and external challenges to its regime survival, economic development and territorial integrity, which the CCP regime has long been obsessed with and increasingly assertive in defending. According to what Chinese State Councilor Dai Bingguo told his American interlocutors, China's number one core interest is to maintain its fundamental system, the CCP regime, and state security, followed by state sovereignty and territorial integrity and, finally, the continued stable development of its economy and society.

Demographic Dividend: The demographic dividend occurs when the demographic transition in a country is at a point when there is a bulge in the productive working-age population such that the ratio of productive workers to younger and older dependents is higher. Such a circumstance opens opportunities for faster economic growth if the working-age population is adequately educated.

East-West rivalry: The military and strategic rivalry between the United States and its allies in Western Europe and the Soviet Union and its allies in Eastern Europe during the Cold War from 1945 to 1989. The conflict was formalized in two military alliances—the US-led North Atlantic Treaty Organization and the Soviet-led Warsaw Pact.

European Union (EU): An association with 27 European member states as of 2011. It began as an association of six European nations after World War II (European Coal and Steel Community). Over the years, its functions and membership expanded. The current membership includes the original six core members plus member states from southern and eastern Europe. In 2002, the EU adopted a common currency—the Euro—for 16 of the member states. Several states, including the UK, opted out of the Euro and a few states did not qualify. The EU is an economic union, but ultimate political sovereignty remains with the member states, which on occasion limits their ability to make decisions that can be executed and enforced.

Eurozone: The member countries of the EU who have met the criteria to be members of the currency union that uses the euro. As of March 2012, the eurozone consists of seventeen countries, the first eleven members in 1999 were Austria, Belgium, Finland, France, Germany, Ireland, Italy, Luxembourg, Netherlands, Portugal, and Spain, which were later joined by, Cyprus, Estonia, Greece, Malta, Slovakia, and Slovenia. Both Denmark and the UK have negotiated opt-outs of the eurozone while Hungary and Poland have made known their preferences to join.

Extended Neighborhood: India's reference to the area outside South Asia covering East Asia, West Asia (Middle East), Central Asia, the Persian Gulf, and the Indian Ocean.

Federal Assembly of the Russian Federation: The parliament of the Russian Federation is called the Federal Assembly of the Russian Federation. It consists of two chambers: Council of Federation (Senate) and State Duma (House of Representatives).

Free Trade Area of the Americas (FTAA): An initiative launched by the United States in the early 1990s to create a free trade area from "Alaska to Patagonia." The project stalled in the early 2000s due to disagreements mainly between Brazil and the United States, the two largest economies in the Hemisphere.

General Agreement on Trade and Tariffs (GATT/WTO): It has provided, since the end of World War Two, a framework for rounds of multilateral trade negotiations. In 1994, during the closing of the Uruguay Round of negotiations, states agreed to the creation of the World Trade Organization, which inherited the GATT framework.

Global Civilian Power: A term that has been used to describe the international role of Germany and Japan after World War Two and that has also been used in reference to the EU. Definitions of what it means to be a global civilian power emphasize: (1) the acceptance of the necessity of cooperation with other states in the pursuit of international objectives; (2) concentration on non-military, primarily economic, means to secure national goals, with military power left as a residual instrument serving essentially to safeguard other means of international interaction; and (3) a willingness to develop supranational structures to address critical issues of international management.

Global Free Rider: A label one Western observer accused China of being, because "Beijing remains highly reluctant to take on more burdens—whether economic, political, or military." Likewise, another scholar criticized China's approach toward international regime as guided by the "maxi-mini-principle—maximization of rights and minimization of responsibilities."

Global Public Goods: Public goods provide benefits that cannot be restricted to a few. Once provided, however, they suffer from the "free rider" problem because many can enjoy the benefits without paying for them. This often leads to a collective action dilemma making the provision of such goods difficult. Who pays and who is willing to pay thus become crucial questions. Global public goods may be provided in crucial areas, such as financial stability, the provision of peace and security, and the protection of the environment. The provision of an open trading system, such as the one facilitated by the United States under the General Agreement on Tariffs and Trade (see WTO) is a case in point.

Great Power: A great power is typically described as a state that has the ability to exert its influence on a global scale. Great powers characteristically possess military and economic strength and diplomatic and cultural influence which may cause small powers to consider the opinions of great powers before taking actions of their own.

Group of 8 (G8): The name given to a collaboration of eight of the largest economies in the world. Created in 1975 as the Group of Six (France, Germany, Italy, Japan, the United Kingdom, and the United States), Canada was added in 1976. For years it was known as the Group of 7 (G7) until the Russia Federation was added in 1997. The G8 also includes the European Union as a non-voting member. The G8 normally holds an annual meeting of the heads of government of the member states hosted by one of the member states. In more recent years, Brazil, China, India, Mexico and South Africa have participated as the Outreach Five.

Group of 20 (G20): This is the name given initially to meetings of Finance Ministers and Central Bank Governors of the world's largest economies. The meetings were launched in 1999 to discuss international economic developments. There are 19 state members plus the European Union: Argentina, Australia, Brazil, Canada, China, France, Germany, India, Indonesia, Italy, Japan, Mexico, Russia, Saudi Arabia, South Africa, Turkey, the United Kingdom, and the United States. The agenda expanded over the years as the leading economic powers attempt to coordinate policy in the financial sector. After the crisis of 2008, the representation has included heads of government as well as the financial representatives of the 20 entities. It was decided in 2009 that major economic issues would be considered by the G20, thus expanding its role. The 20 members account for 90 percent of the world's GDP.

Group of 77 (G77): The Group of 77 was founded in 1964 at the end of the first UNCTAD conference in Geneva by 77 developing countries. G77 sought to provide a means for member countries jointly to articulate and promote their economic interests and enhance their negotiating power on major international economic issues.

Hindutva: A notion of cultural nationalism as advocated by the Bharatiya Janata Party. The concept of hindutva is based on the idea that all Indian citizens, whether Hindu or not, share a common cultural identity and heritage, which should be celebrated and should form the basis of nationalism.

India, Brazil, South Africa Initiative (IBSA): A trilateral initiative launched in 2003. Its objective is to promote a multitude of cooperation projects between three of the developing world's largest democracies.

International Criminal Court (ICC): A permanent international tribunal to prosecute genocides and other crimes against humanity. It came into being in 2012.

International Monetary Fund (IMF): International organization created in the wake of World War Two to provide monetary stability to the economies of its member countries.

Itamaraty: Brazil's Ministry of External Affairs is considered one of the country's most efficient state bureaucracies and concentrates most of the foreign policy decision-making process.

Kyoto Protocol: This 1997 Protocol legally binds developed countries to emission reduction Targets. The Kyoto Protocol came into force in 2005 with 192 Convention Parties (see UNFCCC). The first commitment period started in 2008 and ends in 2012. The United States did not sign the Protocol. Large developing countries like China, India, and Brazil were not required to meet specific targets under this Protocol.

Liangli' erxing: One of the two principles of China's international responsibility that China follows according to one Chinese scholar. It connotes the idea of commitment according to its ability. The other principle is the combination of China's interests with the common interests of the international society.

Liberal International Economic Order: After World War Two, the United States helped in the establishment of a liberal international economic order founded on the pillars of free trade, the gold standard and the free movement of capital. Under the Bretton Woods system, the USA created three multilateral institutions to uphold the liberal economic order: the International Monetary Fund, the International Bank for Reconstruction and Development, and the General Agreement on Tariffs and Trade.

License Raj: The policy of planned industrialization introduced in India in 1951 under the Industries Development and Regulation Act under which the state regulated and restricted the operation of private industry with stringent licensing requirements that covered all aspects of manufacturing from entry and expansion to cost and hiring practices. The dismantling of the license raj (also called the permit raj) began in the mid–1980s and the process was accelerated after the liberalizing reforms introduced in 1991.

Look East Policy: According to Prime Minister Manmohan Singh, the "Look East" policy, launched in 1991, represented a strategic shift in India's vision of the world and its place in the evolving global economy by actively reconnecting with India's civilizational neighbors in Southeast and East Asia.

Middle Power: Middle Power status is usually identified in one of two ways. The traditional and most common way is to aggregate critical physical and material criteria to rank states according to their relative capabilities. Middle Powers simply rank between the countries 'above' (Great Powers) and 'below' (Small Powers) them. More recently Middle Powers have been identified in terms of their foreign policy behavior. Middle Powers are said to carve out a niche for themselves by pursuing a narrow range and particular types of foreign policy interest. This behavioral approach often emphasizes the role of Middle Powers in banding together in the service of international peace and stability.

Missile Technology Control Regime (MTCR): An informal and voluntary agreement established in 1987 to prevent the proliferation of missile technology.

New International Economic Order: In the 1970s, a coalition of developing countries under the umbrella of the United Nations Conference on Trade and Development called attention to the grievances of the developing countries against the developed world and issued the call for a new international economic order to replace the liberal international economic order.

Several proposals were presented to the developed world seeking greater development aid channeled through multilateral agencies; better terms of trade through unilateral tariff reductions by developed countries to exports from less-developed countries; and agreements to increase and stabilize the prices of primary products. By the 1980s, as economic liberalization policies gained greater acceptance, the NIEO movement lost momentum.

Non-aligned Movement: The non-aligned movement had its origin in the 1955 Bandung conference in Indonesia convened by the Prime Ministers of Burma (Myanmar), Ceylon (now Sri Lanka), India, Indonesia, and Pakistan and attended by 29 states most of which were newly-independent former colonies. Determined to resist pressure from major powers and staunchly anti-colonialist and anti-imperialist in orientation, these countries refused to be forced to take sides in the post-World War Two conflict between the USA and the Soviet Union.

Non-proliferation Regime: The non-proliferation regime was established under the nuclear non-proliferation treaty, which was signed in 1968 and came into force in 1970. Under the terms of the treaty, five countries—the United States, the Soviet Union, Britain, France, and China—signed the treaty as nuclear weapons states. All other signatories had to agree not to develop nuclear weapons. In return the nuclear weapons states agreed to provide the non-nuclear states with nuclear technology for energy purposes and to work in good faith toward negotiated reductions of their own nuclear weapons arsenals.

North Atlantic Treaty Organization (NATO): a military alliance formed in 1949 among Western powers and led by the United States to counter the spreading influence of the USSR. The organization exists into the present and since the fall of the USSR has expanded to include some former countries in the Warsaw Pact and several former republics of the USSR. There are currently 28 members. NATO has cooperated to keep peace in Europe and, in a limited way, elsewhere in the world in the post-Cold War era. NATO has succeeded in keeping the United States engaged in Europe and has prevented any one European state from gaining military dominance over the others.

Nuclear Non-proliferation Treaty (NPT): A pact signed in 1968 to establish the framework of the use of nuclear technology for peaceful purposes, foster disarmament between nuclear powers, and curb nuclear proliferation.

Organization for Economic Cooperation and Development: The OECD's members are 29 highly-developed countries.

Pooling Sovereignty: A concept that distinguishes the form of sovereignty states embrace by their membership in the European Union as opposed to traditional forms of sovereignty. "Pooling sovereignty" can be seen as the idea of "giving up sovereignty," in the sense that when member states engage in common decision-making, they increase their ability to make decisions that favor the outcomes they want. Pooling sovereignty is especially relevant to trans-border issues, which cannot be resolved without multinational cooperation.

Real Plan: An ambitious macroeconomic stabilization program that was implemented in Brazil in 1993/1994. By replacing the country's currency and setting sound economic policies, it successfully accomplished its goal to put an end to Brazil's perennial hyperinflation rates.

Responsibility to Protect (R2P): A doctrine based on three principles: (1) that a state has primary responsibility to protect its population from genocide, war crimes, ethnic cleansing and crimes against humanity; (2) that the international community has a responsibility to assist states to fulfill this responsibility; (3) that when a state fails to protect its population or is the perpetrator of such crimes and diplomatic and peaceful means to resolve the problem have failed, the international community should sanction the collective use of force through the United Nations Security Council. At the 2005 World Summit meeting of the United Nations General Assembly, heads of state and government agreed to uphold the principles of R2P.

ROSATOM: State Corporation on Nuclear Energy of the Russian Federation controls the civilian nuclear energy sector (nuclear power stations, civilian nuclear technologies, production of nuclear fuel, uranium enrichment etc.)

Shanghai Cooperation Organization (SCO): was established in 2000. Its members are Kazakhstan, China, Kyrgyzstan, Russian Federation, Tajikistan, and Uzbekistan. This organization superseded the "Shanghai Five" grouping established in 1995 to promote relations of good-neighborliness, mutual trust and friendship, strengthening security and stability in the region, and facilitating common development. The SCO is aimed at developing economic and security cooperation.

Slavophiles: The Slavophile trend in political thinking developed in the middle of the nineteenth century as an alternative to the ideology of Westernization. Slavophiles thought that Russia is a separate civilization and should develop according to its Slavic tradition, culture, and religion. There were various groups and parties within them. They were considered conservative, and though many representatives of the moderate Slavophiles (non-Westerners) were in power structures during the nineteenth century, Slavophile thinking was never dominant among the Russian population and elite. After the 1917 revolution, this term was not used. Sometimes modern Russian Eurasianists are defined as Slavophiles; however it is not quite correct because they see Russia's uniqueness in combination with European and Asian traditions and culture, while acknowledging the existence of a separate Russian civilization. There are no pure types among representatives of both groups (Slavophiles and Westernizers), and the majority of the Russian political elite demonstrate a liberal and conservative mix of ideas and preferences (though in various proportions).

Soft power: A term conceived and elaborated by Joseph Nye in his seminal book, *Soft Power: The Means to Success in World Politics* (2004). According to his classification, soft power exists as a separate category of power in addition to hard power and economic power. The distinguishing feature of soft power is that countries focus on the attractiveness of their political values and policies to foster relationships with other countries to pursue common goals instead of relying on coercion or economic leverage to convince other countries to cooperate with the goals of the power-seeking country.

South American Defense Council (CDS): Created in 2010 under the umbrella of the Union of South American Nations (UNASUR). Its main objective is to provide a framework for exchange of information about military expenditures between the twelve South American countries.

Strategic autonomy: A post-Cold War concept designed to maintain India's freedom of action in the area of security and foreign policy strategy.

Post-independence Indian leaders have been historically averse to joining alliances. The concept of strategic autonomy has taken the place of non-alignment, especially in the context of the Indo-US strategic partnership and India's growing security relationship with the United States.

Supranationalism: A term used to describe a decision-making arrangement in which states voluntarily cede authority to an institution or set of institutions, which, in turn, can make binding decisions on those states. Supranationalism, which literally means "above the nation-state," referred to the transfer of authority to the institutions of the European Coal and Steel Community, the first experiment in European integration, and, subsequently, to the institutions of the European Union, in which the Commission, the European Court of Justice, and the European Parliament are considered among the most "supranational" institutions.

Taoguangyanghui: A policy set by Deng Xiaoping in the early 1990s, which prescribes to the CCP regime the following: to hide its capabilities, to focus on its national strength-building, and to bide its time. Following this policy, China kept its head low and avoided confronting the USA and other Western powers.

The Monroe Doctrine: A policy enunciated during the administration of James Monroe in 1823, which warned European states to stay out of the affairs of North and South America. Pronounced after most of the Latin American states had been granted independence from Spain and Portugal, it was a warning that any interference in North or South America would result in US intervention. There was also a corollary that the United States would stay out of the European spheres of influence. The Monroe has been considered as a core element in US foreign policy for almost two centuries. After World War Two, the United States departed from the corollary aspect of the policy, but continued to consider the core doctrine as a permanent part of US foreign policy.

Treaty of Peace and Friendship between Japan and the People's Republic of China: An agreement signed in August 1978 by Japan and China aimed at strengthening political and economic relations between the two countries. Because of Japan's strong diplomatic ties to the USA, improvements in US-China relations following President Nixon's visit to China in 1972 helped to create an environment in which Japan and China could promote closer ties.

Union of South American Nations (UNASUR): It was created in 2008 and it includes all the 12 countries in the continent. In practice, UNASUR integrates two existing regional blocs, MERCOSUR and the Andean Community. It also provides an institutional umbrella for a wide range of agreements that deal with defense, healthcare, among other issues.

United Nations Framework Convention on Climate Change: An international treaty adopted in 1992 with the objective of considering cooperative ways to limit increases in global temperature and resulting climate change. The treaty came into force in 1994.

United Nations Peacekeeping Mission in Haiti (MINUSTAH): Since 2004 Brazil's Armed Forces has led the UN military efforts in Haiti, with over a 1,000 troops.

United Nations Security Council (UNSC): The ultimate locus of power in the United Nations. It consists of 15 member states, of which five have permanent seats with veto power (US, UK, France, China, and Russia).

Washington Consensus: A term developed in 1989 by economist John Williamson to allude to a package of liberal economic policy prescriptions for developing countries to be followed by multilateral lending agencies such as the International Monetary Fund and the World Bank. These prescriptions called for government debt reduction and fiscal discipline, trade liberalization, deregulation, and privatization of state enterprises, among others. The ideas behind what came to be called the Washington Consensus guided the lending practices of the IMF, in particular, from the 1980s to the mid 1990s. Subsequently, the IMF has adopted a more flexible approach that takes into account institution building along with economic development issues.

Westernizers: Westernization as a trend in Russian political thinking started at the beginning of the nineteenth century after Russia's victory over Napoleonic France (1812) and an unsuccessful noblemen's rebellion against the Russian monarchy (December 1825). The development of the liberal school of thought continued through the nineteenth century. "Westernizers" wanted Russia to follow Western political and cultural traditions and establish a system similar to that of the European political system. At the beginning of the twentieth century, during the democratic revolutions in Russia of 1905 and February 1917, they were the driving force for democratic transformation, the abolition of absolute monarchy, and the development of a parliamentary tradition (State Duma). However they failed to achieve success in stabilizing the political, economic, and social situation in Russia, and lost any influence with and broad support from the population by October-November 1917 when the Bolsheviks took power and started socialist reforms. Westernizers of the Soviet period and at present also declare that Russia should be like a European (Western) state, accept Western values and join into Western organizations even if it goes contrary to historic tradition and culture.

World Bank: At its inception in 1944, the World Bank was established as a single institution, namely the International Bank for Reconstruction and Development (IBRD). The World Bank group is currently made up of five organizations: the IBRD; the International Development Association; the International Finance Corporation; the Multilateral Investment Guarantee Agency ; and the International Center for the Settlement of Investment Disputes. The objectives of the World Bank are to promote economic development and alleviate global poverty.

World Trade Organization: Established in 1995, the WTO is a global international trade organization. As a successor to the General Agreement on Tariffs and Trade, the WTO establishes the rules of trade and serves as the forum for negotiations among member countries to facilitate the free flow of goods and services across state borders.

Yousuozuowei: A supplement to the *Taoguangyanghui* policy, which literally means "striking some points/successes." It prescribes for Beijing a more active or even a leadership role in pursing certain foreign policy objectives, particularly in China's core interest issue areas.

INDEX